The Myth of the Great Secret

Also by Toby Johnson:

In Search of God in the Sexual Underworld:
A Mystical Journey

Plague: A Novel About Healing

Secret Matter

Getting Life in Perspective

A Search for Spiritual Meaning

The Myth of the Great Secret

An Appreciation of Joseph Campbell

BY TOBY JOHNSON

Celestial Arts
Berkeley, California

#24629609

"Pack Up Your Sorrows" written by Richard Fārina and Pauline Marden Bryan.
Copyright © 1964, 1966 Songs of Polygram International, Inc. Used with permission.
All rights reserved.

"Candle of Light" words and music by John Lodge. Copyright © 1969 by Johnsongs,
London, England. Sole selling agent MCA Music, a division of MCA, Inc., New York,
NY for the USA and Canada. Used by permission. All rights reserved.

Excerpt from *The Power of Myth* by Joseph Campbell and Bill Moyers. Copyright ©
1988 by Apostrophe S Productions, Inc. and Bill Moyers and Alfred Van der Marck
Editions, Inc. for itself and the estate of Joseph Campbell. Used by permission of
Doubleday, a division of Bantam Doubleday Dell Publishing Group, Inc.

Excerpt from *The Hero's Journey: The World of Joseph Campbell* edited by Phil
Cousineau. Copyright © 1991 by Phil Cousineau and Stuart L. Brown. Used by
permission of HarperCollins Publishers Inc.

Excerpt from *An Open Life* by Joseph Campbell in conversation with Michael Toms.
Copyright © 1988 by New Dimensions Foundation. Used by permission of
HarperCollins Publishers Inc.

Excerpt from *The Hero With a Thousand Faces* by Joseph Campbell. Copyright © 1949
by Princeton University Press. Used by permission of Princeton University Press.

Excerpt from *A Course in Miracles*. Copyright © 1975 by Foundation for Inner Peace,
Inc. Used by permission of Foundation for Inner Peace, Inc.

Text design by Eric Johnson
Typesetting by Wilsted & Taylor
Cover design by Ken Scott

FIRST CELESTIAL ARTS PRINTING 1992

LIBRARY OF CONGRESS CATALOGING-IN-PUBLICATION DATA

Johnson, Edwin Clark.
    The myth of the great secret : an appreciation of Joseph Campbell / Toby Johnson.
        p.   cm.
    ISBN 0-89087-658-4
    1. Spiritual life—Catholic authors.   I. Title.
    BX2350.2.J642   1992
    248.4'82—dc20
                                                                        91-38777
                                                                        CIP

1   2   3   4   5   6   7   8   9   10 / 96   95   94   93   92

CONTENTS

Nobody knows and you can't find out.
JOHN BROCKMAN

There is an environment of minds as well as of space.
The universe is one—a spider's web wherein each mind
lives along every line, a vast whispering gallery where
. . . though no news travels unchanged yet no secret can
be rigorously kept.
C. S. LEWIS

Weaving a Tapestry
of Meaning

The Myth of the Great Secret was originally subtitled "A Search for Spiritual Meaning in the Face of Emptiness." It might well have been subtitled "What I Learned from Joseph Campbell." The book first appeared in 1981. Its companion book, *In Search of God in the Sexual Underworld*, was published a year later. Together these presented a theory of religion—and an application to such real-life issues as teenage prostitution and the so-called sexual revolution—based on the ideas of Joseph Campbell. While the two books developed a small following (I still get letters from readers who've found copies in used bookstores), they were in some ways ahead of their time and soon went out of print.

In the early 1980s, Joseph Campbell was relatively unknown. Of course, he'd already published a shelf of books and had devoted fans all over America. But it was not until after his death in 1987 and the subsequent appearance on television of the six-part series of interviews with philosopher and television commentator Bill Moyers that he caught the fancy of the American people. PBS channels discovered that the airing of the series, titled "The Power of Myth," during annual fund-raising appeals brought enormous success. Apparently this was the kind of television the thinking and contributing public wanted on the air.

Perhaps by the end of the decade of Ronald Reagan and the Moral Majority with its unfulfilled promise of restoring the righteous moral values and deadly serious religious certainty of the 1950s, Joe Campbell's sensible approach to religion and his infectious, good-natured laughter were a breath of fresh air. There was something reverent and sacred even about his irreverent and sarcastic accounts of Christian teaching and history. Even when he complained about the abuses and spiritual aberrations of religion in the West, it was as though he understood the secret truth behind it all—and that that made it okay to joke about the most serious and sacred of topics. Somehow, you always knew God would be laughing along with Joe.

As early as 1966 I was one of Joseph Campbell's devoted fans. After being assigned *The Hero With a Thousand Faces* for an undergraduate course in Jungian literary interpretation, I discovered my whole world view and spiritual attitude transformed. I was in Roman Catholic religious life at the time and the transformation had serious practical implications.

In the early 1970s, out of religious life, living in San Francisco, and pursuing a degree in comparative religion, I had an opportunity to hear Campbell in person. That opportunity blossomed into much more than attendance at a lecture. I got to know Joe personally and began a correspondence that continued sporadically over more than ten years.

The transformation Campbell's ideas produced and its consequences in my life were recounted in *The Myth of the Great Secret* and *In Search of God in the Sexual Underworld* (this revised edition of the former includes some of the most notably Campbellian portions of the latter). This recounting necessarily included episodes from my life. But this book is not properly an autobiography. I'm hardly important enough to warrant an autobiography. My life is important only as an example. For one has to have concrete examples. That's an important part of Campbell's notion of myth and religion, that inherited traditions provide us with symbols and metaphors for interpreting and enriching our individual lifestories. In fact, he titled one of his books *Myths To Live By*. Abstract, transcendental truths can only be told in terms of concrete, everyday examples, and the examples must not be mistaken for truths.

What has made my story interesting is how Campbell's wisdom helped me to face the very difficult religious crisis that confronts the modern world. Essential to that wisdom is the notion that each of us is a storyteller and it is in telling the story of our lives—even if only to ourselves—that we utilize the myths of religion and that we place ourselves in the divine context. This seems to be what religion is really all about.

This book weaves together metaphors—in the style of my teacher. These are the metaphors of my life, of course, but just as the metaphors of Joseph Campbell's life have inspired millions with awe and wonder, understanding and enjoyment, so I hope those of my life and my generation may also inspire in readers some wonder and enjoyment.

I'm pleased to report that Joe liked the original of this book. He wrote, "*The Myth of the Great Secret* is a jewel of a book. I have read it with deep fascination, enchanted not only by the graceful style . . . but also by the skill of your presentation, giving us your message at the start, in a prologue, and then illustrating it with increasing force, to the end, in a sort of narrative-and-expositional crescendo. And, of course, it was with very great pleasure for me to learn of my own contribution to your dark-forest adventure. The episode of the blank slide that time at the Mann Ranch! And I think the way you have put together all that we have been learning from each other in those meetings and encounters, up and down the state of California, is really wonderful. The book is the definitive chronicle of our 'Queste del Saint Graal' of the seventies." (The story of the blank slide—a joke Campbell played on me and on his audience—is told in Chapter 3.)

One of the issues that concerned Campbell more and more in the seventies and eighties was the question of "the new myth." His audiences began to ask him what would replace conventional theism now that science had undercut so many of its foundations. He always replied that one could no more predict a future myth than one could predict tonight's dream. Yet it seemed to me quite obvious that Campbell's own thought predicted what would be the new myth. And it's seemed quite obvious that the popularity of his thought has borne this out. That he didn't realize the implication of his own work seemed to be a blind spot in his understanding—a blind spot, by the way, probably indicative of the message in the episode of the blank slide . . .

Joe Campbell was a man. He had his successes and his failings, his strengths and his weaknesses. Other people may write about those. Though I knew him as a man, I was most interested in his thought and how his writings had affected my experience of my religious compulsions. This is what I've written about in my appreciation of Joseph Campbell.

That is not to say that Campbell's personal life was not important to his thought. That he was raised a Roman Catholic; that he was fascinated as a child with Native American lore; that he was a successful track runner in college; that he went to Europe in 1924 and met Krishnamurti on the boat; that he experienced the difficulties of the Great Depression and spent several years in Woodstock, New York, in seclusion studying; that he was invited to teach at Sarah Lawrence College; that he married Jean Erdman, an accomplished dancer; that he came under the tutelage of Heinrich Zimmer and studied Indian culture and religion; that he met Carl Jung and edited six volumes of the Eranos papers from the Jung Conferences at Bolligen; that in the 1970s he came to California to lecture; that he lived in the cultural and ethnic melting pot of New York City—all these were the events of his own lifestory. They influenced his personal experience and colored the wisdom he gleaned. But the wisdom to be learned from any person's lifestory is, hopefully, always greater than the sum of events.

What Campbell tells us in his prolific writings is that the events of our lives can make us heroes and teach us wisdom that arises from far beyond the individual, and that understanding life in this way can help us cope with the daunting difficulties and frustrations of daily life and, in fact, raise us into a realm beyond the everyday.

This is what Campbell meant when he said the great myths of the human past can open us to a heightened experience of being alive. And it is what he summarized in his now familiar dictum: "Follow your bliss." This means to pursue that which inspires one with a sense of wonder and connectedness, full of the rapture of life. It doesn't mean pursuing simple materialistic happiness or middle-class (even academic-class) fulfillment, though it may incidentally result in those. Bliss is a technical term in Buddhism, *ananda,* for being enraptured in enlightened wonder and living in harmony with truth and being. This doesn't mean being narcissistic in the sense of being concerned only with one's own happiness and satisfaction, though it does mean following one's own path and not looking to "what other people think" for the measure of one's success. It means paying attention to what life is telling one one ought to be doing, paying attention to the promptings of one's soul, to the urgings of compassion, and to one's sense of being part of the grand process of life.

Carl Jung identified the psychological themes in the religious and mythological traditions. He called these "archetypes." One of the archetypes was the "wise old man." It referred to the character in one's lifestory who teaches wisdom and points the way to discovery of the deep secrets of that grand process of life.

Joseph Campbell was for me—and, through his writings and lectures, for many—the "wise old man." He opened my eyes and pointed me toward my bliss. Through my lifestory, I've discovered how to gently leave behind the naive—and now discredited—religiousness of my youth and find wonder, meaning, and bliss in a new mythic consciousness.

I strongly believe Joseph Campbell is one of the instruments by which this new mythic consciousness is being born. It doesn't come from him. One might say it comes from the mind of the planet and he has been one of its voices—one that happened to get publicity because as an individual he happened to be at the right place at the right time and happened to have the personality to get noticed. One might also say that because he was following his bliss he was especially attuned to the urgings of that planetary mind.

◈

Joseph Campbell was by birth an Irish Catholic. That heritage helps to explain why laughter and storytelling were part of his intellectual explanation of things and part of his personal style. Joe loved to tell stories. He had a great voice and was constantly modulating his tone, demeanor, and vocal character. He made people laugh, even as he made them think. One such story succinctly summarizes the message of this present book. And it reveals the religious predicament of the modern day.

Campbell told that he'd been lecturing on mythology, explaining how the various religious traditions influenced one another, how certain doctrines developed, how the various gods around the world reflected one another, and how they and their followers differed from one another—the stuff of Campbell's lectures that's become so familiar to PBS viewers these days.

During the question and answer period, Campbell told, a rather stern woman stood up and explained that only one religion could be right and that all the others are therefore mere myths. "Mr. Campbell," she concluded, "I've been listening to you all night and . . . and . . . well, I think you're an atheist!"

"Madam," Joe said he replied, "anyone who believes in as many gods as I do can hardly be called an atheist."

That kind of not being an atheist is precisely what the new myth is about and it's the secret I learned from Joseph Campbell.

Intimations

Peace is at the heart of all because Avalokitesvara-
Kwannon, the mighty Bodhisattva, Boundless Love,
includes, regards, and dwells within (without
exception) every sentient being.
(The Hero With a Thousand Faces, *p. 160)*

Discovery comes less often from learning and thinking than from intuition. I was in graduate school in Theology on the way to the priesthood; I'd learned about the truths of Roman Catholic Christianity. I'd also studied C. G. Jung and Alan Watts and Joseph Campbell; I'd learned about the truths of the world's religions, especially Hinduism and Buddhism. I'd thought a lot about God. But once when I was living in the Servite Priory in southern California, I experienced intuition. Though it lasted only a moment, it has come to influence all my thinking since.

The monastery, house lore had it, was built during the 1920s by an ex-gangster who needed to disappear into the California desert where enemies would never find him. To gratify the whim of his wife, who had loved the Alhambra at Granada, he constructed a Moorish castle complete with moat, minaret, domes, and hanging gardens. After his death (of perfectly natural causes) the property, like so many other such odd estates, ended up in the hands of the Church, in this case, the Order of

Servants of Mary. To counter the Islamic influence, the Servites had erected a huge fountain depicting Our Lady's bodily assumption into heaven right in the middle of the hanging gardens. And to house some fifty novices and students they'd added two dormitory wings on the crest of the hill above the castle.

By the time I arrived at the castle it had been a seminary for years, but it still retained some of the original exotic flavor. The road into the property bridged an arroyo euphemistically referred to as "the moat," then dipped down to pass under an arcade which upheld a terrace over-looking the arroyo, and finally circled a rock-walled garden in front of the main entrance. From there a huge doorway led into a marbled an-techamber, up a few steps, and into the great hall, which the Servites were now using as a chapel. Lining both sides of the huge room were glass doors painted with brilliant icons depicting the Catholic sacra-mental system; on the right these opened onto the terrace above the moat and on the left, onto a central tiled court, where palm trees and tall cypresses shaded the Shrine of the Assumption and what was left of the gardens of cypresses, succulents, and cactuses.

It was no longer a hideaway. The sprawl of Los Angeles had reached all the way to the desert and surrounded the property. And there was no need for hiding anymore. Indeed, the seminary maintained a very visi-ble presence in the middle-class suburb of Riverside. We had a large crowd of followers and friends of the community. And we conducted very popular and well-attended liturgies on Sunday mornings. This was in 1969 when progressive Catholics were spiritually exhilarated by folk guitars and still expected that the Mass in the vernacular was going to make religion more relevant in their lives. It was after one such liturgy, toward the end of the first summer I lived there, that my life changed.

After Mass, I had gone back to prepare lunch for the community. Being pretty good at it and enjoying cooking, that summer I'd taken on responsibility for the kitchen duties. The room was a mess. The pre-vious night the arrival of visitors from the Midwest had inspired an im-promptu party. Now dirty dishes from the coffee-and-doughnut social following the morning Mass were piling up atop the remains of that party. To add to the confusion, during the evening one of the visitors had fallen against a lavatory in one of the upstairs rooms, knocking it off the wall. The pipes burst and rained water into the refectory adjoin-ing the kitchen. As part of the late-night repair, the water had been mopped up, but in the morning the floor was still dirty and streaked.

The Prior of the house, a gentle, saintly, and somewhat reclusive man named Father Peregrine Graffius, assumed the job of waxing and buffing the refectory floor. (I think he wanted to avoid all the hoopla surrounding the arrival of the visitors.) I set out to straighten up the kitchen and wash the dishes. It seemed like an endless chore. More dishes were being brought in from the after-Mass social than I could keep up with. And nobody was volunteering to help. I grew first angry, then philosophical, then despondent. The previous school year I'd been quite taken by the moral philosophy of Immanuel Kant with its insistence that for human actions to have moral significance they had to be done out of duty and not desire. Even before discovering Kant, I'd read Joseph Campbell's account of the Buddhist saint Avalokitesvara who overcame personal desire and saved the world by vowing to take upon himself the suffering of the world. Swept with zeal in the fervor of Campbell's words, I'd made the bodhisattva vow myself. And so that morning I'd kept reminding myself of my commitment to duty and to overcoming personal whim.

Just as I finished in the kitchen, the Prior came in and asked me to help him replace the tables in the refectory, then to put away the buffing machine for him. That would be my last chore. The house was quiet now. All the guests had left. The brothers, for whom it turned out I'd unnecessarily fixed lunch, had gone off with the visitors from the Midwest. All morning I'd been alternately cursing the makers of this mess and berating myself for not accepting my religious duty more gracefully. I was exhausted and emotionally drained.

I rolled the buffing machine out into the courtyard. It caught on a tile and the brush fell off. As I was replacing it, the machine slipped and fell on my fingers. Then, when I pushed open the door to the chapel, a pile of folding chairs that had been carelessly leaned up against the door frame crashed down, and the brush fell off the machine a second time. I stacked the chairs properly, reassembled the machine, and managed to get it through the door and down the aisle to the back closet where it was kept. I found there was no room in the closet because folding chairs there had also been stacked improperly and in order to get the machine inside the door I had to position it precariously on the edge of the brush. It slipped and fell on my fingers again.

I slammed the door to the closet. I almost screamed I was so angry. But then a curious peace descended upon me. As I started to walk back toward the front of the hall, I realized that despite my resistance I had been behaving correctly. I had indeed been doing my duty. And, I realized, that was how God would be acting in my spiritual life. I saw that all that had been happening that morning, including all my complaining and resisting and fussing, had been the instrument by which God was shaping and molding my spirit, by which I was being taught to accept things the way they are and not just the way my ego wanted them to be.

And then, in a flash, I saw that these events had not been the *instrument* of God, but had *been* God. And I knew in that moment that I was seeing the face of God. All my life, I had prayed to know what God looked like, to see the face of God. And I knew then that I'd always been seeing it, that I had always been in the presence of God because God had always been my present experience. The chapel turned to God all around and stretched out endlessly. The universe opened up to me. Everything was obvious. My sense of ego disappeared. There was only God and whatever was left of me, I realized, was also God and had always been God. I sank to my knees on the steps of the sanctuary, amazed that suddenly I seemed to be seeing the divine so clearly, and that it was all so simple.

It lasted only a moment. A quizzical voice inside my head asked if I was having a mystical experience. With that self-reflection, the walls of the room slammed back into place. I was me again, imprisoned in my ego. Shaken but elated, I staggered out of the chapel and across the courtyard. As I was ascending the walkway that led up to the novitiate wing, again for a moment the stairs turned into God bearing me up— as they had always been, but which I'd never understood.

❧

The experience can be explained away. It may have been simply the effect of coffee and doughnuts and stress and too much adrenaline decaying in my brain. And yet . . .

The experience changed my life. I have since then never quite doubted that life is the vision of God's face—though my measuring and evaluating ego continues to veil it from me—and that such a God is very different from the one I'd been taught about in catechism or that is preached about by television ministers or talked about in mainstream churches.

As I said, I'd been moved spiritually and intellectually by my reading

The Hero With a Thousand Faces a few years earlier. Joseph Campbell had explained to my satisfaction how the myths of the world's different religions are all metaphors for the qualities of God. He had inspired in me a fascination with the Buddhist myth of the bodhisattva Avaloki-tesava. He had sown seeds in me, I understood, for the realization of the meaning of that—and of all—myth. He had set me up for the discovery of a secret.

That is how I discovered that there is a Great Secret that is every-where hidden and everywhere revealed. Listen, let me tell you a secret . . .

CHAPTER ONE

Belief in Crisis

*. . . the democratic ideal of the self-determining
individual, the invention of the power-driven machine,
and the development of the scientific method of
research, have so transformed human life that the long-
inherited, timeless universe of symbols has collapsed. In
the fateful, epoch-announcing words of Nietzsche's
Zarathustra: "Dead are all the gods." (Hero, p. 387)*

We are all looking for something that will make our lives rich, interesting, and meaningful. Yet most of us have so lost touch with the search
that we wander aimlessly, feeling only an occasional restlessness which
reminds us that there ought to be more to life than there seems to be.

In the past, religion provided the belief systems and rituals that
helped individuals and communities understand experience and shape
decisions. Religion was the source of understanding in the face of ignorance, solace in the face of disaster, hope in the face of despair. Religion once guided the search, pointing to a reality that made human
lives significant and providing a language of symbols for expressing
how. But today religion has lost most of its power to move us. The underlying epistemology of religious belief has shifted. People are having
trouble believing as they did in the past. The discoveries of modern science and, more important, the attitude of scientific skepticism that has
penetrated every level of society have undermined religious faith.

As far back as 1949, when *The Hero With a Thousand Faces* was published, Campbell could observe the reality of Nietzsche's sad, but sobering, declaration cited in the epigraph above, which even made the cover of *Time Magazine* in the 1960s. In 1981, when *The Myth of the Great Secret* first appeared, I framed my presentation of the wisdom I learned from Campbell's approach in the crisis that seemed to be confronting religion. Ten years later that crisis is just as real. The question we have to ask—in the context of what we now know about religion and the religious traditions of all humankind—is whether this crisis tolls the death knell of spiritual wisdom or if it rings the announcement of a new spiritual consciousness: a consciousness shrouded in secrecy.

The truth we had all as children expected to support us seems to be slipping away, leaving us suspended in the void. There is a great need today for something solid to hold on to. The involvement of preachers and evangelists in the politics of the latter twentieth century indicates the yearning of many Americans for something to believe in. Unfortunately, this "moral majority," in its zeal, has too often overlooked the real roots of the religious crisis and blamed other people's immorality instead of their own lack of faith. Thus what has appeared on the upswing in these decades is not spirituality and faith but righteousness and religiosity. Yet how to increase church membership or which sectarian doctrines are right or wrong are not the serious questions in religion today.

Plato discovered long ago that the important philosophical questions are ethical, but that to understand ethics one must develop a metaphysics and to understand metaphysics one must develop an epistemology. In order to decide what to do, one must first know what is true. One must know what truth is. That is the issue of epistemology. And the epistemological stance of most Americans is too simple and too threatened to support an ethic that can deal with the complex questions of the modern world.

But perhaps there is something hauntingly significant about our epistemological vacuum. Perhaps, in order to find a resolution, we need simply to reverse our attitude toward our confusion. Perhaps what seems so to threaten belief is instead the condition in which insight can be achieved. Perhaps the crisis of religion can be the source of spiritual transformation. That has been a progression I have seen in my own life and this is why my story may be of some interest.

From unquestioning belief I moved into confusion and dismay as the religious tenets I held so dear seemed to conflict with the rational, sci-

entific principles I knew to be correct. My effort to be both a holy and
virtuous man and an intelligent, clear-minded thinker seemed doomed.
That confusion pushed me to grapple with the epistemological issues
that founded the problem. I saw that religion is only superficially concerned with doctrine and behavior and much more truly with spiritual
awareness. I glimpsed the mystical substratum on which belief rests and
saw that the confusion and sense of the emptiness of all truth need be a
source less of apostasy than of ecstasy.

And I saw that this awareness of a mystical reality—not unlike the
critiques of modern philosophy—points beyond itself and beyond its
gods to a deep stratum of consciousness, the experience of which for
many has been the fruit of the mystical quest. For even in religious language, this has sometimes been described as an experience of emptiness. Thus, paradoxically, the sense of emptiness and meaninglessness
which has resulted from the attenuation of faith brought about by the
scientific age appeared to be, with only a slight twist, the goal of religious experience. The twist, I discovered, is that where for modern humankind the experience of emptiness is frightening and demoralizing,
for religiouskind it has been metaphorized in ways that make it enlight-
ening and liberating.

෬

Today few of us feel enlightened or liberated. Few of us—though
there are a few—long for the embrace of the Void. Most of us instead
feel—perhaps a little as I did that exhausted afternoon at the castle—
helpless, powerless, and angry. All too often we feel the urge to throw
open our windows and shout the slogan from the movie *Network:* "I'm
mad as hell and I'm not going to take it anymore." But in fact we just
keep on taking it.

In spite of the thrilling embrace of democracy all around the world,
the political system of our own nation hardly seems responsive to the
public need. The economy is collapsing for reasons we cannot understand. Over and over again we hear our leaders confuse democracy and
freedom with capitalism. The political party that came into power in
1980 promising to bring prosperity and reduce the size and expense of
government has instead brought a dramatically increased national
debt, a terrible problem of homelessness, popular but expensive and
ecologically disastrous military adventuring, and the transfer of the sav-

ings of the middle and working classes into the hands of super-rich bankers and unscrupulous financiers. The gap between the rich and the poor is expanding.

Whipped up by a "war on drugs," crime and violence are ever increasing. Conservative forces that are dead-set against permitting adults to possess euphoria-producing drugs even in small amounts for their own use are just as dead-set against prohibiting even children from possessing weapons capable of killing whole crowds in a single burst. The leader of the free nations of the earth turns out to keep more citizens locked in prison for crimes against popular morals than any other country.

Both American presidents and the Roman pontiff of the 1980s have called for a return to a stability of economics, belief, and morality that seems only anachronistic. A new Christian fervor has been proclaimed, but its aims seemed more focused on cutting taxes for the rich and enforcing a middle-class way of life than on promoting Jesus's gospel of love and care for the downtrodden. The Church, which once taught irrefutable doctrine and offered answers to every troubling question, has now proved to be but one of many institutions proclaiming ideas that often seem in conflict with hard scientific knowledge and good sense. Modern social scientists have popularized the idea that the religious institutions are bureaucracies like other bureaucracies, governed by petty concerns that cannot claim divine authorization. A multitude of religions offer a variety of "right answers." There are too many gods clamoring for attention and demanding total conviction for thinking people to accept any of them seriously.

The amount of information about human psychological functioning, social dynamics, economic variables, metaphysical systems, political ideologies, spiritual paths, and mythic traditions that confronts the average person today is staggering. There is literally too much data to process into any sort of meaningful synthesis. This phenomenon has been called the "knowledge explosion." One of its consequences is the loss of a unifying framework within which to place or from which to retrieve information. Only computers are able to manage all the data, and, at least presently, they are incapable of creating paradigms that make the information intelligible.

Paradoxically, truth, once so sure and simple, has become ever more elusive and shifting as information has proliferated. Our world seems to be slipping out from under us. Life seems controlled by forces no one can quite determine. Truth evades us. The media seems to edit and shape the news to suit its own social and financial ends. People don't know if they can believe the reports on the six o'clock news or trust the editorial page of *The New York Times*. How can they deal with an encyclical from the Pope or a position paper by the National Council of Churches? Almost all of our unifying beliefs have been dismissed as "myths" by scientifically minded men committed to "objectivity" and reason. What has resulted is an epistemological malaise—confusion about the nature and meaning of truth and deep existential despair.

❧

Several developments are responsible for the modern predicament and the concomitant epistemological malaise. The first of these is simply progress. History has begun to move past us with dizzying speed. Only the knowledge explosion itself stands as a limit to technological development, and then only by promising a future miasma of inefficiency and confusion. Stimulated by the mass media, social change accelerates unprecedentedly. Schools of opinion arise, inspire believers, create political and cultural turmoil, and then evaporate as new ones replace them. "Isms" of every sort compete for political, social, economic, and intellectual influence. And everything seems to be happening faster than anyone can keep track of. Each day's news is guaranteed to report a new fad, a new medical breakthrough, a new scientific discovery, a new disaster, a new scandal, a new international crisis, a new solution to yesterday's crisis.

Indeed, scientific breakthrough and technological advance seem to create only new demands for more of the same to solve the problems they produce. The development of atomic power promises cheap energy but has produced only more expensive electricity, radioactive waste, and the threat of disastrous reactor meltdowns, made all too real by the Chernobyl explosion. Air transportation is fast and relatively inexpensive but squanders fuel and requires methods of controlling noise pollution and more and better safeguards as more lives are jeopardized by potential crashes, collisions, and terrorist attacks. The proliferation of automobiles promises personal freedom but has created traffic congestion, drunk driving and highway carnage, pollution, and urban sprawl, and threatens to rapidly exhaust fossil fuels. The space program has taken us to the moon and the planets but has filled the heavens with surveillance devices, debris to fall on our heads, and the potential for real star wars. Computer intelligence and microcircuitry make data processing possible on a vast scale but require ever more sophisticated efforts by individuals to protect their privacy. Television makes possible mass entertainment and immediate exposure to world events but threatens to produce passivity, illiteracy, and artificiality in our citizens. Universal vaccination and wonder drugs, like major tranquilizers and antibiotics, have alleviated mental illness and wiped out many human diseases, but have opened the way for chemical mind control to threaten freedom, overpopulation to raise the specter of mass starvation, cancer to emerge as a major killer, and mysterious diseases, like AIDS, to appear. Technology seems unable to recognize its own consequences. There seem always to be ever newer and bigger problems for society to deal with.

❧

Pure science at the "cutting edge" of knowledge has developed sophisticated philosophies and made epistemological distinctions between the "real plane" and the "construct plane," between "reality" and "paradigm." But, unfortunately, such perspectives have shaped the modern sensibility far less than a naively simple understanding of scientific method which can be called scientific literalism. This is the second development I suggest as responsible for the contemporary epistemological malaise.

Methods used in scientific investigation involve several pragmatically selected assumptions. They are: 1) that the only access to information is through the senses; 2) that accurate information must be verified by experimentation; 3) that for the purposes of experimentation, the number of variables to be considered can be reduced to a minimum; 4) that experiments must be replicable by any other experimenters; and 5) that experimentation verifies causal relationships among discrete variables.

Though useful for practical problem-solving, these assumptions, when generalized, suggest that the world is made up only of autonomously existing entities which are related in simple, mathematically describable ways and which can be isolated from one another and from their interrelationships. The reality implied by experimental method is one-dimensional, simple, and discrete; the only world view assumed to be reasonable is focused, objective, and causal. By the researchers in too many laboratories and by the man and woman on too many streets, these practical assumptions are unthinkingly taken as Truth.

As seen by the average person—whose reality is often a haphazardly constructed composite of high school science rendered out-of-date by the acceleration of progress, misunderstood news stories, and private extrapolation—the modern world appears a collection of concrete, lifeless, external objects, devoid of any "meaning" beyond blind obedience to mechanistic scientific principles.

There has been serious criticism of both the nature of scientific method and the focus of scientific research. Philosophers, inside as well as outside the scientific community, have suggested that experimentation only verifies its own original assumptions. Niels Bohr's Principle of Complementarity and Werner Heisenberg's Uncertainty Principle recognize that the observer can never be divorced from the phenomena under observation, because the choice of perspective and the technique of observation affect the phenomena.

An old Sufi parable illustrates part of the problem. It tells of a drunk late at night searching the ground around the base of a lamp post. A passerby stops and offers to help. The drunk explains he has lost the key to his house and asks the passerby to join in the search. But after a momentary look around, seeing that there is no key near the lamp post, the passerby asks, "Are you sure you dropped it here?" "Oh no," says the drunk. "I dropped it down the street a ways, but it's too dark down there to see it, so I came up here to look where the light is better." The rational investigation of common sense reality may well be like that drunk's. The answers sought may lie out in the dark, in elusive, nonrational, or socially unpopular phenomena, not in the easily investigated light.

"New paradigm" philosophers and critics of science, like Joseph Chilton Pearce and Theodore Roszak in the 1970s, suggested that the universe is in itself amorphous and shaped by human consciousness. New paradigm scientists, like Rupert Sheldrake, suggest that the world is alive and the shape of the world is determined by psychically and behaviorally influenced fields that change with repetition. Thus the focusing, intentionality, and replication involved in scientific experimentation perhaps alters the nature of reality itself and so guarantees the success of the method.

At any rate, often the focus of research is determined less by a will to discover truth than to meet the economic needs of modern society. There is no such thing as pure research. Scientific investigation requires vast amounts of money. That money comes from business, from government, or from foundations funded by business. And it is available only after carefully prepared research proposals are submitted to and approved by committees well aware of the sources of this money. Technology necessarily focuses on the economic needs of the society that hosts it, and, like any good guest, it seldom insults its host.

While some of this questioning has filtered down to the populace, it has only exacerbated the modern malaise. Some wise scientists may understand that they are working only to expand the area of light beneath the lamp post and that their explanations of reality may never be complete and will never be absolute. But ordinary citizens have not been able to keep up with the great paradigm shifts that have accompanied progress. Most people today are still dealing with the issues that were current when scientific method was first developing.

In a sense, many people are still dealing with Galileo's trial. Rather than understanding the acute dilemma in which the Inquisitors found themselves, they tend to condemn the Roman Church as venal, pigheaded, and totalitarian for having questioned Galileo's observations through his telescope. They fail to see that the issue was not whether Venus had phases and the earth orbited the sun, but whether truth was determined by revelation or by observation; whether the accesses to truth ought to be controlled by anointed guardians who would provide only the information necessary for salvation or be opened willy-nilly to anyone who claimed to have performed a successful experiment. Revelation had given purpose to humankind's place in the universal process and indicated the existence of level upon level of reality and richness beyond the surface of the world. Observation showed the world only a surface that seemed to have little purpose but obedience to the principles of physics. The real question was whether life would be better lived if there were only One Revealed Truth or many.

Even today the skeptical public tends to imagine the theologians desperately clinging to power, fearing that the new science will undermine their control of the masses. They fail to see the parallel between Albert Einstein and other morally inspired scientists asking Franklin Roosevelt not to continue the Manhattan Project and the Church asking Galileo not to publish. Certainly the post-Galilean shift in focus and priority from the spiritual world, shaped by revelation and tradition, to the physical world, verified by empirical, sensory evidence, was as significant a turning point in history as the development of nuclear weaponry.

We have sided with Galileo. That choice has resulted in enormous progress and technological invention. We have leisure and material abundance today that prescientific men and women could never even have dreamed of. But in rejecting the traditional, authoritative, "divinely inspired" arbiters of truth, we have also brought upon ourselves the modern predicament. We are barraged with data and diverse frameworks of interpretation. No one can tell us what we should or shouldn't believe. To alleviate the strain on our faculties and to cope with the immensely complex world around us, we are forced to become reductionists.

And yet that is no solution at all. For the strain and complexity are inescapable. This is the third factor that feeds the contemporary malaise. In its most positive form it is the acceptance of pluralism, the recognition that many expressions of truth stand side by side. In its negative and troubling form it is the confusion born of a multitude of conflicting world views, a loss of orthodoxy, and the triumph of heterodoxy.

Throughout history different belief systems have existed side by side, but leaders in each culture have worked hard to keep orthodox teaching pure. Most of the commandments in the Bible—from the dietary laws of kosher to condemnations of homosexuality—were originally designed to prevent syncretism and to protect Judaism from the encroachment of unorthodox religious beliefs and practices. What the gentiles practiced as religious acts, the Jews condemned as abominations in order to keep Jewish culture separate from gentile.

Despite efforts to ensure orthodoxy, the feared influences of foreign ideas did occur. Merchants and travelers carried their myths and transported their gods along major trade routes. At least some of the similarities between popular legends and mythological systems around the world can be explained by the spread of stories from one culture to another. In recent times, the spread and reach of cultural diffusion has expanded as never before. Modern communications and transportation have made every place and every idea accessible. The world that was once made up of tiny, sometimes isolated cultures has become, in Marshall McLuhan's words, a "global village."

A major manifestation of this has been the spread of once regionally limited religious and philosophical systems. There are now probably as many Hindu and Buddhist missionaries in the West as there are Christian missionaries in the East. The sacred texts of all the religions, plus books on every social and political philosophy, are available in most bookstores. Universities in America, in the interest of freedom of thought, teach philosophy or religious studies survey courses that present no particular doctrine or explanation as correct. One consequence of this has been general familiarity with ideas that would once have been alien. Another has been that the plurality of answers causes questioning of the very notion of truth. It seems that everything is true and nothing is true.

For a polytheistic religion that has always recognized a plurality of gods and devotions, like Hinduism, this presents no great problem. But for the monotheistic religions of the West, like Christianity and Islam, pluralism poses a major challenge. And for the West, so long nurtured by monotheism, the triumph of heterodoxy, inconsistent with naive realism, demands a major shift in metaphysics and epistemology.

The concomitant of heterodoxy is relativism, the fourth factor of the epistemological malaise. Relativism—and its 1990s cultural spin-off multi-culturalism—suggests that there is a plurality of expressions of truth because truth looks different from different perspectives. But this is in direct conflict with the experimental requirements of objectivity and replicability. It suggests that even sensory data may not be consistent from time to time, place to place, and person to person. To recognize the relativity of truth is to recognize the interdependence of all phenomena. Nothing remains as a standard against which all else can be judged.

The ancient Greek Archimedes, who described the mechanics of leverage, said that given a place to stand and a point to use as fulcrum he could move the world. The search for the absolute space—which could provide such a fulcrum—against which all motion could be measured was an obsession of classical physics. Newton believed he could prove it is possible to determine motion relative to the fixed stars, independent of any observer, with his famous spinning bucket. He declared that the tendency of water to rise up the sides of a bucket suspended from an untwisting rope (due to centrifugal force impelling the water outward as the torque from the rope spins the bucket) shows that the bucket is spinning in relation to absolute space regardless of the motion of the observer. An observer rapidly circling a stationary bucket would see the same apparent motion of the bucket, but would not see the water rise up the sides. The movement of the water proved to Newton the existence of an Archimedian point of view from which to know the world.

Two hundred years later, Einstein argued there is no justification for positing an absolute space. He explained the rise of the water as the result of gravitational drag caused by the spinning of the universe around the bucket as much as by the bucket spinning within the universe. Einstein maintained that *all* motion is relative. The only constant, he said, is the speed of light—the speed of exchange of information—and it remains constant only because motion so distorts space around it that the factors of distance and time, by which velocity is calculated, change. Measuring sticks shrink slightly in the direction of motion. Time gradually slows as speed increases.

Einstein's hypothesis holds that the presence of activity in space distorts space around it. That is to say that the universe looks different from every point of view because each point of view distorts its own immediate vicinity. In a relativistic perspective, the same is true of facts. Each fact seems to influence other facts around it. There is no absolute truth against which all facts can be evaluated, for there is no absolute vantage point from which to view the interrelation of facts. No Archimedian point is possible. Hence relativism and pluralism have undone the notion of a single, knowable truth. Truth appears different from every vantage point, and each person's life gives him or her a unique vantage.

꩜

The modern predicament, then, is characterized by a desperate need to find something definite in a flood of information and by a malaise brought on by the suspicion it can never be found. Investigation has revealed that the rock upon which the world is founded is, after all, only sand, and the sand seems to be washing away with each new wave of scientific discovery or cultural exchange. Perhaps the universe appears, in Sir James Jeans's phrase, more like a great thought than a great machine; yet that thought seems so complex that no mind can grasp it. With no possible perspective from which to view it and no mind outside it to conceive it, this great thought appears to pull itself into existence by its own bootstraps, hanging over the abyss.

What we are left with is a sense of nothingness, of the arbitrariness and changeability of truth, of the emptiness of the universe.

CHAPTER TWO

Emptiness, Peregrination, and the Spirit of Mendicancy

. . . whether small or great, and no matter what the stage or grade of life, the call rings up the curtain, always, on a mystery of transfiguration—a rite, or moment, of spiritual passage, which, when complete, amounts to a dying and a birth. The familiar life horizon has been outgrown; the old concepts, ideals, and emotional patterns no longer fit; the time for the passing of a threshold is at hand. (Hero, p. 51)

The ability of the mind to turn back upon itself has been cherished as the conscious reflection that makes human beings different from other forms of life on Earth. But this ability is, in part, responsible for so much of the confusion that has been wrought in our systems of belief today. Modern thought has so challenged its own sources that it has stripped them of truth. We observe that most every explanation of phenomena believed in the past has been supplanted by a better explanation. We are able to enter into infinite regressions of questions questioning questions, denials denying denials.

Bertrand Russell, father of set theory, made famous the problem of how to catalogue a library, asking if the catalogue of books itself belongs in the library. Then logically there should be yet another catalogue that contains all the books plus the catalogue of the books. But then does this metacatalogue belong in the library? These discussions gave rise to a whole series of philosophical questions in mathematical theory about whether knowledge can ever be complete. Kurt Gödel is credited with the theorem arguing that there can never be a complete set of mathematical theorems because the final theorem—that the set is now complete—wouldn't fit in the set (like the catalogue of the library). In the early 1980s, Douglas Hofstadter popularized this kind of thinking about thinking in the bestselling *Gödel, Escher, Bach: An Eternal Golden Braid*. (This modern fascination with self-referential, recursive thinking has shown up in the arts in so-called postmodernism.)

The familiar example of the problem of self-referential statements is the sentence: "This statement is false." If the statement is true, then it's false. If the statement is false, then it's true. The only way to make sense of such a statement is to move up a level to a metastatement observing the problem of self-reference. While the example seems mere sophistry, the problem really has profound philosophical implications. And these manifest the problem of modern consciousness's ability to be conscious of itself.

While this has become a problem of modern times, it's actually quite an ancient phenomenon. Those Hindu and Buddhist icons and statues of gods and buddhas with multiple heads layered one upon another are depictions of the experience in meditation of watching oneself watching oneself watching oneself ad infinitum. That these depictions show up in such a context indicates the religious implications of such questioning. There was, for example, a time when many of us were satisfied with the argument that the Bible must be the true revealed Word of God since it says so right there in the Bible and the Word of God can't lie. But as soon as we got sophisticated enough to understand self-referential statements, that polemic might have begun to seem as strong an argument against the literal truth of the Bible as it had previously been in support of it. We were forced up a level to a metaquestion.

A sense of emptiness arises from such questioning of the explanations of reality that we have traditionally held. For they force us to suspect, at least, that the explanations, especially religious explanations, are merely images, fairy tales that satisfy specific needs but that possess of themselves no real truth.

This questioning has been done in the past not only by the opponents of religion but, as well, by religious mystics and visionaries. These were men and women not satisfied with the simple, superficial beliefs of their families and neighbors. Fascinated with what seemed to lie behind conventional religious teaching, they sought some direct experience of Truth and of God instead of mere images. They might have said that

God had called to them from behind the stories and images that those around them accepted complacently as Truth.

Some of these seekers then tried to explain how their experiences of God were different from what they had been taught and how the images had both helped and hindered their mystical quest. Some, trying to cut through the use of myths and images altogether, used words like "emptiness," "nothingness," and "the Void" to describe their experience of the Ultimate. Thus some of the most famous religious figures sounded very much like modern skeptics who declare that the myths of religion are false, that the gods do not exist, and that Ultimate Truth is empty—if only because it seems to go on forever.

❧

I was born in San Antonio in early August 1945, at a time when history was being changed forever by the detonation of the bomb at Hiroshima. I grew up fascinated by the power of the atom and aware of the coincidence of my birth and the birth of the atomic age. My parents, whose stories of our family dramatized the fact of that coincidence, cared deeply for their two sons. I was the older, in some ways special to my mother, for she had lost infants in childbirth before I was born successfully by cesarean section. She attributed that success not only to the intelligence of the obstetrician who recommended the cesarean, but also to the intercession of the Blessed Mother, to whom she had prayed the rosary each night. My mother, an intelligent woman and herself a kind of mystic, taught me to feel a debt to the Divine Mother. My father, a hardworking and competent businessman, taught me to be competent also, to know how to think through problems and to handle the day-to-day tasks of life simply and efficiently.

As a child, I was fascinated by the phenomenon of the Pet Milk can. The label of the can showed a can of Pet Milk with a label on the can showing a can of Pet Milk. And on and on. As a teenager, I became deeply intrigued by the idea of emptiness and infinity such self-referential recursion implied. The emptiness appeared to me appealing and promising, even as it seemed stark and frightening. I think it sparked in me something similar to the sense of grandeur and alluring mystery that I'd discovered reading science fiction stories of exploration into deep space, to strange worlds where the rules of terrestrial life did not apply, where mystery and adventure lurked, where beauty stalked forlorn landscapes, transfiguring the peaks of alien mountains. In the stories of strange worlds and even stranger life-forms and disembodied intelligences, I experienced the same sense of the sacred and the wonderful that, I suspect, ancient and medieval peoples must have experienced in the tales of the gods and the stories of the saints, recounted by shamans or depicted in mosaics of stained glass.

☙

I was blessed with a mother who read to me and taught me to love reading and with a teacher who showed me how to write and taught me to think of myself as a writer. The year after I turned fourteen my father died, ending my childhood and leaving me suddenly aware of mortality and of the responsibilities of adulthood. Also that year, beginning my discovery of the life beyond childhood, I entered high school, where I met the Brothers of the Society of Mary whom I would join, on my birthday four years later. During those four years I came under the influence of Brother Martin McMurtrey, the man who, through a three-year course in expository writing, taught me the significance of metaphor, symbol, foreshadowing, and allusion. From Brother Mac I learned to express thought rationally and linearly, and yet also to invest it with complex levels of meaning conveyed through subtle references and interconnections of images. Thus I began to see the world as made up of the interweaving of intricate patterns and leitmotifs.

My reading, especially of science fiction and the actual science that founded it, taught me a sense of wonder and appreciation of life on levels beyond the mundane and trivial. It called upon imagination to force open the horizons of mind, to believe in orders of reality quite beyond the world of the immediate senses. It suggested that there were secrets about the universe that, if discovered, would tie together and explain the events of life and that these secrets existed on other levels or dimensions of reality than we could see with the naked senses.

That reading gave me a trust in scientific curiosity to seek the multiple levels of existence I had glimpsed. I knew that rationality and common sense and experimentation and investigation could figure things out. But, even then, I knew enough about Einstein to know that for these methods of science to work, one had to have a broad enough model to include all phenomena. And that meant moving up to a higher level of reality.

Religion and science both seemed to be about achieving a more expansive model of what's real. My upbringing in a good and religious
home taught me a respect for knowledge and wisdom and for the moral
and mythical tradition of Roman Christianity. Education in the Catholic school system inculcated a disdain for literal, fundamentalist, anti-
intellectual religious thinking. Catholic education, after all, is good,
intelligent, solid education. Yet Catholic education taught a curiously
realistic approach to divine reality that somehow didn't jibe with solid
scientific reality. Indeed, there seemed to be in the Church a stubborn-
ness and a refusal to examine basic metaphysical and epistemological
assumptions. Once for a high school religion course I wrote a paper interpreting the doctrine of the Trinity in terms of Einstein's theory of
multidimensional space. Of course, in ways it must have been sopho-
moric, but it was also daring and inventive. Yet for my efforts I was kept
after and sent to the school chaplain to be counseled in orthodoxy.

෴

As I would learn a few years later from Joseph Campbell, the spiritual
life is aptly metaphorized as a journey. The journey begins with a call.
In religion I sensed a call to a vision of the universe that piqued my sense
of wonder. After all, if I could not pilot a spaceship to Mars or be a mis-
sionary to a planet of Aldebaran, perhaps I could learn to walk the
heavens with God and find other stars—more bright and splendid. God
was the only image I knew that seemed a worthy goal. And the only God
I knew at the time was that of the Roman Church.

Pursuing that goal by entering the Catholic religious order that
taught at my high school, a group of Brothers called the Marianists,
meant leaving home, entering the world, and journeying far away, from
Texas to Wisconsin. That journey began in earnest the day my best
friend throughout high school, Larry Goodwin, left for novitiate with
an order called the Passionists. We had together made the decision to
enter religious life, though we had chosen different directions in which
to go. It was still a month before I was to leave myself. But Larry's departure certainly signaled the beginning of this new phase of my own
life.

Already my adolescent religiousness—and the lessons from Brother
McMurtrey about literary technique—had me finding "meaningful coincidences" and messages from God in daily events. I had, after all, been

raised in the magical-mystical world in which making the Nine First Fridays guaranteed the grace of a happy death and in which the Blessed Virgin Mary routinely appeared to children and wrought miracles in the sky: a few coincidences were nothing for God to arrange. Years later I would learn to call those perceptions of meaning "synchronicities" and to explain them as hints from the deep unconscious of psychodynamic and spiritual verities. As a Catholic teenager, though, I was happy to accept unquestioningly the signs God sometimes seemed to vouchsafe graciously.

The local radio station to which, as a teenager, I listened religiously (pun intended) was running a contest. Each day they announced a "secret word." The listener who caught the word when the disc jockey used it later could win a prize. The day Larry was leaving the secret word was "peregrination." I knew what this obscure word meant because I'd come across it in a classic science fiction novel, *A Canticle for Leibowitz,* in which the word was used in a recurring technical way to refer to a group of monks who leave Earth by spaceship as futuristic missionaries to carry human wisdom to the stars.

We were not exactly going to the stars, but I knew that on that day both of us were beginning a long peregrination.

&

The first year of religious life is novitiate, a year of monastic training outside the formal educational system. It is focused on spiritual development and initiation into the styles and lore of religious life. For that year I lived on a farm in the Mississippi River bluffs of Wisconsin, a life wonderfully monastic, prayerful, and peaceful.

We rose early to spend a couple of hours at prayer before breakfast and housework chores each day. During the morning we attended classes in theology, prayer, and asceticism (the practice of religious discipline). After lunch we played soccer or softball for an hour or two and then worked around the property, picking apples in the orchard, bringing in bales of hay from the fields, clearing brush, doing laundry, preparing dinner. The late afternoon was taken up with spiritual reading and prayer. The recitation of the rosary was followed by dinner. Most of our meals were eaten in silence while one of the novices read to us. Over breakfast we were usually read the life of some saintly character; over lunch, news and social commentary; over dinner, a religious but

often entertaining novel. To celebrate special occasions the rule of silence was dispensed and we were allowed to talk.

And at any rate, every evening after dinner we'd always have an hour
or two of recreation when we could do as we wanted and talk as we
pleased. (Usually every week or two we'd get an all-day recreation to go
on an outing, climb a mountain, swim in the Mississippi, or ice-skate
on the lake near town.) After recreation the evening generally consisted
of meditation, study period, night prayers, and bed. Except during the
recreation periods, we were supposed to maintain silence and at night
we were bound under a strict "grand silence," which was not to be bro-
ken for any but the most extreme emergency.

Our nights were quiet. The presence of God hung over the house,
bearing us into solitary sleep and away into our dreams. I especially
liked the nights. I remember lying in bed watching the clouds blowing
over the river-worn bluffs across the valley from the novitiate. I cherished the solitude of that time. During the day we had very little time
alone. Despite the silence, we were together, the thirty-some novices
and about six faculty, almost all the time. We grew very close to one
another that year.

The Novicemaster, Father Pieper, was a wonderful old man with the
quick mind and mentality of a rebellious teenager. He taught us to cherish the styles and rules of religion and monastic life not out of fear of
punishment but out of personal responsibility. And he introduced us to
some of the most avant-garde ideas in modern biblical scholarship. He
taught us that the Scriptures had to be interpreted in the context of their
own times and according to the genres and literary forms in which they
were written. It may seem obvious in an English literature class that
poems should be studied as poetry, novels as fiction, and literary criticism as expository prose, but that's not how the literature of the Bible
has traditionally been studied: the poetry, fiction, cultural commentary,
theater, history, and legalities have all been lumped together and treated
as though they were all alike with the same subject matter and same
rules of interpretation.

Father Pieper's presentation of modern Scriptural exegesis, for instance, showed that the Book of Job was a Hebrew attempt at a Greek
tragedy; Job was no more historical than Oedipus, though, like Oedipus, a kind of Everyman dealing with important human issues. This
"form criticism," as it was called, revealed that many of the stories in
the life of Jesus were recounted in an ancient Hebrew allegorical style

called *midrash* which applied traditional cultural symbols to current events in order to place the events in a larger context. The visit of the Wise Men to the Infant Jesus was a prime example. According to modern scholarship, the story of the Magi was never intended to describe an historical event; it wasn't written in the literary form of an historical account. It was an allegory about the universality of Jesus's wisdom which his followers would later recognize applied not only to Israeli Jews but to Greeks and Persians and Egyptians. Indeed, the gospels themselves were epic poetry more concerned with meaning than with news reporting. These were heady thoughts, radical discoveries for eighteen-year-old boys.

I was house librarian, recataloguing a library of devotional literature of several thousand volumes. (At the time, I wasn't yet worried about whether the catalogue of the library belonged in the library.) I was able to spend long hours, in the dead of the starkly beautiful Wisconsin winter, reading and studying the books. I discovered a God much grander and more worthy of interest than the moralistic and doctrinaire God I'd learned about in catechism. I discovered the mystics. I discovered the appeal of the divine wilderness, where no one is at home save God. And it was not unlike the wilderness of stars that I had for so long yearned to traverse.

I read Saint John of the Cross. I fancied myself a disciple and fellow traveler of Thomas Merton, the 1930s communist-radical turned Trappist monk and social commentator who'd become a spokesman of American Catholicism after his spiritual autobiography, *The Seven Storey Mountain,* was chosen by the Book of the Month Club. I even discovered the then-suspect writings of Pierre Teilhard de Chardin, the Jesuit paleontologist who'd been silenced by the Church for his mystical interpretation of biological evolution.

I considered myself progressive and open-minded, willing to deal with the problems of religion in the modern world. In my studies I'd come across an admonition that theologians working to make religious thought contemporary had to be "radical," that is, they had to investigate basic assumptions and not merely restate old formulae in new guises. That is, they had to look at the roots. And it was the mystics and visionaries who had personal contact with the divine reality that they sometimes spoke of as God who seemed to have done just that radical investigation.

My second year, now a freshman in one of the colleges run by the Order and a physics major, I was much less interested in dogmatics (except as a kind of rational exercise rather like the mathematics at which, as a budding scientist, I was becoming proficient) than I was in mystical theology. I was something of a troublemaker. I was one of what priest-sociologist-novelist Andrew Greeley was then calling "the new breed" of religious. I believed taking personal responsibility for our lives was more important than blindly obeying regulations. I objected to the way rules were enforced. I was convinced that in our superiors we needed not disciplinarians but spiritual leaders who would inspire us to pursue the spiritual life in new, self-motivated ways.

Years later I learned that my Marianist superiors had been alarmed by a paper I'd written discussing the mystical meaning of those relatively familiar words in Saint Paul's Epistle to the Philippians: "Let this mind be in you which was also in Christ Jesus, who, though he was by nature God, did not think Godhood something to be clung to miserly but emptied himself, becoming a servant and being in the body of a man like us. He humbled himself, becoming obedient, obedient even unto death, even unto death on a cross" (Phil. 2: 5–8). I'd seen that as an exhortation to each person to empty themselves, to give up Godhood for incarnation, to honor the body, to accept suffering, and to affirm life. I think the superiors sensed both an unorthodox mystical tendency and a taint of sexuality in my interpretation.

Even more years later, when I first watched the Power of Myth videos and honored the memory of the man who'd become my teacher and inspiration, I was elated to hear him quote those very words and to interpret them as an invitation to come into the world and accept the suffering inherent in being alive and to affirm life.

After two years of religious life, I was told to leave the Order. The Brothers were basically high school teachers, I was counseled—intelligent men in their teaching fields, good men but, by and large, not mystics, simple men whose religious faith was already being shaken by the turmoil in the Church. They didn't need me with my rabble-rousing and my odd mystical fascination. I wouldn't really be satisfied with them, said one of my superiors, a wise and astute counselor. It's providential, assured my spiritual director, a man with a most appropriate name: Father Search.

I left the Society of Mary in 1965 and transferred to Saint Louis University in St. Louis, Missouri. While the school was run by the Jesuit Fathers and steeped in Catholic tradition, it was there I was exposed to ideas that began to challenge my Catholicism. In the class on Jungian literary interpretation, I discovered Joseph Campbell's brand of comparative religion.

The professor had given us a list of reading he proposed we do over the summer in preparation. The first book I found was *The Hero With a Thousand Faces*. I struggled through that beautifully written, but very dense and difficult book, dealing with ideas quite new to me. The basic theme spoke directly to my already established notion of the spiritual life as a peregrination. I was fascinated to discover that this notion was not only deeply established in my own Western tradition, but had correlates around the world. All of a sudden Hinduism and Buddhism seemed to me not "pagan religions" but carriers of mystical truth. I was amazed at the way Campbell recounted the various religious myths in terms of each other. I saw that they seemed more like different languages for similar ideas than competing systems of indoctrination.

I remember being literally "blown away" by the chapter titled "Apotheosis." The word means "to become God" and that was the goal my mystical leanings had taught me a few years before and that was the goal Campbell said was the high point of the hero's journey. It is in this chapter that Campbell tells the story of the bodhisattva Avalokitesvara and tells of the three wonders of the bodhisattva.

The first wonder is the androgynous character of the bodhisattva. "Male-female gods are not uncommon in the world of myth. They emerge always with a certain mystery; for they conduct the mind beyond objective experience into a symbolic realm where duality is left behind," wrote Campbell (*Hero*, p. 152). The second wonder is that he/she perceives that time and eternity are one. The bodhisattva myth annihilates the distinction between life and release-from-life. And the third wonder is that these two wonders are the same. That is, that the key to achieving apotheosis is to overcome polarity and to see that this is eternity here and now.

I was dumbstruck. The story of Avalokitesvara choosing to give up nirvana in order to save others moved me to the quick. It seemed to resonate with my Christian upbringing. And it seemed to remind me of transpersonal memories of making that vow myself in some other kind of lifetime. And, of course, the myth explained that memory, for it suggested that indeed the life in me was the bodhisattva for the bodhisattva has taken on all lives. That memory, then, was a kind of direct experience of my oneness with Avalokitesvara, the god to whom "go the millionfold repeated prayers of the prayerwheels and temple gongs of Tibet. To him go perhaps more prayers per minute than to any single divinity known to man" (*Hero,* p. 150). He is the ultimate god. Reading the chapter had indeed produced in me an apotheosis. The myth had worked.

I suppose it was partly because of the intensity of that intuition that I became a "follower" of Campbell's. Something in what he wrote rang true in me. I can see, of course, that it was his affirmation of life, his announcement that things are great just the way they are. That intuition produced in me an experience of bliss and, in Joe's dictum, I was following my bliss by understanding the world of religion—which was such a major issue in my life—in his way.

And I think that myth spoke directly to me because there's something in that myth that is especially appropriate for modern humankind, in spite of its antiquity, and I'll come back to this myth at length later.

The story of Avalokitesvara brought together my deeply Christian sentiments about self-sacrifice and my thoroughly modern enthusiasm for the adventure of the world. In short, by being willing to sacrifice himself for the sake of saving the world, Avalokitesvara discovered that the world became divinized. As he vowed to give up entry into nirvana, good Buddhist though he was, and to take on himself the sorrows of all sentient beings, he was transformed. And the world was transformed. As he said yes to the world with all its inherent suffering, he realized he somehow was the world and had no need to flee into nirvana. Indeed, he discovered that there was no difference between the world and nirvana. In Christian terms, he saw that "the Kingdom of God is within you."

During my first year at Saint Louis University, along with a number of other students, I began to regularly attend "folk masses." During those years the Roman Church was just beginning to loosen its restrictions on the form of liturgical services. A certain amount of experimentation was being allowed, and these liturgies seemed to be experimenting just the other side of the tolerated limits. The folk masses, held in a remodeled dining room of an old hotel the University had taken over, were conducted by a religious order called the Servites who, I was pleased to discover, appeared to embrace the kind of progressive, radical thinking I had been calling for—and gotten in trouble on account of—with the Marianists.

I was strongly drawn to them. I knew I wanted to be a Servite, but I'd only recently been expelled from one religious order, and it seemed precipitous to join another. And while I did make inquiries and exhibit interest in joining, I did not make a real decision until one day in May of the second year I'd known them.

It had been a particularly intense day. I had been thinking about the story of the bodhisattva who embraces all human experience and says yes to life. I was trying to understand just what I was called to, how I was to say yes to life, how I, like a bodhisattva, could embrace life with all its sorrows and all its joys. I felt that I had to remain open to whatever came to me, taking from my experience whatever clues I could find to point out the way to me. I felt like a wanderer, in some ways lost, yet with all the road signs before me if only I could see to read them. I was trying to understand where next my peregrination would lead me. I felt I had made my decision to say yes, but I still did not know what proposition I was agreeing to. I wanted to see the road signs on my path.

As late afternoon came, it was time for the Servite Mass. That was always a joyful occasion and I was looking forward to it. My commitment to say yes to life and to herohood had left me feeling more anxiety than joy about my future. Before Mass one of the Servite students, a young man named Allan Pinka, taught us a folk song to sing during the liturgy. The song was Richard Fariña's "Pack Up Your Sorrows." As I listened to the words we sang I realized the song was about the bodhisattva vocation: "If somehow you could pack up your sorrows and give them all to me, you would lose them, I know how to use them; Give them all to me." The verses spoke of the emptiness of the universe around us, of the burden of life, and that refrain spoke of the vision that could take that sorrow and transform it.

Allan explained that the song had been chosen because it was a special day for the Servites, the feast of one of their own members who had been canonized a saint. This Servite, he explained, had been a Florentine playboy until he was stricken with melanoma in his left leg. He prayed fiercely that the cancer would be healed and that he would not lose the limb. In his fervor he promised, not unlike Martin Luther during the lightning storm, to join the fledgling Servite Order that was growing in Florence at the time. Fatigued from his entreaties, he finally fell asleep. When he awoke, the cancerous lesion was gone. He joined the Order and, maintaining the zeal of his conversion, labored among the poor and suffering, taking their sorrow and transforming it. Thus this modern folk song, which spoke of the lonely pilgrimage through life, seemed an appropriate way to commemorate this man. His name, which typified the mendicant spirituality of the Order, was Peregrine Laziosi.

Well, Saint Peregrine was a Servite.

That day, in the coincidental coming together of patterns, I saw clearly the next step of my peregrinations. What was on the surface a mere happenstance of words inspired me with decision. The next school year I moved in with the Servites and the summer after was invested with the habit of the Order and took for myself, as my patronymic in religious life, the name Peregrine. (By the time I joined the Servites most of the men had stopped using religious names and had gone back to their baptismal names. In fact, I'd never used my baptismal name, Edwin, but all my life had gone by "Toby," an affectionate name my parents had begun calling me even before I was born. I never used Peregrine as an actual appellation, but certainly in my heart, and between me and God, I knew I was Peregrine.)

&

My interest in the Servites was founded on more than just that coincidence, of course. I, like so many of my generation in the late 1960s, was questioning the values of our society. The war that so affected all of us in those days seemed to be rooted in a materialist economy that appeared to have pushed the nation into actions inconsistent with the American spirit of freedom and tolerance. And my experience with the Society of Mary had already taught me to value religious poverty as an antidote to materialism.

Poverty seemed intrinsic to the challenge of conventional values posed by religious life. Religious poverty means living simply, consuming as little as possible, sharing what you have with others and accepting their sharing with you, and thereby being freed from the constant struggle to accumulate things. It has always been an essential element in religious life in the West. The first Christian religious were anchorites who went to live in the desert countryside of the Near East and northern Africa. Long before Christianity, of course, there had been anchorites.

In India, yogis had lived in caves or groves or had sat in meditation atop piles of rock since before recorded history. What all these early religious shared was the choice of simplicity and voluntary frugality.

Many of these ascetics, in both East and West, for whatever reasons they chose their style of living, achieved altered states of consciousness through their poverty and renunciation. Perhaps some of them just went crazy from listening to the wailing of the wind, night after night, blowing across the opening of their cave. But others saw beyond the surface of experience to a divine reality which they were able to communicate to students and disciples. They were revered as saints and miracle workers. And their life of simplicity was proposed as an ideal because it seemed to facilitate the search for the Ultimate.

Many people were drawn to the life dedicated to the spirit. Some chose to imitate the anchorites' simplicity, but not their extreme isolation. They lived near one another, met together for meals, and gradually shifted the predominant form of religious life from eremitic to communitarian. This certainly made sense for Christians, whose religious doctrine so celebrated interpersonal love. In the sixth century, Saint Benedict established rules of conduct and procedures for these communities to follow. And from those rules monasticism grew into a great social, political, and economic force in Europe.

Though there was a rule of obedience to the abbot, monastic life was always basically democratic, and rules and practices varied from one community to the next. In the early days of monasticism, monks could move from one community to another. Thus they often traveled around looking for the most agreeable arrangements. These traveling monks became a source of scandal and a threat to discipline. A monk who transgressed community policy or violated basic rules of religious life or took advantage of the community could simply up and leave whenever things got uncomfortable and move on to the next monastery. The introduction of the vow of stability, which bound a monk to a single house and forbade this pilgrimaging from one community to another, was a great reform. Stability had far-reaching effects. As a result of it, monasticism became institutionalized.

From the time of the Apostles, Christians living in community held ownership of property in common. Jesus had urged his followers to sell all that they had and give to the poor. Despite the contemporary claim that Christianity advocates the right of private property, such was not the case in the early Church. Indeed, in one of the most curious of the

New Testament stories, Saint Peter struck dead a man and his wife, Ananias and Sapphira, for holding back money from the community. As the Church grew, common ownership proved unworkable and was abandoned. But among religious, the evangelical ideal was still viable. The desert fathers proclaimed the importance of simplicity and poverty. The communities that followed Benedict's Rule practiced common ownership. When a person vowed stability, he disposed of all his personal property, often ceding it to the order.

By the thirteenth century, because of common ownership, the monasteries had become practically the largest landowners in western Europe. They produced cheeses, wines, liqueurs, breads, and other foodstuffs for their own consumption and sold what was left over. They had the longevity and economic stability to become vast institutions. Especially because they were usually tax-exempt, they had grown rich. In renouncing individual ownership, the monks had assured themselves financial security and relative affluence. The state of religious life was far from the austerity and dependence on Providence chosen by the early anchorites. Those first holy men and women, seeing the riches and luxuries that had crept into the Church and especially into a religious life that still professed to be practicing poverty, would no doubt have been appalled.

One contemporary who was appalled was a young Florentine named Francesco Bernardone. He was the son of a textile merchant who had achieved a comfortable position in class status among the newly developing bourgeoisie. After experiencing a dramatic visionary conversion, Francesco renounced his father's wealth. Not unlike some of his spiritual descendants seven hundred years later, who, in the Summer of Love, came to the northern California city named after Francesco, Saint Francis of Assisi went off to live a life of simplicity.

Around him he assembled a small group of followers—most of them also disillusioned children of the middle class. They wanted to devote their lives to seeking God but were dissatisfied with the monastic life. The Church seemed just as affluent as the families they were abandoning. They left Florence and set up a community in the countryside. Then, once established, they began to return to the city to work among the poor and the sick. In keeping with the legalities of their time, after a while they sought official recognition by the Church. To do so they had to present the rule by which their group would be governed. And in creating that rule, they instigated a new reform in Christian religious life.

The Franciscan reform, called mendicancy, added the renunciation of ownership of property by the community to the monastic renunciation of ownership of private property by each monk. Mendicancy cut directly into the root of the monastic institutions, advocating not flight from the world into prosperous and secure monasteries but service to the poor and an insecure life like theirs. The religious, called friars, would live like the lilies of the field which Jesus had offered as the model of those who love and trust in God, owning nothing, making no plans for a secure future, living for the good they could do, and trusting in God and in fellow human beings for their sustenance.

Mendicancy exploded in Christian Europe. Multitudes hastened to throw off their possessions and devote their lives to service. If, after all, religious consciousness strives for a vision of transcendent reality and vitality not limited to the surface appearance of the everyday world, then the values of that world must be challenged. If indeed life will support those who are open to it, people reasoned, then must not they relax some of their tight control over their future? If they really chose to believe and say that God is good, that love will prevail, then didn't they have to live as though those propositions were true?

Five religious orders, both of men and of women, grew out of the reform: the Franciscans, Dominicans, Carmelites, Augustinians, and the Servites. Of course, it wasn't long—even within Francis's own lifetime—before the rule was moderated. Mendicancy as an ideal and model was profoundly appealing and challenging, but it was very difficult and unrealistic. The history of mendicancy shows that institutions have a difficult time following these ideals.

The seven men of Florence who left their homes in the spirit of the Franciscan reform and went to live on Monte Scenario and establish the Servite Order lived their ideals on the mountainside. But after a time of isolation, they felt they should be doing good works and so went back into the city to work in a hospital. Their zeal and example attracted followers and the Order grew. But the second generation found the rigors of mendicancy severe. Often they had no food. One of the legends of the Order tells that after the friars prayed to Our Lady for help one day, there was a loud knocking at the door of the chapel and they opened it to find baskets of bread mysteriously left for them. But institutions cannot depend on such miracles. Soon all of the mendicant orders began to allow some collective ownership of property, and by the mid-sixteenth century the Council of Trent had virtually reversed the original reform so that programs of apostolic work could be established and future security would not always be in jeopardy.

The spirit of the original reform has resurfaced occasionally throughout the history of Western civilization. The young people who stood by the side of lonely highways hoping to get a ride to San Francisco from a fellow hippie, probably driving a beat-up Volkswagon van (and not a trip to jail in a Highway Patrol car and a shaving by an overzealous barber) were mendicants. What is important about mendicancy, as spiritual practice, is not the institutionalization within the Church, and less the actual lack of money and the austerity that such lack imposes, than the willingness to be open to risk and to an uncertain future. Such openness is almost inherently contrary to institutionalization and formalization. In that, the spirit of mendicancy manifests a key element of the spiritual life.

☙

By the time I'd become a mendicant and was living as a Servite friar, I'd given up a long-standing ambition to be a physicist. In choosing to enter religious life in the first place, I'd turned down an opportunity to go to the Massachusetts Institute of Technology. It wasn't long into my college career that I changed my major from physics to English and then to theology. My fascination with mystical consciousness was gradually supplanting other interests. Soon it led me into religious psychology. Obviously the religious experience was a psychological phenomenon. And my generation, the counterculture of the mid-sixties, was obsessed with psychology.

In that course on Jungian literary interpretation in which I'd first come across Joseph Campbell, I began to find a "radical" approach to religion. Jung had identified patterns of religious thought that seemed to prevail all over the world. He pointed to deep archetypal patterns that made more sense as symbolic images of the mind than as doctrines about metaphysical reality. My interest in Jung was to have major consequences and to create new sources of spiritual turmoil and confusion in my life.

During my first year with the Servites, I found that something in me had changed. I came home one afternoon to my room in the dorm where the Servites lived, feeling a little perplexed by a statement about the historical uniqueness of Christianity that had been made in a theology class I'd just attended. From Jung and Campbell I'd learned that Christianity was far from unique in being the "One, true religion" and maybe even wasn't the best of world religions.

My room was small, a room in a once-grand hotel that had slowly deteriorated and then been bought by the University for a dormitory, mainly for graduate students and members of religious orders who attended the school. The walls were an old battleship gray. I had tried to improve the appearance of the room by adding brightly colored accessories. Among them were a number of psychedelic posters, including the Richard Avedon photographs of the Beatles. (A year before I had had my first experience with LSD, the easy access to mystical consciousness Timothy Leary had promised.)

I stood for a while looking out the window at the traffic moving below, wondering what was happening to me. Here I was a Roman Catholic religious, yet somehow I knew that I had seen through the external teachings of that religion. I no longer believed that that man Jesus who lived in Palestine two thousand years ago was so different from the other world saviors—from Prince Gautama, Mohammed, or Lao-tse, or, for that matter, from any of the rest of us who struggle with deep spiritual questions about the nature of our lives.

I turned and looked at a crucifix hanging on the wall. Even biblical scholarship told us we could never really know what happened that day in Jerusalem. We could only learn of it through the filter of myth and metaphor and the conventions of mystical poetry of the Near East. Common sense told me Jesus was a man who'd taught about goodness and the meaning of life and used those very conventions to talk about God. He was caught up in the swirl of politics of his day and died a martyr to his gentle message of love and respect preached to a culture based on military power and patriarchal, legalistic dominance. In the poems about him he was deified, as symbols were used by the writers to give significance to the events of his life. Jesus wasn't a god exactly who incarnated to save the world by his death in order to repay a sacrificial debt to an angry father-God. I no longer believed in the historicity of such mythical, supernatural events. They were true as metaphors about the Self in every human being, not as historical events.

I understood that Jesus's crucifixion was important because of the

faith of two thousand years of believers who found in the religious poetry a significance for their own lives and their own experience of Self.
I knew this was a religious sensibility, but how did it fit with my identity
as a canonical religious?

I turned away from the crucifix. My eye was caught by the poster on
the wall opposite: Beatle George Harrison, in orange and green high-
lights, a blazing psychedelic vision, his eyes upturned and his hand,
marked with a glyph of the all-seeing eye, raised in benediction, the mu-
dra "fear not." And I realized that though I no longer believed in a specific religious truth, I still believed in religious experience. I believed in
the possibility of mystical vision. And I saw what my identity as a religious really was.

The point was not whether Jesus Christ was God, whether he rose
again on the third day and would lead us all into heaven in the end, but
whether the thought of him and his spiritual acts could lead us to the
kind of vision he had had and that was symbolized by the poster of
George Harrison. Somehow, in the moment of losing my faith, I found
my faith restored. Somehow I had seen beyond the surface of religion
to roots that sank deep into my soul and into the collective soul of
humanity.

Within a couple of weeks of that experience the universe confronted
me with it again in what I'd expected to be simply a good science fiction
movie. I found in Arthur C. Clarke and Stanley Kubrick's *2001: A
Space Odyssey* a spectacular reiteration of my realization. In those
flashing, undulating lights, strange landscapes, and the even stranger
time-distorted bedroom sequence with which the film ends, I saw again
the message that enlightenment, apotheosis, comes from meeting the
incomprehensible. And thus I saw that it was not merely in religious images that the mystical vision could be conveyed. I left the theater, literally dumbstruck for a couple of hours, acutely aware of the dazzling
appeal of the emptiness of specific truth and of the promise of transcendence therein.

The following summer I spent at the Servite Priory at the castle in
Riverside. It was near the end of that stay that I had the dramatic experience I described in the Prologue. The next September I started graduate school in theology with the Servites in Chicago.

I continued to pursue the writings of the mystics, though now it was
not just the medieval Catholics I read. I saw that my realization about
the nature of religious truth and my vision of the face of God was very

close to the deep epistemological propositions of Buddhism. And so I found myself drawn more and more toward Buddhist thought. I was not alone in that: My monastic model, Thomas Merton, was making a similar journey through Christianity to Buddhism to the transcendent truth beyond, deeper than either religion. The year I was in Chicago, Merton passed altogether beyond the world of specific truths, the perhaps not unwilling victim of a fatal jolt of electricity in Bangkok.

☙

In religious life I discovered that Truth was not something outside to be acknowledged, but something to live, something that had to be molded and adjusted to fit the reality of one's own life. I found, surprisingly, within the Church a certain flexibility with doctrine and discipline. I soon perceived that this was a rather natural product of expertise and commitment to dealing with religious and theological issues.

Later in my life, I was to find a similar flexibility of policy in the mental health profession. There, this was a product of expertise with issues of psychological functioning and medical care. The implications of the flexibility were, however, less controversial in psychiatry than in religious life.

An example of the flexibility in psychiatry was the use of minor tranquilizers. Since a large number of the complaints that bring patients into the offices of medical doctors in general practice have no clear-cut physical cause and are most likely idiosyncratic symptoms of anxiety, mild tranquilizers like Valium or Xanax often bring effective relief. And so doctors sometimes prefer them over either a specific symptomatic treatment or a time-consuming explanation of the psychosomatic nature of the problem (which may not help anyway). Mental health professionals, on the other hand, recognize that the proper way to treat such symptoms arising from anxiety is through psychotherapy. They know that minor tranquilizers can create psychological, if not physical, dependence. They often decry the overuse of such drugs and warn against their addictive potential. Indeed, they begin to suspect that every distressed soul who appears at the doorstep of their clinic asking for Valium, having heard perhaps from friends that it helps them sleep, is really driven by Valium dependency. Thus, especially in community mental health centers, there are policies against the routine use of minor tranquilizers.

During the mid-seventies, I worked in a psychiatric emergency clinic in San Francisco. I found that many of the professionals who did not like to prescribe Valium for clients had few problems with taking it themselves. After a particularly harrowing experience in the crisis clinic—like, for instance, when a PCP-crazed maniac threatened us with a twelve-inch-long butcher knife—we'd often break out the Valium. Because we understood the problems of anxiety and the limitations of drug treatment, we felt confident in our own use of these antianxiety agents. In fact, I found that most mental health professionals, though they often had a restrictive and narrow view of the use of any kind of recreational drug by clients, had a fairly liberal view of their own use of drugs like marijuana or an occasional insight-producing psychedelic.

While on the one hand this seems like a hypocritical double standard, on the other it makes sense. None of us objects to an electrician giving us overcautious instructions about handling live electrical wires, even though we understand that electricians need not follow them quite so rigorously themselves. When one knows what one is doing, one can take shortcuts. That is what expertise means. It is why we hire experts for jobs instead of amateurs; it will take them less time and trouble. Experts are simply more experienced and knowledgeable in their field and thus can make informed decisions that nonexperts cannot.

I had found a similar double standard in religious life, not so much with drug use (alcohol, not illicit drugs, is the chemical of choice among the Catholic clergy), but with doctrine and the exercise of religion. These, of course, can create just as life-distorting compulsions as drugs.

Religious professionals, like any other experts, have a sense of the real point behind the doctrine and discipline of religion. They generally do not have the magical notions about religion that some lay people do. Thus they may feel competent to make decisions about their own belief and behavior that they would question in people they consider less informed than they.

One of my theology professors, for instance, once explained to us the "real" meaning behind the modern doctrines of the Blessed Virgin Mary. Both the Assumption and the Immaculate Conception (the only two dogmas that have actually been declared under the rubric of papal infallibility), it seems, contained historico-political subtexts.

Pope Pius IX came into office in 1846 a great supporter of the liberal cause in Italy. He supported populist movements to redefine the relations of power in society. A major event of his papacy was the First Vatican Council which set out to redefine the power in the Church itself. The Council had only completed the first part of the task, the role of the papacy, when it was abruptly forced to disband because of the invasion of the Papal States by the populist leader Garibaldi. The Papal Secretary of State was assassinated on the steps of Saint Peter's and the Pope became a virtual prisoner in the Vatican. Betrayed by the very forces he'd supported, Pius, in disguise as a physician, fled to Sicily where he polled the attendees at the Council, all now returned home, about the wisdom of exercising the newly defined papal infallibilty to declare the doctrine of the Assumption of the Blessed Virgin Mary (B. V. M., as she is referred to in the shorthand of the Missal).

The Assumption is the doctrine that at the end of her life, the mother of Jesus was taken body and soul into heaven so that she did not suffer the rending of soul and body and the corruption of the flesh that ordinarily accompany the end of life. To those in the know, Pius IX's declaration, following an affirmative response to his poll, meant the Pope was saying that even though he'd made a strategic political mistake in supporting Garibaldi, the Church, symbolized by the B. V. M., remained uncorrupted in its physical, institutionalized form.

The doctrine has meaning beyond the historical, of course. C. G. Jung thought the Assumption celebrated the sanctity of the flesh and finally acknowledged the femininity in the Catholic God. But, at least according to my theology professor, Brother John Totten, its real significance is only understandable in its political context.

Pius XII came into office in 1939. He had to carefully balance the priorities and teachings of the Church with the political realities of his day which were, of course, the rise of German Nazism and Italian Fascism. Following World War II, with the defeat of the powers that had threatened him and to which he had made major concessions, Pius was forced to admit he'd made serious errors. At least some of the guilt for the Holocaust was saddled on him because of his silence and willingness to acquiesce to Fascism. In 1954, specifically in commemoration of the defining of the Assumption (to make sure the connection with his predecessor was established), Pius XII declared the doctrine of the Immaculate Conception of the B. V. M.

The Immaculate Conception is the doctrine—so often confused by

Catholic and non-Catholic alike with the Virgin Birth of Jesus—that, in anticipation of the sacred role she would play in the incarnation of Christ, Mary was exempted by God from the human heritage of original sin. From her conception, Mary was free of the stain on the soul of sin. Immaculate means pure, containing no flaw or error. To those in the know, according to Brother Totten's historical analysis, Pius XII's declaration of the Immaculate Conception meant the Pope was saying that even though he'd made a strategic political mistake in signing Concordats with Hitler and Mussolini, the Church, again symbolized by the B. V. M., had always been in soul free of flaw or error and remained so.

Curiously, the laity are seldom let in on these historico-political subtexts. They seem expected to just take everything on face value. When I was growing up it was routinely said that Catholics were required to believe in both the Assumption and the Immaculate Conception, though, as I observed above, many Catholics didn't understand what these notions were. They just believed them. And such believing Catholics are often dismayed by changes in Church discipline. They say how unfair it was to condemn to hell someone who ate meat on Friday fifty years ago, when today Friday abstinence has been abandoned. The non-experts fail to see that the sin of eating meat on Friday fifty years ago had nothing to do with the evil of meat or the sacredness of Fridays; it had to do with obedience to Church discipline enforcing a particular bit of symbolism.

The experts understand that very few human acts are evil in themselves. What is sinful is the attitude with which acts are done. It is not actions that are irreligious, but attitudes toward life. Religious professionals often understood this and were far less likely to feel violated if, halfway through a bowl of mushroom soup during Friday's dinner, they found a small piece of chicken. They were likely to trust that God's justice is more understanding than Church discipline and that no souls are burning in hellfire because of a technicality of discipline.

A clear and not very controversial example of the application of this double standard I discovered in monastic life regarded attendance at religious services. Catholics, of course, have traditionally been required to attend Mass on Sundays. To one trained in doctrine it was apparent that the attendance at Mass on Sunday was not a divine, absolute imperative but, like abstinence from meat on Fridays, a simple disciplinary rule of the Church designed to keep people at least miminally involved in the activities of the institution. What was important was that one maintained one's devotion, not that one obeyed the letter of the law. That, after all, was the main point of Jesus's reform of first-century Judaism.

I must admit, however, I was quite appalled when I first discovered that some of my fellow religious in the Servite Community in Chicago were not attending Sunday Mass. Yet as I thought about their behavior, I came to understand that for many, their lives were so filled with religion that concern with minimal observance was superfluous. I cannot say, of course, that all the religious who dispensed themselves from specific disciplines were doing it out of the abundance of their zeal—as I cannot say that all the psychiatrists who took Valium were prudent in their consumption. But from considering their behavior I learned the important lesson that most rules are pretty arbitrary and that this is understood even—or perhaps especially—within the Church.

A much more controversial application of the double standard concerned sexuality and the obligation of celibacy. Celibacy (which is the obligation imposed by the vow of chastity) is the state of not being married. It concerns social and juridical status. It only indirectly concerns sexuality. But because traditional morals require that sex be engaged in only in legal marriage—mainly to guarantee that inheritance pass only to legitimate, biological heirs—celibacy excludes sexual behavior.

The Church, as a matter of discipline, asceticism, and symbolism, requires that religious observe celibacy. Symbolically, celibacy was intended to witness to the life lived unfettered by the ordinary demands of family and social obligation. It was to choose such a life that Sören Kierkegaard reneged in his engagement to marry Regina Olsen, lest he fall into "domesticity." For the domestic fetters could confine the imagination and strangle the spirit. Moreover, in the world in which the notion of celibacy developed, when it was virtually unheard of for a person not to contribute to society's need for new members by marrying and raising children, for one to reject one's place in the social order for the sake of God was a powerful statement of commitment to a greater reality.

In the discourse in which Jesus disallowed divorce, he praised those who made themselves eunuchs for the sake of the Kingdom. This statement in Matthew's Gospel (9: 10–12) is the basis for the monastic obligation of celibacy. But eunuchs were not men who were nonsexual. Many of them were temple or court prostitutes, emasculated so they *could be* sexual without reproductive consequences. What they were was men who could not reproduce. That is perhaps the choice Jesus was praising. Since for most people immortality was achieved through off-spring, choosing not to reproduce was a declaration of faith in eternity, in the reality of the Kingdom within, here and now.

Of course, Christianity has been notoriously antisexual, and that may have been a result of a long period of domination by a celibate priesthood (as Uta Ranke-Heinemann argues in her book *Eunuchs for the Kingdom of Heaven*), but that has not been the purpose of celibacy. The point of disavowing marriage has not been that sex is evil, but that altering one's relation to sex can alter one's experience of life and of God.

The vow, as it was explained to me by my superiors and as I spoke it, was a promise to God and to myself to use my sexuality for the sake of my spirituality. Of course, when I was first in religious life, I did take that to mean total abstinence. And that exclusion of sexual activity produced in us young religious an almost hysterical intensity. It turned us toward our spirituality and it produced within the community a power and depth of interpersonal relationship, free of possessiveness and jealousy, that simply would not have been there had we been functioning less abnormally.

Later, I found that that intensity could not be sustained. Sexuality crept back into our lives, though usually only in veiled ways. Occasionally one of the brothers would fall in love with a woman student at the university or a couple of the brothers would fall in love with each other; when I was living in the seminary in Chicago, the Prior of the community was openly maintaining a relationship with a married woman. Whatever the situation, the religious status of one or both parties so influenced the relationship that it still remained abnormal. And that really was the point of the vow. The repression of sex has been a familiar practice worldwide for inducing unusual states of consciousness. And, in the end, that was what was important about celibacy. Even when it was clear to us that sex was going on in the monastery, most of us felt that our vow curtailed most sexual activity and, even when we were acting sexually, continued to focus sexual energy toward religious aims.

Of course there was sex going on in the monastery. Those who'd be scandalized by that revelation are simply denying their own sexual feelings. The sex was usually innocent and harmless. Perhaps it was often beneficent, for it was an occasion for prayer and realization. The questions most of us dealt with, which we agonized over through many hours of prayer, were less whether our sex was sinful than how our emotional, sexual involvement fit into our spiritual lives and what were we to learn from these feelings. More often than not, the feelings were of frustration, rejection, inadequacy; occasionally, they were of ecstasy, intimacy, and true love—the same mix felt by the ordinary young person just discovering love and sex.

Discretion concerning any sexual activity was expected. Monks didn't brag about conquests—that kind of sex really was forbidden. They did talk about positive feelings of love, affection, and mutual support, but little was ever said about actual physical experience. Even so, the monks were not unaware that some of their number were functioning sexually. And the Order was surprisingly honest and just about that. In the provincial annual financial statement of one of the orders I was in, there was a line item: child support payments. If one of the monks fathered a child, the Order assumed responsibility. They may not have liked the added expenditure, but they recognized their obligation in justice and they reported the expense honestly.

The religious hurt by celibacy were seldom those who had the love affairs or who fathered the children, but instead were among those who never acted sexually at all. Some became embittered old men, resentful that other people could enjoy themselves. Others renounced their vocation altogether; as soon as they felt sexual urges or fell in love, they left religious life to marry or to become profligate. They couldn't rise above the legalistic interpretation of the vow and couldn't sustain the psychological pressure. These men may have been obeying the law, but they weren't dealing with their sexuality as a part of their spirituality.

The Order, of course, had also to deal with the members' sexuality, somehow placing it in the spiritual context. Sometimes this was done in ways that were positively medieval. By the time I had joined my second religious order, most of the medievalisms had been supplanted by a psychological sophistication in the spirit of the late 1960s. But the Order had made those changes in a remarkably short time. Friends of mine remembered that things had been very different only a few years before.

Then, when rumors began to fly across the country that the novices were sleeping with each other, a hue and cry would arise and the provincial would hasten to investigate. On one such occasion described to me, the provincial and his tribunal, in a medieval tour de force, descended upon the student house with pomp and seriousness. For several days they conducted an investigation. Each postulant, novice, and scholastic was called before the visitors and asked about his own behavior and about that of others. No one, of course, knew what anyone else was saying about him, for each was bound under strict obedience to reveal nothing of what transpired in the interview. A great emotional charge built up throughout the whole house. Everyone feared that he had been betrayed, even when there had been nothing to reveal. (Inquisitions have been notorious for eliciting false charges.) Everyone expected that his name would appear on the list of those branded homosexual and expelled from the Order. Hysteria mounted.

Then the tribunal completed its questioning. A morning passed while they pondered their findings. In the late afternoon a house chapter was convened. All of the religious gathered in the chapel. A pall fell over the room. The meeting began with solemn and somber ritual. With the ancient hymn *Veni Creator Spiritus,* the Holy Spirit was implored to watch over the proceedings. Then the provincial spoke. He expressed great concern about the souls of the young religious in his charge. He sermonized on the beauty of innocence and purity and grew enraged at the evil of sin and pollution and the scandal of leading another into degradation. Everyone was quaking in his seat, wondering how he could endure the humiliation of calling his parents and asking for the money to come home, a reject from the seminary.

Then, in a grand gesture of forgiveness and magnanimity, the provincial absolved everyone. The chapter was dismissed. A huge dinner was served, with pitchers of martinis and manhattans waiting at the tables as the students, greatly relieved, filed in and took their places in the refectory. Silence was dispensed and celebration continued into the night.

No one ever learned if anything had actually been discovered by the investigation. And, of course, it didn't matter. The message was clear. The symbolic, ritual role of the life of a monk is more important than the actual life of the individual living as a monk. How the individual deals with his own day-to-day living is his own business. His superiors can offer him guidance, but they cannot live his life for him. A monk's actual behavior has to fit into his spiritual life—that is his vow. How he achieves that is between himself and God. But when rumors of sexual activity in the novitiate had come to the provincial's attention, for instance, the discretion necessary to preserve the symbolic function was in jeopardy.

When, in my day, those rumors began to fly—and I was the subject of them—the provincial quietly asked me about them, sympathetically listened to my story, kindly counseled me, and then, under their vow of obedience, silenced the men responsible for spreading the rumors. For the rumors were more a violation of celibacy than whatever innocent sexual activity might have been going on.

This is not exactly hypocrisy. And if there is scandal in it, it is not so much in the existence of a double standard as in our failure to make that standard available to everyone. Laity and religious alike could understand spirituality in more than superficial and legalistic ways. The solution is not to destroy the carriers of symbolic meaning, like Friday abstinence, Sunday Mass, or the vow of chastity, but to educate all people to understand these things *as* symbols which they can inflect in their own ways to enrich their experience of life.

Thinking that God is concerned with external observances, with day-to-day human concerns like sex or politics, trivializes the divinity. God has never been concerned with sin. For God, everything that is made is good. Sin is a concern of humankind. We rightly make rules for life in society. Without them civilization would disappear. We need traffic lights to prevent accidents, but nobody thinks that God is personally bothered by someone's running a red light. God is concerned with our spiritual lives, with our willingness to be open to life and to one another.

That openness was what I understood mendicancy to be about.

⁊

By the end of the sixties, a cultural revolution was sweeping America. The Church was renewing herself. Or collapsing. We weren't really sure which. Organizational turmoil within the Order was beginning to threaten many of us. The Servites were splitting in two. Confusion about the meaning and place of monastic life in the mid-twentieth century was spawning a reactionary movement to get things back to the way they used to be. Most of those I'd joined the community to be with were leaving. My radical perspective caused me discomfort with the attempts to preserve the past. I couldn't articulate my realization about the nature of myth without sounding like a heretic or an apostate. And I was, after all, a member of a generation of troublemakers, fussing about the war, decrying American middle-class values, and wearing our hair too long, blurring the lines of differentiation between the sexes.

My own hair was too long: in imitation, I explained to the provincial, of that picture of George Harrison that still hung on the wall of my room. Of course, for none of us did the length of our hair really matter. But in those tumultuous days of the close of that decade, long hair had developed symbolic significance. For an older generation, long hair seemed to suggest the end of values and morals, the patriotism and faith on which they had founded their lives. For the younger generation it seemed to promise a new and transformed future, free of war and hypocrisy—we hoped. For me, because it simultaneously identified me as a hippie in all the best senses of that movement for peace and love, and called to mind the realization I'd had that day when the poster of long-haired George Harrison reanimated my faith, my long hair symbolized my vision of religion not as history but as transcendental insight.

When, after a year in Chicago, I transferred back to the castle in southern California, I was told to cut my hair. The superiors feared that the appearance of long-haired seminarians around the houses of the Order in Orange County, a bastion then of reactionary, pro-war, anti-progressive thought, would alienate contributors. And the Order needed their money, if for no other reason than to support the fleet of automobiles with which its men navigated the southern California freeway system. Ironically, there was a statue of Saint Peregrine in one of the Orange County churches of the Order; the statue wore its hair in exactly the same style I did.

And long hair was not the only counterculture style I championed because I saw it as fundamentally spiritual. I had written an article in the provincial newsletter suggesting that, in the spirit of mendicancy and in the spirit of the times, Servites should hitchhike rather than drive. Then we wouldn't be so dependent on those contributors. Well, I was certainly making myself a troublemaker again.

I wouldn't cut my hair. The provincial didn't order me to do so, but it was pretty clear that my wanderings were about to lead me out of my second religious order. I knew it was time for me to put myself on the side of some lonely highway, hitching into a future I could not guess. It was 1970, the beginning of a new decade. I was in California. And I was going to stay true to my identity as Peregrine the wanderer.

CHAPTER THREE

The Mystical Insight

It is miraculous. I even have a superstition that has grown on me as the result of invisible hands coming all the time—namely, that if you do follow your bliss you put yourself on a kind of track that has been there all the while, waiting for you, and the life that you ought to be living is the one you are living. When you can see that, you begin to meet people who are in the field of your bliss, and they open the doors to you. I say, follow your bliss and don't be afraid, and doors will open where you didn't know they were going to be.
(Power of Myth, *p. 120*)

In the spirit of mendicancy, I was trying to stay open to new ideas about the spiritual life. After a summer on the road, following my leaving the Servites, I settled in San Francisco and enrolled in a graduate program in comparative religion at the California Institute of Asian Studies which I'd learned about from reading Alan Watts, the Episcopal priest turned Beat-missionary of americanized Zen Buddhism. (The school is now called the California Institute of Integral Studies.)

I pursued my favorite topic: religious epistemology and the notion of emptiness. I was still looking for the secret, still trying to find what to empty myself of as Christ Jesus had emptied himself.

During my first year at the Institute of Asian Studies, I discovered a flier on the bulletin board announcing that Joseph Campbell was going to be giving a seminar at a place about seventy-five miles north of San Francisco called the Mann Ranch. I was eager to meet him in person. I wrote immediately, got the registration forms, and signed up.

Fortunately I applied for a work scholarship and so was asked to come up a day early to help get the place in shape. Apropos of the times and consistent with the mendicant spirituality I'd been preaching to the Servites, I hitchhiked up Route 101 to Ukiah. I called when I got to town and Larry Thomas, owner of the Mann Ranch, drove down out of the hills to get me. I spent the rest of that day and the next helping Larry and his partner Barbara McClintock clean the house and prepare food for the fifty-some guests who'd be arriving.

The first person to arrive, of course, was Joseph Campbell himself. He flew from New York to San Francisco and then, in a propeller-driven commuter plane, to Ukiah where Larry picked him up and drove him back out to the property which was high in the coastal mountains between Ukiah and Mendocino.

I remember that I was immediately entranced by Campbell's voice and manner. Even when he came into the kitchen to ask for a glass of water, he seemed masterful and brilliant and, at the same time, warm and affable. He looked so handsome and dignified, yet so youthful and eager. He laughed easily, I recall. And he insisted we call him "Joe." No "Professor Campbell" or stiltedly formal "Joseph."

At the same time, over lunch I was quite taken aback when, out of the blue, he began complaining about a political bumper sticker he'd seen on a car on the way out to the ranch. This was in the spring of 1971 in northern California. The country was in turmoil over the Viet Nam War. Almost three years before, Richard Nixon had taken over the Presidency when Lyndon Johnson declined to run again in order to bring the war to a speedy conclusion. Nixon had promised results. But the war was still raging. In the spirit of the times and of the geographical locale, that bumper sticker had said "Impeach Nixon."

Joe Campbell turned out to identify as a Republican and to be a supporter of Nixon and the war. I was aghast. One of my favorite quotes from *The Hero With a Thousand Faces* had shorn up my belief that my radical politics and antiwar sentiments were consistent with my spiritual hero quest: "For the mythological hero is the champion not of things become but of things becoming; the dragon to be slain by him is precisely the monster of the status quo: Holdfast, the keeper of the past . . . he is enemy, dragon, tyrant, because he turns to his own advantage the authority of his position. He is Holdfast not because he keeps the *past* but because he *keeps*." (*Hero,* p. 337.) Didn't Campbell understand?

Later in that conversation Larry got to asking Joe about drug-

induced mystical experience. Larry himself had had a very profound experience a few years before in London with a motherly crone of a psychiatrist who'd fed him tea and tongue sandwiches and then guided him
through a life-changing session with pharmaceutical LSD. Joe listened
interestedly to Larry's story and then said that under no circumstances
would he ever take LSD and that he thought doing so was like driving
your car over a cliff, hoping you'd have an interesting experience. It
sounded like he'd been listening to too much Art Linkletter.

Was this man the champion of things becoming?

Over the weekend seminar, my skepticism gradually abated. Regardless of what his politics were, when he started talking about myth and
religion he shone. He was so natural, sometimes he sat on the floor. He
did not seem to be delivering a prepared speech. Especially when he was
answering questions from the audience, he demonstrated an incredible
wealth of knowledge at his fingertips. He even sometimes footnoted his
references, mentioning page numbers of citations, during his talks. And
however brilliant and supernally intelligent his presentation was, it was
always entertaining. He told stories, did jokes, recited myths, and always he was interesting and often funny.

One of the techniques of storytelling he used to great advantage was
anachronism. He loved to blend the mythical language of the world of
eternity with the vernacular of today. In recounting a tale, say, of an ancient Babylonian hero, he'd put modern slang into the characters'
mouths so that Gilgamesh might call out to his friend Enkidu "Hey,
buddy" or the buffalo god coax an Indian maiden into elopement with
the words, "All right, girlie, off we go." In discussing the Exodus, he
might say that Moses was following the course of the plagues he'd
called down upon the Egyptians in *The New York Times*. The blending
of ancient and modern syntax, of course, functioned not only as a hu-
morous device, it exemplified one of Joe's primary insights: that the language of myth is about eternal truths, not historical events, that the
gods are here and now. Yahweh might speak in the beautiful cadences
of the King James Bible, but he also speaks in the lingo of the modern
street.

By the end of the weekend seminar, I was enamored enough of the
man and his knowledge and his message of eternal verities, that his
seemingly antediluvian take on American politics became forgivable.
After all the guests had left and the old rambling ranch house was put
back in shape, I recall one last dinner with just the staff at which Camp-

bell was present. I don't know that anyone specifically challenged him on his pro-Nixon comments, but he explained his reasons for thinking of himself as a conservative that put his Republicanism in context.

Joe explained that he was staunchly individualistic. He said the real danger of modern society was its threat of swamping personal freedom with collective need and responsibility. How could there be heroes if government meddled in everybody's life? Joe insisted this was what true conservativism was all about, the freedom of the individual. I agreed with him strongly enough that I didn't object that the Nixon government seemed to meddle in the lives of my youthful generation at every level with laws regarding drug use and sexual behavior and policies that threatened to drag us out of our homes and schools to send us to Viet Nam to be cannon fodder for its know-nothing anti-communism. (It really wasn't till Ronald Reagan came to power on the shoulders of biblical fundamentalists that conservativism lost connection with individualism and championed greed instead.)

Joe called himself a classical conservative. He cited the story of the commencement of the Grail quest as the exemplar of truly Western religious consciousness in which the knights agree among themselves that it would be unseemly to follow in another's footsteps and that they should each pursue their own paths, beginning in that place in the forest which was darkest and most alone.

Joe Campbell occasionally prided himself on not really being part of the modern world. He didn't watch television and didn't keep up with popular culture. He lived, after all, in that place in the forest that was darkest and most alone and always pursued his own path. In that sense, he really didn't fit into the polarities of modern American politics. And it was as easy for reactionary Republicans to laud his conservativism as for radical counterculturalists to praise his regard for freedom and adventure.

One more note about Campbell's style and delivery: over several years of hearing him at the Mann Ranch, and later at a series of seminars managed by Barbara McClintock at Dominican College in San Rafael, and then hearing him most recently on television, I've seen that in fact his words were not nearly as extemporaneous as they had sounded. And, of course, that would be true. He was a college professor; he taught this material semester after semester, year after year. He gave the same lectures over and over again. It's no wonder he could cite footnotes and references. It's no wonder that he knew long passages by heart or could retell involved and intricate stories with such facility.

What, for me, the recognition that I've heard this or that story before has meant is not that Joe was not the brilliant lecturer I first thought, but that there are themes and ideas that were especially dear to him, that he must have thought important, and so he managed to get them into his lectures because they were an integral part of his message. In telling my own anecdotes about Campbell, I am frequently relying on my memory of the repetitions in his presentations. These are the points that stuck with me. These are the points that I think meant something to him.

❧

Not only did I meet Joseph Campbell and develop a friendship and correspondence with him, I was also invited to join the staff of the then-forming Mann Ranch Seminars. I'd made good friends with Barbara McClintock, one of the organizers. In fact, it was through Barbara that I maintained much of my contact with Joe over the years. For she remained a very close friend of his, and acted as agent and virtual amanuensis when he was in California. She is now Executive Director of the Joseph Campbell Archives and Library at Pacifica Graduate Institute in Carpinteria, California. For several more summers I worked there, as cook and host to the many visitors who came to listen to the workshops we organized in Jungian psychology and religious and mythological thought. It was an ideal place for me to pursue my burning question about the nature of religious truth. During those summers I met and listened to many of the leaders of the newly evolving sense of religion, science, and social values in the modern world that was being called the "new consciousness" and "new paradigm science."

When I wasn't cooking, entertaining the guests, or attending the lectures myself, I was studying for my master's thesis on mythological consciousness. And when I wasn't studying or writing I was wandering around the property, cultivating and observing mythological knowledge in myself.

I was living in a little cabin about a mile down from the big house. Sometimes, as I'd head back there late at night after the evening's lecture, I'd stop and wonder at the beauty of the night. When the moon was out over the valley, I'd sometimes put on my religious habit and go sit on a fence post and sing Gregorian chants to the moon goddess. Though I was no longer officially a monk, I'd kept the black full-length tunic, scapular, cowl, and full cape. I'd sit on my perch, my habit billowing in the wind, and experience the vast depth of the sky above, the emptiness of space all around, and the eternity into which I as an individual ego faded into insignificance.

The Mann Ranch was a magical place. The main building, a rambling Victorian ranch house built by Abner Mann, an executive of the Southern Pacific Railway, around the time of the great San Francisco earthquake in 1906, was nestled halfway down one side of a bowl-shaped valley. Following a meandering stream some twenty-five miles to the west, the valley opened out of the hills onto the ocean near Mendocino. At night the Pacific Ocean coastline fog would often flow up the valley, filling the bowl almost up to the level of the house. Under a full moon that fog-filled valley looked like an ocean of milk.

There is a Hindu myth that the world originated in the stirring of such an ocean of the milk from the breast of the Great Mother. Perhaps some ancient visionary, I thought, sitting on a fence post, gazing upon such a valley full of cloud in the Himalayas, had had an intuition of the dynamics of creation. And when he told his insight to the townspeople they incorporated the image of his meditation into their mythology.

Down the road from my cabin the path made a sharp turn into a dark little hollow where a wooden bridge crossed a dry stream. When there was rain, the stream would fill with water roaring down the valleyside, crashing between rocks that lined the stream bed. There, where my path crossed the bridge, was a pile of such rocks. And on those rocks, especially late on very dark nights, there would sit a demon I named Grendel, after Beowulf's antagonist. During the day, of course, it was obvious that the shadows that comprised Grendel's features were but tree branches, and that the sudden drop in temperature I'd feel as I approached his perch was just cool air slipping down the stream bed toward the bottom of the valley below. But at night I was happy to experience those rocks, trees, and cool air as Grendel, the boundary guardian.

I'd actually been frightened the first night I encountered him. Two fireflies had settled in the branches of his face and made a most convincing pair of eyes for him. It didn't take visions of bridge-guarding trolls to frighten me. After all, here I was, a city boy, for the first time living in a cabin in the woods. It made sense to me to symbolize that free-floating fear as something specific I could grapple with. That first time I met Grendel I talked with him, and agreed to occasionally bring him presents—a leftover morsel of dessert or a candle—if he would protect me while I was pursuing my studies. Creating the Grendel myth was a good exercise in what I was studying.

When the valley wasn't full of clouds, when the night was bright with moonlight or with stars, or when the sky was brilliant blue and the sun poured summer down on us, to the east stretched out a vista of blue-green hills fading into the distance. The space was enormous. It was a special place for me, where I could deal with vistas in my mind and grapple with questions about the spiritual life that had haunted me for years.

ॐ

The major focus of my work at the California Institute of Asian Studies was the notion of emptiness (*sunyata*) in a second century Buddhist sage named Nagarjuna and what I saw to be a parallel concept, the notion of disinterest, in the medieval German Dominican preacher called Meister Eckhart. Both of these men had denied any absolute truth to metaphysical and religious propositions. In the terms of their very different conceptual frameworks, they had both urged avoidance of specific viewpoints and concrete formulations. Nagarjuna, in the tradition of Mahayana Buddhism which he is credited with initiating, and Eckhart, in the tradition of Neoplatonic mysticism, both used the words that so fascinated me. They spoke of emptiness and the Void. They denied substance to God and the gods.

Of all the world's religions, Buddhism has been the one most concerned with such issues. Buddhism is essentially atheistic, insisting that no god has real, substantial, self-subsistent existence. The Buddha taught that the aim of religion ought not be the appeasement of an angry deity or obedience to law that promises immortality or even the achievement of consistency with nature, but rather transcendence of the whole dynamic by which human knowing creates the world of experience. The Buddha likened the life of the ordinary person to a dream from which, he had discovered, it was possible to wake.

Buddhism was a reform religion that grew out of the highly mythologized system of Hinduism. The historical Buddha, Prince Siddhartha

Gautama, taught that salvation would not come through belief in and worship of a plethora of gods, or from living out extraordinary ascetical practices, but from waking up. Maintaining that as long as consciousness merely rearranged the symbols and metaphors within the dream there could be no release from the hold of the dream, the Buddha focused on the suffering of the dreamer as a motivation for struggling to break free of the dream. He taught that any belief in the substantial reality of the dream or the dreamer would necessarily result in suffering. His fundamental teachings are summarized as *anatman, anitya,* and *duhkha:* There is no self, there is no permanence, there is only suffering.

Gautama was in effect a behaviorist. He did not preach a metaphysics or a world view. He never tried to ascertain or to describe how things were. He preached only that the sense of self and of the world must be illusions because they produce suffering, and thus life should be lived moderately according to Four Noble Truths: All existence is suffering; suffering derives from desire; there is a possibility of release from suffering; and this release comes through living the eightfold principle of moderation (i.e., right understanding, right purpose, right speech, right conduct, right vocation, right effort, right alertness, and right concentration).

As time passed, the gods slowly encroached again. It was not long before Buddhism developed a mythological system. However, the myths were never quite believed as literal. Descendants of the Buddha used the gods to personify psychological and spiritual faculties, but they denied them substantial existence.

The Buddha's original teachings were stark and life-denying. They cut through myth by focusing entirely on discipline and behavior. They were not exactly puritanical in the way that the life-denying sects of Western religion would be years later. But they were austere in their simplicity. The later teachings of Buddhism developed a much less severe approach which recognized that the existence of the gods (and of "eternal truths") was an epistemological issue. This reorientation of Buddhist thinking came, in part, from the influence of Nagarjuna, who lived some six hundred years after Gautama Buddha.

Explaining this reorientation, the myths tell that the Buddha had discovered certain truths that he believed human beings were not yet ready to hear. These he disclosed only to the nagas, the serpent gods who live in the depths of the sea, which is to say, to unconscious guides in the depths of the psyche (what Jung called archetypes). Once the early teachings had prepared humankind for a subtler awareness of religion, there came along a character seeking after ultimate truth called Arjuna. He was so named because he was born under an arjuna tree—born under a tree just as Gautama had been born under a tree and was enlightened under a tree. Arjuna was taken away to the Iron Palace of the nagas in the netherworld where the secret wisdom of Gautama was revealed to him. Thus the full doctrine of Buddhism was not taught until about A.D. 150 when it was expounded by Arjuna of the Nagas who is regarded as the father of life-affirming Mahayana Buddhism.

I was first exposed to Nagarjuna's writings in a course taught by an old Japanese bishop who, like the holy men described in Zen literature, simply laughed in answer to most of the logical questions we put to him. Nagarjuna was difficult to understand, the translations of his works intricate and convoluted. Yet for all that, the way Bishop Syaku talked about him made Nagarjuna's secret wisdom seem somehow immediately relevant to the issues I was asking about.

Nagarjuna's teaching grew out of the two major schools of Buddhist thought which had developed in the six centuries between the Buddha's teaching the possibility of escape from suffering and Nagarjuna's proclamation of the secret wisdom.

The first of these was the *Abhidharma,* which had devised an elaborate atomic theory—not at all unlike the Monadology of Leibnitz some fifteen hundred years later—to explain *anatman* and *anitya.* This atomic theory maintained that there is no self and no permanence because all that really exists are minute, discrete quanta of experience (called dharmas) which flicker in and out of existence. Since both objects and perceptions are composed of dharmas, they are, in fact, illusory. Thus, the Abhidharma philosophers reasoned, meditation on and rigorous analysis of the nature and activity of the dharmas would bring about release from illusion.

The other major current of Buddhism was elaborated in a massive body of literature known as the *Prajnaparamita* (The Perfection of Wisdom). The Prajnaparamita focused on religious sensibilities not metaphysical designations. The Prajnaparamita held that compassion for all beings caught in the round of suffering and death would bring about release. It told the story—which had been so influential in my own spirituality—of the bodhisattva, the holy being who out of compassion set aside his own enlightenment in order to bring all other sentient beings to enlightenment by transforming their suffering through his transcendent vision.

In his major work, the *Mulamadhyamakarikas* (Fundamentals of the Middle Way), Nagarjuna cut through the distinction between the Abhidharma and the Prajnaparamita by denying that either doctrine had any substantial reality. Nagarjuna taught the principle of *sunyata*. Sunyata is usually translated "emptiness," or "nothingness." In writing the thesis on Nagarjuna, I proposed that a more intelligible way of translating sunyata would be "contentlessness." For in Nagarjuna's thought it meant that the metaphysical and religious notions of Buddhism are only temporarily useful concepts that have no content and that refer to no objective existence—in the contemporary lingo of Marshall McLuhan: no message, only medium.

Nagarjuna taught that all ideas, philosophies, and beliefs are empty because everything is relative. According to his principle of "mutual co-origination," no experiences are more basic than any others because all are intelligible only in terms of each other. He maintained that, since the very existence of the world itself arises from the mutual interaction of the relations within the world, enlightened consciousness should not focus on individual objects and experiences. Thus Nagarjuna's reality shifted from the world of nouns to a world of verbs or, even more properly, to a world of adverbs, devoid of substantives.

What was significant about Nagarjuna's teaching was not his elaborate and convoluted refutations of Buddhist thinking. These seem merely like clever sophistry. But the implication of this teaching was that what is important about religious doctrine is not what it teaches about the universe, but how it works to bring about release from illusion. Nagarjuna taught that the distinction between nirvana and the world of suffering exists only in the mind. He maintained that nirvana—the state of not clinging to anything, including belief in the Buddha and in nirvana—was achieved when one realized that there is not the slightest difference between samsara (the world of flux) and nirvana (the state of release), between time and eternity. This was the transforming vision of the bodhisattva. Indeed, in the end, the bodhisattva would discover the emptiness on which his whole sensibility was based and would see that there had never been any suffering beings, nor any bodhisattva to save them.

Nagarjuna concluded that the aim of Buddhism was not the achievement of some holy ideal but the destruction of all viewpoints. From there, enlightenment would follow of its own accord. This is the kind of thinking responsible for such curious Buddhist ideas as that if one meets the Buddha on the road, one should kill the Buddha, and that sitting in meditation can no more make one enlightened than polishing a floor tile can make it a mirror—and this in a religion the major practice of which is sitting meditation. A Zen drawing depicts a bullfrog sitting on a lily pad, with the caption: "If sitting could make a Buddha, I, foolish old frog, would have been enlightened long before now."

According to Nagarjuna, enlightenment comes from seeing that all views and opinions are just views and opinions and have no real substance. They are empty. Truth is empty. It is appreciation of this emptiness that brings release.

꙳

The Asian mind apparently had an easier time. grasping that the forms of religion were mere symbols—powerful but empty. The Western mind has had a much harder time with such notions. It has been said that the Western mind is more reality-oriented than the Eastern: Western thought is more logical, rational, scientific, concerned with the manipulation of objects in the world and the behavior of the natural world; Eastern thought is nonlogical, nonrational, introspective, concerned with the patterns of mind and not of space. The West has been traditionally life-affirming in its doctrinal stance, though often life-denying in practice and application of doctrine; the East has been life-denying in its doctrines and cosmologies, but often in practice quite affirming of human experience.

Thus, while cutting through the dynamics of mythologization seemed the heart of the mystical experience, few Western mystics were able to articulate or escape from those dynamics. One who did, I found, was a fellow mendicant, Meister Eckhart.

Eckhart's thirteenth-century Europe was very different from Nagarjuna's second-century India; it was a world invaded and pervaded by the personality of the Christian God. Though some underground secret traditions carried on ancient wisdom from the pre-Christian and Gnostic mysteries, mainstream thought was realistic and exclusive. There was little room for the thought that God was a symbol for some transcendent experience which was inflected in many different ways for many different people. There was one God; the way to God was through the Church; there was one Church and one way to get to God.

Though the Church was monolithic, both in its government and in its influence in the lives of its adherents, it was not then as defensively dogmatic as it was to become after the threat of the Reformation. As a syncretic religion, early Christianity had incorporated into the "Communion of Saints" many of the local gods and traditions it encountered as it spread across the face of Europe. (In fact, up until recently, under the names of Saints Barlaam and Josaphat, the Roman Catholic Church celebrated the feast of the Buddha each year on November 27.) But despite sophisticated theological notions of analogy and allegory, which were similar to our modern-day understanding of metaphor, the myths were taken literally. And, in contrast to the East, few seemed aware that they were supposed to point to something that utterly transcended them.

So it was in an unreceptive environment that Eckhart tried to deal with the dynamics of mythologization by which metaphors and symbols came to stand for the transcendent reality. Though he was trusted and respected, and held several important offices within his religious order, he spent his later life dealing with accusations of heresy. This was serious stuff. Eckhart lived in a time when theological heterodoxy brought condemnation and possible execution at the heretic's fiery stake.

Shortly before his death he went to Avignon, the seat of the papacy during the mid-fourteenth century, to answer charges of heresy. Eckhart preached and wrote in his vernacular German, but at the Papal Court he answered the charges in Latin and, in Latin, acknowledged the authority of the Church and agreed in principle to retract any propositions deemed heterodox. He was apparently saved at least temporarily by the language difference.

He escaped learning of his eventual condemnation, however, thanks only to the slowness of travel between Avignon and the Rhineland and the swiftness of natural death. For Eckhart died sometime before the delivery of the bull condemning his theology.

Despite the papal condemnation, Eckhart's thought played an important role in the development of Western philosophy. Some of which was simply because he wrote in German and the conquest of vernacular languages was an important step in the growth of Western culture, but also because he linked the mystical thought of Plotinus and Dionysius the Areopagite with the German transcendentalist thought that later spawned the *Critiques* of Immanuel Kant, and thus modern philosophy. In Eckhart's mysticism is the root of Kant's distinction between noumenon and phenomenon, between the world as it exists in itself and the world as it is perceived by the human mind.

Eckhart was prematurely feminist. His thinking was influenced by "feminist" religious women of his time called Beguines. And, if only as a linguistic peculiarity, in both Latin and German, while God *(Deum, Gott)* is masculine, Godhead *(Deitas, Gottheit)* is feminine. So in his preaching Eckhart would sometimes call God He and sometimes She. So-called "inclusive language" has become an issue in contemporary, feminist-influenced society. Actual sexual distinction, of course, has nothing to do with God. (This was often signified in the East by portraying gods as androgynous.) The nongendered plural might be the most accurate convention to use in contemporary American English, though pluralizing the pronoun seems to suggest another non-applicable quality, number. One of the solutions of the inclusive language debate has been to avoid pronouns altogether, always using the word God. There is a powerful wisdom underlying this solution which is that "God" really is always a pronoun, for "God" is not the name of any person, place, or thing, but is always a substitute referring back to something uncertain.

The fundamental notion of Eckhart's mysticism was that there is a radical distinction between God as He (or She) exists in people's minds and God as God actually is. He held that it is possible, by virtue of a divine spark that dwells in the soul and gives it its awareness, for people to experience directly God as God actually is—which Eckhart called the Godhead. What is impossible, according to Eckhart, is to experience the Godhead through ideas; indeed, the moment individuals begin to grapple with ideas about God, they are deterred from experiencing God as God actually is. In that sense, Eckhart's fundamental distinction was self-denying, for even to allude to the Godhead is to create an idea in the mind and so be deterred from discovering God as God actually is in Godhead.

In short, Eckhart maintained that all people ever know are ideas—that is, myths and symbols are concepts about reality, not reality itself. Absolute Reality, the Godhead, is always beyond grasp. Absolute Truth is unknowable. It is empty of intelligible content.

In the same way that the Godhead is absolutely beyond all thought and all distinctions, so also are the Godhead's opinions of things. In the Godhead there are no opinions, views, or values. Those, then, who have ideas or values in their minds thereby exclude the Godhead. And so the highest virtue, which Eckhart said is what Jesus praised when he blessed the poor in spirit, is to be like the Godhead—free of all ideas and values. This virtue Eckhart called disinterest. (The German word is *Abgeschiedenheit*. The traditional translation is "detachment." Raymond B. Blakney, whose translation I used in my graduate work, chose "disinterest." Modern day radical Catholic mystic and Eckhartian scholar Matthew Fox, O. P. translates *Abgeschiedenheit* as "letting go.")

According to Eckhart, disinterest frees one from the limitations of a viewpoint, so that life can be experienced immediately, in the Now-moment, without theories, opinions, or concepts. Disinterest is what "gives God his status as God." It is an attitude toward life that accepts things just as they come. The object of disinterest, Eckhart said, is ". . . neither this nor that. Pure disinterest is empty nothingness."

Eckhart, of course, urged the practice of religion. He used the religious images and language he had inherited from his culture, but he recognized that they were arbitrary. "All paths lead to God and he is on them all evenly, to him who knows," said Eckhart. "I am well aware that a person may get more out of one technique than another but it is not best so. God responds to all techniques evenly to a knowing man. Such and such may be the way, but it is not God." (Blakney, p. 250)

Believing that Absolute Truth was unknowable, Eckhart maintained that even the Godhead could not know itself, because it could never occupy an Archimedian perspective on its own existence. Hence, Eckhart's God—the foundation of all knowledge, forever veiled in the mystery of its own transcendence and able to know itself only in the relative, multifarious world of human perspectives—resides in emptiness. For Eckhart, as for so many mystics, that emptiness became an object of fascination and longing, because it was seen as the source of the attitude of disinterest that could free one from viewpoints and opinions and thus release the soul from suffering and from fear.

Though Eckhart was perhaps the best known Western religious figure to call into question the entire mythologizing process by which religion and philosophy spoke of truth and knowledge, Christian theologians from Dionysius and Erigena onward occasionally spoke of mystical experience in terms of negation and emptiness. The goal of the mystical quest was frequently described as emptiness, a barren desert, an unfathomable abyss, a nescience, a Divine Dark. Thus John of the Cross, in allegorizing the spiritual life as the "ascent of Mount Carmel," declared that the way of ascent is through nothingness and that the goal is nothingness: "nothing, nothing, nothing, nothing, nothing, nothing, even on the Mount nothing." In his poem "The Dark Night of the Soul," Saint John said that the seeker is drawn, through that which he knows not, "To a place where he (well I knew who!) was awaiting me—A place where none appeared."

To be sure, the mystics found joy and supernal love and ecstatic bliss at the end of their quests. The dark night was simply a stage along the way. It was important because it represented the acceptance of ignorance and of the incomprehensibility of divine experience. The mystics discovered the contentlessness of all knowledge, they realized in their ecstasy that correct information does not matter very much, and what they were seeking—and what they recommended as a goal for human life—was not an education of the mind, but an experience of the heart and the spirit. They declared that the emptiness upon which consciousness rests is the real source of wonder and salvation.

☙

Nargarjuna's conflation of samsara and nirvana and Eckhart's distinction between reality and idea suggest that scientific truth and religious truth are so different that they conflict no more than apples conflict with oranges, than the mathematical theorems of Euler conflict with the paintings of Leonardo da Vinci, or the truth of Danish history conflicts with the truth of *Hamlet*. That is, science is realistic, religion sort of poetical. Science is about things, religion about states of consciousness. And, to the extent that there is such a thing and that it's meaningful to talk about it, Ultimate Truth is about something else which transcends both of them.

That science is realistic and religion poetical is a very radical thought. This discovery was a fruit of the mystical life that only the few were supposed to make. People, Giordano Bruno for instance, were burned at the stake for saying things like that. Even today it woud be considered grossly heretical and the churches don't want you thinking like this. And yet, of course, it seems almost obvious.

But I want to be very clear I'm not coming down on the side of science against religion. The mystical discovery isn't just that religious truth is poetic and metaphorical. The mystics weren't just discovering that their religious ideas were wrong. They were seeing—as the philosophers of science would also see—that truth is multidimensional, revealing itself only through partial, evanescent appearances. It is forever shifting, eluding all but the most superficial grasp. Because their concerns are with things, science and technology have championed the superficial, practical grasp. To mistake those concerns with the meaning and purpose of life is to lose hold of vast layers of significance beyond.

Knowledge requires a viewpoint and because, by definition, no viewpoint is possible from which to know the Ultimate, such truth cannot exist as a knowable, objective reality awaiting discovery through the implementation of the proper tools and methods. Instead, Truth appears as the face of a vast and shifting interplay of subjective experience and interpretation that looks different from different perspectives. And meaning—the personal experience of Truth—changes with individual and collective needs and intentions.

To mistake the surface that science can measure and predict for the greater truth does a disservice to both the scientific and the visionary truth and, even more importantly, to the gradually dawning awareness of the scope of human consciousness itself. And that is what all this is about: the evolution of consciousness.

≈

The role of metaphor was, of course, a central concern of the disciplines I had been studying, comparative religion, mythology, and philosophy: to observe patterns of similarity and to discern the intent of the metaphors that have been used to convey wisdom and understanding.

Some authorities have said that the religious and cultural metaphors are revealed by God; others, that they reflect primitive tribal social and cultural needs and conflicts; and yet others, that they manifest unconscious urges and neurological drives. What is certainly so is that throughout history men and women have observed phases and patterns in life and in nature—the cycles of planting and reaping, of the waxing and waning of the moon, of the rising and falling of the sun in the heavens. Occasionally they have had so-called peak experiences in which these phases appeared to have deep significance. From the patterns of nature seemed to flow intuitions about the meaning and purpose of human life.

My own observation, corroborated by Campbell's testimony, was that these fundamental experiences and intuitions of the people were made sense of by teachers and tribal leaders. Some of these were primitive shamans who inhaled burning herbs, ate mushrooms, fasted, and scourged themselves in order to induce trance consciousness. Others were medieval theologians who prayed, meditated, sang Gregorian chants, and engaged in learned debates with one another. Some were witches who worshipped the Great Mother out on the moors under the full moon. Others prophets and hermits who lived in the rarefied atmospheres of high mountain passes. And today these are scientists, psychologists, cultural commentators, and even politicians.

These community leaders interpreted fundamental experiences and intuitions and placed them in the context of their own understandings of the significant needs and desires of their peoples according to their perceptions of what their own lives were about—based on personal experiences, including those that made them leaders, and on what they had learned from their teachers. Thus they created and transmitted guiding metaphors—symbolic images that could capture collective experience and intuitions and move the populace in directions the leaders believed to be important.

In the most accurate sense, myths are not falsehoods but are the patterns of these images, symbols, and metaphors which have been used to understand and to convey human experience. Myths are structures of thought, frameworks for making sense of experience, that rise along with cultures and shape their evolution. They are the media through which individuals perceive and pass on collective beliefs. In *The Power of Myth* interviews Campbell says, "One could say that the images of myth are reflections of spiritual and depth potentialities of every one of us. And that through contemplating those we evoke these powers in our own lives to operate through us." (*Power of Myth*, pp. 217–218)

These collective beliefs concern everything from anxieties about economics to major political doctrines, from definitions of public scandal to intuitions about the meaning of existence. They may be as fleeting as worry about a temporary drought or the popularity of a social hero or movie starlet, and as substantial as belief in democracy or in the working of Divine Providence even in disaster.

Religion is that class of collective beliefs that deals with practical questions about moral behavior and, more important, with questions about the meaning of life and the purpose of human existence. As

Campbell explained, religion has dealt with four major areas of concern: how the world is structured (cosmology), how society best functions (sociology), how the individual matures and prospers (psychology), and how consciousness perceives its own nature (mysticism). (This was a model Campbell used repeatedly in his talks. One interesting presentation of it appears in *The Masks of God, Vol. 4: Creative Mythology*, pp. 609–624.)

Religious myths reflect both the experiences of ordinary people trying to live full lives and the sensibilities of leaders trying to capture common experiences in metaphors. While many of these leaders have been kings, politicians, and bureaucrats, or churchmen behaving like these, those who developed the basic religious myths were the mystics and visionaries. Through a vast variety of disciplines and practices—some of which seem appalling and inhuman today—these spiritual leaders achieved states of altered consciousness in which they saw beyond the surface of everyday reality. In psychological terms, they saw deep into the layers of the unconscious; in metaphysical terms, they saw into the constituents of being; in spiritual terms, they saw through the limitations of physical existence into the primordial nature of life and consciousness itself.

They then worked to explain their insights and intuitions to disciples and students and, through them, to the populace. Such mystical experiences as they had are almost always ineffable—incredibly difficult, if not impossible, to describe. Of course, ineffability of this sort is not limited to mystical experience. Most people have felt frustration with trying to explain why they find something particularly beautiful. Those who have taken psychedelic drugs know how difficult it is to convey the insights they had while tripping. The only way to describe beauty or psychedelic experience is to say: "Well, it was like this or like that."

"It was like . . ." That is precisely what the shamans, mystics, prophets, oracles, and visionaries have said. They described their experience in terms of things that seemed familiar; they used familiar metaphors and symbols in the hope that these would help others achieve similar insights. Over time, certain metaphors came to be regarded as most effectively capturing and communicating ineffable mystical experience. Thus these were revered and passed down through generations and were canonized as "true." Particularly in the West, where people were prone to think literally, the metaphors and symbols of the mystics came to be mistaken for the ineffable reality they were intended to convey.

Gradually they were concretized and formulated. It was forgotten that these mythical metaphors and symbols originally came from someone stammering out of a trance, "It's like this, it's like this . . ."

❧

In modern times this mistaking of metaphor for literal truth has become pronounced. Scientific method is founded on the assumption that there is a reality outside the observer. As the assumptions of scientists have shaped popular consciousness, they have given rise to the belief that it is possible to divorce the observer from his or her observation and to pinpoint exactly what is going on "out there" whether anybody's watching or not. This is the sense of the familiar philosophical conundrum: Does a tree falling in the forest, with no one to hear it, make a sound?

Many people today are sophisticated enough to know that the sound is really the act of perception, and they are not reluctant to answer no. But they are usually quick to affirm that there do occur the waves of disturbance in the air which, impinging upon an ear, would *be* sound. They certainly think the trees in the forest exist whether or not there are people around. And they believe that the qualities of the trees can be described accurately even when one is sitting in a philosophy classroom far from the actual forest.

This is the modern realistic sensibility that has obscured the metaphorical and subjective quality of religion. For when early believers said that Jesus (or Buddha or another of the multitude of world saviors) was born of a virgin, they meant that for them there was something as marvelous and special about Jesus's coming into the world as if he had been born of a woman who had never had sex. It was later believers who mistook the metaphor so badly that they began discussing the gynecological dynamics by which Jesus's mother could remain "intact" *pre, in, et post natum.* That somehow missed the point. The image of the virgin birth was not supposed to describe obstetrics but to inspire awe and reverence and a sense of the personal and collective significance of Jesus's place in history.

Most of the religious metaphors have meaning on a variety of levels. The virgin birth, for instance, also means that the savior is born into material existence directly from the creative power itself (the primordially feminine Great Mother) without the agency of the rational mind (the masculine Father). The virgin birth also means that the savior is born through the conjunction of opposites and thereby transcends the logical demands of non-contradiction. Such "feminist" interpretations of the mythic image need not carry all of the antisexual implications that have made the virgin birth currently so unpopular.

One of the biblical sources for the virgin birth of Jesus, for instance, is the verse in Isaiah: "Behold, a virgin shall conceive and bear a child and his name shall be called Emmanuel." (Isaiah 7: 14) Of course, Isaiah was talking about his own immediate times. He was rebuking King Achaz for not following his advice to stay out of conflict with a coalition of neighboring nations. The prophecy continues, "He shall be living on curds and honey by the time he learns to reject the bad and choose the good. For before the child learns to reject the bad and choose the good, the land of those two kings whom you dread shall be deserted." The "prophecy" was a poetical way of saying that by the time a child born to a woman of marriageable age would be old enough to know right from wrong the foreign relations threats worrying the King would have resolved on their own.

Isaiah didn't know he was supposed to be predicting the birth of Jesus. It was only in retrospect, when the doctrinal content of Christianity was being established, that this reference was applied to the birth of Jesus. But, at any rate, biblical scholars tell us that the word in Isaiah translated as "virgin" really meant something more like "young woman who has not yet had a child." We don't have such a word in English that applies to humans, though we do that applies to cattle: a "heifer" is a cow that has not calfed. In this sense a virgin is a "non-mother," not a sexual innocent.

The virgin birth signifies that the savior is born of a mother who is not a mother, i.e., his origin violates/transcends the laws of non-contradiction. In Christianity, this is obviously the point since the essence of the Incarnation is that Jesus was simultaneously God and man, i.e., God and not-God. Sex wasn't the issue. The issue was the void between God and man. The myth of Jesus's incarnation signified that that void was being bridged through the wisdom Jesus preached.

The resurrection of Jesus or of Osiris reveals the cycle of the eternal return of the transcendental Self—the promise that no life is ever totally wasted, that life conquers death, and that death is a natural part of the process that allows new life to grow up, phoenix-like, from the sadness and fear we feel at our mortality. It need not be limited to the historicity of certain rather remarkable physical resuscitations. The myths of creation indicate the inventive power by which consciousness engenders the world and maintains it in experience. The myths of afterlife indicate that individual existence, fleeting and truncated as it always is, is but the surface of the deeper reality that gives significance to the individual life. Indeed, the one level on which all the myths have little, or debased, meaning is the literal one.

Yet referring to the great religious myths as images, symbols, and metaphors for collective human experience could seem reductionistic, suggesting that all there is to myth is a poetical/fantastical description of the real world. There are those who use this reasoning to debunk mythical consciousness. Elucidating the metaphors, seeking to find the "metaphorands" (Julian Jaynes's useful neologism for the "something" that is the object of the metaphorizing/mythologizing process) has been called "demythologization." In fact, it only offers new myths, more familiar metaphors for our own times. Explaining the metaphorands of myth, using rational, scientific-sounding words to explain what the myths mean, simply reinterprets them into current mythology. For the naive scientific world is the popular myth structure of today.

In the eyes of those who have seen through to the nature of existence, nothing really means anything on the literal level, for *all* human experience is necessarily mediated by metaphors. It appears that the "real world" itself is a metaphor, built up over centuries and gradually concretized, for some direct experience of consciousness. The primordial experience is simply being conscious, or just being, and this experience has been shaped into the world by the attempts of many, many people to communicate their experience to one another.

The direct, unmediated experience is unintelligible. It is occasionally achieved—sometimes through ingestion of drugs that anesthetize or stupefy the faculties that order experience into intelligible patterns (i.e., the metaphors), sometimes by dint of strenuous effort, sometimes through trauma or illness, sometimes by sheer accident. Those who have had the experience often report that it seemed to undo the world, and sometimes transform their values. They say, with William James, that the world appears to be, in itself, a "booming, buzzing confusion," within which ego operates as a reducing valve to limit and sort out the mass of input.

Those who have a strong faith in the solid existence of the world are often bewildered by such experiences. Having thought that the meaning and significance they experience in their lives came from the outside world, they are dismayed when confronted with the realization that they themselves are the source of the meaning they find and that they must take responsibility for the world they experience.

This discovery does not deny the reality of the world outside the mind. It is neither simple nihilism nor naive idealism. It says only that nothing intelligible can be said about the outside world because intelligibility itself—like the sound of the tree falling—exists only in the mind of the perceiver and because the world is meaningless outside of a mind which can perceive meaning. Thus statements like "The world is real" and "The world is not real," "God does not exist" and "God does exist," are meaningless in themselves.

Those who have a sense of the mystical dimensions of life tend to be fascinated by such ideas. They experience a sort of delight and wonder in the realization that the world around them is arbitrary, that there are no fixed rules except collective consensus, and that nothing need be taken *too* seriously. Sensing that there is something they ought to know but don't, they are lured ever deeper into their own experience of consciousness.

The myths that religious leaders and teachers use to structure consciousness are often fascinating to these mystical types because, once literal meaning has been divorced from them, the myths appear as maps with which to chart a way toward and through the direct experience of consciousness. Thus they appear useful not as descriptions of reality but as descriptions of the mind that over millennia has generated the world of reality as each of us knows it.

We look back on the medieval interest in astrology, magic, and alchemy as poor substitutes for our astronomy, technology, and chemistry, yet from another perspective the poverty is ours not theirs. For we, with our prosaic interpretation of their symbols, have lost the sense of coherence and connectedness with the environment around us that their metaphorical "pre-sciences" taught them.

The geocentric, Ptolemaic universe was—as northern California comparative religion professor Jacob Needleman has observed in *A Sense of the Cosmos*—far less a scientific statement than a psychological one. That the sun and stars went around the earth meant that human lives were influenced by the powers of heaven, a fact clearly visible in the effect of the seasons. Centrality was not better; it made this life subject to the whims of fate manifested in the night sky. But it made life meaningful. The geocentric system was less megalomaniacal, claiming the earth to be the center of the universe, than it was humble and self-effacing, recognizing that life on this plane of existence was dependent, conditional, and contingent, that human life is created from levels of complexity and meaning that elude grasp.

What spirituality can do that secularism, at least so far, has not done is to restore life-affirming meaning to our world. For the spiritual life is the life lived vitally on as many planes of interpretation and understanding as possible. Indeed, life is perhaps most spiritual when we are least attached to specific notions and ideas about God and about reality and most open to the plurality of metaphors. If so, then the meaning of religious truth is very different from what the churches popularly teach.

Many people today understand that religion is metaphorical. Few of these, however, value the religious metaphors. They observe that the churches have taken the myths seriously in ways that seem foolish and used them to inculcate guilt and perpetuate divisiveness. These skeptics are often correct, though they may fail to see that taking secular symbols seriously may be just as foolish.

In giving ourselves over to a literal approach to life, we fall prey to a boring and debilitating interpretation of experience. Life becomes one-dimensional. The myth of Madison Avenue-driven consumerism, the myth of the good life in southern California (a two-car garage, a patio with a barbecue pit, and a boat in a world where it never rains), the myth of upward mobility—these status symbols within the material, three-dimensional world become the substance of secular devotion. These are meager myths on which to base a life.

Religion might be able to protect us from such banality, but we have first to save religion. And the salvation of religion hardly lies in a return to old doctrines or even in construction of new doctrines parallel to those of the past. It is unlikely that a new messiah could arise, able to sweep the world in the way that the messiahs of old could sweep small nations. We cannot go back to the prescientific past. What we require is a guiding myth, free of polemic, that cuts right to the root of religion, recasting it. Then perhaps we can begin intelligently to value the vast system of symbols and metaphors that our predecessors employed to give meaning to their lives and rediscover the many levels of meaning and significance that are conveyed in the mythic traditions. Then we can begin to *believe* rather than *know* the truth that is important for us.

In the scientific world, knowing is considered more valid than believing. Many modern Christians—and members of quasi-religious groups—insist that they know rather than believe the propositions taught by their groups. (Even someone as steeped in mythical thinking as C. G. Jung could say, in an interview for the BBC, that he didn't believe there was a God; he knew.) Belief is taken to imply lack of certainty.

There is, however, a deeper sense of belief. Ursula LeGuin, science fiction writer and modern mythopoet herself, describes this sense of belief: "The poet Rilke looked at a statue of Apollo about fifty years ago, and Apollo spoke to him. 'You must change your life,' he said. When the genuine myth arises into consciousness, that is always its message. You must change your life." In this sense, belief does not mean "positing certainty," but "opening oneself up to being changed."

In *Religious Language: An Empirical Placing of Theological Phrases,* Ian Ramsey, a British churchman, spoke of myth in this same spirit as: ". . . odd language"—"and we might even conclude in the end that the odder the language the more it matters to us"—that is designed to make "the light break," that is, to produce transformative experience. Writing in the tradition of British linguistic analytic philosophy, he pointed to the indefiniteness of myth, which he observed is different from fact because there is not necessarily any fact upon which the content of myth is based. Also in this spirit wrote Frederick Streng, a professor of religion whose interpretation of Nagarjuna was the basis of my own understanding of Buddhist Madhyamika philosophy and the whole sense of emptiness. In *Emptiness: A Study in Religious Meaning,* Streng says that the truth of religious doctrine is its ability to "save," i.e., to produce religious experience.

The sense of Jesus's resurrection, for instance, is only tangentially related to the archaeological fact of an empty tomb: The miracle of resurrection is already outside the historico-scientific world frame. Resurrection has to mean more about the life of the believer than it does about an alleged event two thousand years distant in time. The verification for a myth is its saving power and not its mapping with history.

When *Credo in unum Deum* is taken to mean "I know there is a God," it means little more than "I know that so-and-so is president of the United States." When *Credo* means "I believe in God," it can mean "I will allow this idea to change my life." Believing means letting the religious metaphors influence one, letting them become not Ultimate

Truths but, in Protestant theologian Paul Tillich's words, "ultimate concerns."

Knowing requires a perspective and assumes certain laws of logic. One cannot know both A and not-A to be true at the same time and in the same manner. But one can believe in both A and not-A, in the sense of being open to being affected by both propositions. Knowing is what the experience of emptiness and the plurality of truths calls into jeopardy. Believing is the healthy response to that experience. If nothing is true, we can believe in everything. We can allow all the mythic images and symbols to affect our lives. We can look for those that speak to us as Apollo spoke to Rilke. We can say, like Joseph Campbell said to the lady: "Anybody who believes in as many gods as I do can hardly be called an atheist."

∾

My study of Nagarjuna and Meister Eckhart had shown me that the teaching of emptiness declares that Divine Reality—Ultimate Truth, upon which all other truth is based—is not a suitable object of knowledge. The mystics who spoke of the divine emptiness, or of the unknowableness of God, or of nirvana, were trying, in the language forms available to them, to call the minds of their students and listeners beyond the views, opinions, and beliefs they held unthinkingly, because such, the mystics had seen, were impediments to spiritual vision.

From Nagarjuna and Eckhart and Campbell, I learned that opinions are like baseball cards. They're something to collect, to bring out at the right times to show other people, perhaps even to enjoy mulling over in private. Opinions (like Joe Campbell's Republicanism, of course) are just opinions. They're like myths and stories in that regard. They set a context within which to view new information. They do affect a person that way. But they're not right and wrong in the way that mathematical information is right or wrong. They are definitely not something to take seriously or to identify one's ego with. And ego is precisely the problem.

Part of the spiritual effort is getting over the daily attachment to ego. And one of the major ways of doing that is learning not to take our opinions seriously. In that regard I remember at that first appearance at the Mann Ranch, Joe was asked about meditation practice. He answered in a challenging way that raised a variety of points, saying something to the effect of: "You must understand that yoga and meditation come out of the Eastern mind. They're designed to shatter the ego and so free the soul of the individual.

"What an Eastern ego is is so different from what a Western ego is. I've been to India and I've seen it for myself. These people were never taught to be strong individuals. Children are not given any choices. They're told by their parents what kind of ice cream they like. And the parents are told by their culture. And they don't question this.

"What ego means in a traditional culture like that is the individual's resistance to doing what the culture says to do. It's an entirely different thing from the West.

"That Eastern, traditional-society ego," Joe said, "is like a little Christmas tree ornament, a little glass bubble. Yoga is like a a delicate, very precise silver hammer. And when you tap the glass bubble with the little hammer, the bubble just shatters and the individual is freed from the pulls of ego that distract the individual from fitting into the culture.

"The Western ego-person, on the other hand, is like a big solid rock. Parents have taught their children to make educated choices and to value their right to choose. When you tap that solid rock with your little silver hammer, well, nothing happens.

"That's not to say yoga and meditation aren't good things to do, but it is to say that the struggle to transcend ego and the suffering that goes with being an isolated, individual ego is something else."

A familiar line Joe always repeated was his answer once to a question from the audience, "What is your yoga?" He'd always laugh and say: "I told that fellow my yoga was rare roast beef, good Irish whiskey, and a hundred laps every day around the pool at the YMCA."

Ego is not personality. In the West, it refers to something akin to perspective; in the East, as Campbell observed, it refers to a retrograde, uncooperative tendency within the human being. This was something I asked him about in one of my first correspondences with him. In a letter to me, dated April 27, 1971, Joe wrote:

> First, then, I think of "ego" as an organ of the psyche, somewhat as the eye is an organ of the body. Freud describes it as the organ of the "reality function"—"reality" here meaning "empirical reality." Jung writes of "ego" as an "autonomous complex": it can be overthrown permanently or temporarily, by other autonomous complexes, as in Jekyll and Hyde transformations of the personality, in amnesia, in psychoses, etc. It is the

binding center of a continuity of consciousness and, as such, not the "self," the "psyche," or "soul." Our question, then, is not properly of "ego" and "godhood," but of "self" or psyche and "godhood"; and yet "ego" does play an important role in the argument, since "ego" is the conscious subject of knowledge, and is the "knower," consequently, of "God."

"God," as known, is Object for a Subject. But only "God" can know "God" fully: that is the meaning of the doctrine (is it not?) of the Second Person of the Trinity as the "Knower of the Father." Short of the Knowledge of the Father that is possible to the Son, there is, then, no true "knowledge of God"; there are only such "knowledges" as "egos" can entertain. But "ego knowledge" is dualistic. As long as there is thinking, there is ego and there are categories. It is improper, therefore, to " *think*": "God and I are one!" However, if the *experiencing* subject can be dissociated from the *thinking* —if one can say with Paul, "live now, not 'I' but 'Christ in me!' "—then (it would seem to me) the whole question of duality, "I and Thou," etc., will have dissolved; and what will remain will be the question of the metaphysics of all this, which, as Kant points out, is beyond knowledge; or, perhaps, a question as to whether Paul and the mystics may not perhaps be overstating their experiences. Eckhart states, "It is of more worth to God that Christ should be born in the virgin or good soul than that he should have been born in Bethlehem" [or something to that effect]. This statement and that of Paul would seem to suggest that human consciousness can indeed become identified with that of the Son and become capable of truly knowing the Father. That would also imply, however, that, like the Son, one has become "One with the Father," as the Son is "One with the Father."

For Meister Eckhart, ego referred to the failure of the individual person to see the identity which is real with the Father. In that sense, the sought after "ego-loss" of yoga, meditation, and contemplative practice is not at all a renunciation of the Western accomplishment of personal responsibility, dignity of the individual, and worth of the human being, but an awareness of the divine identity. What we need to lose are those opinions and ideas that make some things good and others bad, the opinions that we use to divide ourselves from other people and from our true identity.

⟨⟨⟩⟩

It is a familiar theme in religious stories that people fail to see God when he appears to them because he is not what they are expecting.

They already have a clear conception of what God is like, and when he or she confronts them directly, they turn away because "that just couldn't be right."

The description of the dying process in Tibetan Buddhist myth illustrates this. One summer at the ranch I was assisting Joseph Campbell at a lecture on the *Bardo Thodol,* the so-called *Tibetan Book of the Dead.* My job was to operate the slide projector. Campbell had given me a loaded carousel and asked me to change the slides at his signal.

As the lecture began, slides appeared of the Tibetan mountains and countryside, then paintings of Tibetan priests like those who might be attending the dying soul on its afterlife journey, and then finally of the dying person. At Campbell's nod I clicked in the next slide. The screen was flooded with bright white light; no slide had entered the projector. Something's wrong, I thought, and clicked the advance switch again. This time a mandala of the bliss-bestowing Buddhas appeared. And even as I was relaxing, Campbell explained my error. I had demonstrated his point.

The immediate experience of the soul on entering the afterlife is of the Clear Light. This is the direct experience of nirvana, of ultimate consciousness. Yet the soul bypasses it, looking for some expected image— even though it has been taught over and over that the Clear Light is the first thing it will see. I'd studied Tibetan Buddhism. I knew that the Clear Light would be the first vision after death. Yet when the slide that was no-slide appeared as the bright white light on the screen, I panicked and switched it off.

Now the first teaching of the mystics is that God or nirvana is never what one expects. One's opinions always get in the way. What one must empty oneself of is opinions. The reason for teaching emptiness is to call the mind past its opinions. That is true, in some ways, of all religious doctrines. By undermining the belief in the obvious sensible material world, doctrine breaks one bond to views and opinions. If, however, the belief in the spiritual world takes on the same simple solid character that it was designed to undermine, then the spiritual teaching has been lost.

Perhaps we moderns who believe nothing are closer to the Light than we have ever imagined!

CHAPTER FOUR

The Great Secret

*Whether dream or myth, in these adventures there is an
atmosphere of irresistible fascination about the figure
that appears suddenly as guide, marking a new period,
a new stage, in the biography. That which has to be
faced, and is somehow profoundly familiar to the
unconscious—though unknown, surprising, and even
frightening to the conscious personality—makes itself
known; and what formerly was meaningful may
become strangely emptied of value . . . (Hero, p. 55)*

Driving across the Oakland Bay Bridge one afternoon, I was wondering about Nagarjuna and Eckhart. I was feeling confused about the whole notion of Truth, frustrated, even angry, that the God who seemed so important was, instead, so elusive. I was wondering why God was not more accessible and responsive.

Suddenly I realized that that—the confusion, the perplexity, the frustration, the mystery—was precisely what the whole thing was about. God was being responsive. And that was what I had seen at the castle: That is how God is revealed. The point of religious Truth is not to make explicit the multiple levels of reality, but to make them appear demanding and fascinating, to pique curiosity, to lure the mind beyond the surface. The whole religious enterprise, I saw, points beyond itself to a fundamental quality of consciousness that affects everything we know and every approach we take to knowledge. And, of course, this is where it meets science—not at the level of explanation, but at the level of imagination.

Revealed in every aspect of the universe—on all levels of existence, from the simple material to the most advanced cosmological or most bizarre esoteric presentation of it—there is a secret. Consciousness itself, I saw, is the striving to discover that secret. For secrecy is the fundamental epistemological category. And it can only be spoken of in myths. Those individual myths manifest the myth of the Great Secret.

I had wanted to understand what the mystics meant by emptiness. I'd thought it would help me discover the Ultimate Truth behind the modern confusion. But I had been caught in a self-contradictory regress. That afternoon on the Bay Bridge I realized that emptiness is the metaphor for this infinite regression. The mystical quest pursues a fundamental secrecy upon which the experience of consciousness rests. What the mystics meant by emptiness is what in myth is metaphorized as the hidden knowledge the hero seeks after. Truth is ultimately secret, conveyable only through metaphors and myths which are used for speaking of Ultimate Truth, not because they are pretty or stylish, but because they are all one can use. The mystical statements about emptiness are not metaphysical, but epistemological.

As I realized that it was not ultimate metaphysical fact I was dealing with, but the nature of human knowing, reality began to appear to me made up not of solid objects but of experiences and thoughts. My mind was being called beyond the everyday world. And that was, I saw, the point of mystical doctrine: not to convey truth—at whatever level—but to induce openness of mind and to inspire wonder. It doesn't matter whether what inspires wonder is true or not, only that it is effective.

This insight did not give me a new vision of Truth. I saw nothing that others before me had not seen. But I did achieve an awareness of the mythologizing faculty; I glimpsed how the mind creates the universe of experience and then reveals to itself that creation. And that, I realized, was the basis for a guiding myth that could for me, and I believe for others, make sense of religion in the modern world.

☙

Throughout the world's great religions can be found the intimation that there is a secret which founds life, gives it a reason for being, and draws together all its elements. The traditions all declare that the world of sight and sound is but the surface of a greater reality, that behind the events of the visible world there is another reality of which this world is but a manifestation and feeble reflection.

Christianity teaches that the world is the creation of God the Father, made for his delight, into which, because of sin, his only begotten Son has been incarnated. Beyond this world, perceptible only through the delicate experience of personal motivation, the greater reality proceeds as the economy of grace. Guardian angels watch over each of us, guiding us toward salvation. Those who have already been saved, the saints, stand waiting to attend to our spiritual needs and to pass our prayers on to God. In a dramatic and tangible way, the infusion of grace in our souls is manifested through the ritual actions of the sacraments that the Son, incarnated in the person of Jesus of Nazareth, left behind to maintain his presence within history.

Hinduism tells us that the world of our experience is *maya* (illusion). We are in fact curiously individuated bits of Brahman, the creative power, who have lived and died in this world countless times. Surrounding us, and offering their aid in our dealing with the illusion, are the innumerable ranks of gods and goddesses and all sorts of divine and demonic beings who enter into the world in subtle ways. Fellow human beings who have worked diligently to free themselves from the karma of their past lives and to improve their concentration on, and awareness of, deeper reality can teach us techniques for following them up the ladder of reincarnation into a state of timeless bliss.

Judaism observes that the world is the garden of God's creation, into which men and women were placed to tend and enjoy the delights of the garden. Through disobedience to the Law, we have lost sight of the garden, but the contractual relationship with God goes on. Yahweh God is the Lord of History, and in his incomprehensible ways he continues to work to re-create the world through the lives of his chosen people. For reasons known only to God, his people have suffered enormous hardships and ignominy and yet have survived and, despite all the odds against it, have continued to produce leading figures in the history of human thought.

Buddhism declares that the world of ordinary mortals is but a dream. The dream is fraught with suffering and misery because of desire, which clings to the dream, and of ignorance, which prevents us from observing its nature. The universes of heavens and hells, peopled with gods and demons, are but figures in the dream, yet they have dream reality enough to help us through. Within our world there are teachers, at least some of whom are incarnations of divine beings who have, as humans, vowed to remain within the dream to help fellow sufferers endure the arduous task of awakening. The most important of all teachers for this present age was Prince Gautama, who, in working for his own release from suffering and death, discovered the nature of suffering and ignorance and taught a way of salvation characterized by mildness, compassion, and avoidance of extremes.

Islam calls us back to submission to God. It calls us to pay attention to God's presence, to obey God's command that we care for one another, to pray daily in concert with other worshippers, and to spread the word that all people must obey God's will. Masters and holy men who have dedicated themselves to do more than the Law requires live among us as teachers and channels of grace. Some of them have seen that the fundamental revelation *La Ilaha El Allah Hu* (There is no god but God) means, indeed, there is nothing but God.

Confucianism and Taoism, the two sibling traditions that influence Chinese and Japanese thought, offer practical wisdom about life in the real world of men and women. They reveal the dynamics that proceed on a level above individual human lives. Matters of state and matters of nature are determined by the interaction of great archetypal forces—the yin and the yang, the creative and the receptive—that are manifested in multiple ways in human experience. These traditions, in practice, are mingled with local folk religions that recognize the presence of angels and demons in our lives and that call us to honor our ancestors that they may live on in memory and so that we, in turn, may be remembered and afforded some degree of immortality.

And religion is not the only medium through which this news is presented. Modern science tells us that things aren't what they appear to be: The writing desk is both a solid piece of furniture and a nearly empty space occupied by minute, rapidly moving particles that seem to be but evanescent whorls of energy flow, the form and behavior of which are determined by the geometry of space-time. Psychology tells us that our experience of the world is massively influenced by our past experience, from which we have learned how to sort out sense data, and by such dynamics as repression, sublimation, and transference which further separate us as conscious entities from the world of exterior things. The social sciences tell us that our behavior is determined far more than we realize by external forces and patterns.

Parapsychology and the occult sciences (variations on religion, yet based on different sources) tell us that there are occurrences in the world that just don't fit our commonly agreed-upon conventions and assumptions about reality: Plants respond telepathically, cancer can be cured through visualization, healers can instantaneously restore function to crippled limbs, psychics can "read" people's lives from the invisible light around their bodies, people's intentions can influence the outcome of events in the external world.

Even the evening news occasionally runs a story about inexplicable phenomena. Strange things are happening. Sometimes these are accounts of bizarre acts of violence—by serial killers, for instance, who cannibalize their victims—which can be "explained" as the insanity of particular, peculiar individuals. (Though, even so, we have to wonder what kind of a world a person like Jeffrey Dahmer, the "body parts killer" of 1991, lives in and how he ever got into a state of consciousness so totally different from that of the rest of us.) Sometimes the news stories are of events that don't seem to have *any* explanation. The most common of these are the lights in the sky called UFOs. Others range from such seemingly benign phenomenon as the appearance of crop circles in farmers' fields in Great Britain, in which rings or perfect circles appear during the night where the grain has been bent and flattened inexplicably, to such troubling phenomenon as cattle mutilations in the southwestern United States in which livestock are apparently killed, also during the night, by having their internal organs surgically removed. Such phenomena suggest that there are "secrets" about the world we haven't been told.

In fact, it seems these last two examples have been explained: crop circles as the work of a couple of old English countryside pranksters and cattle mutilations as that of birds of prey going after just the prime parts of the animal. But, however well science explains odd phenomena, the mind always conjures up some more. At the edges of the village compound there are always protective guardians; beyond them there are always fearful monsters. Both support the boundaries between the known and the unknown, the apparent and the mysterious. The archetypal images reveal that at the fringes of the consensual world there are fuzzy areas where the rules of reality don't hold. And that fact challenges our whole notion about rules.

☙

Not only in the external world which we share with other conscious beings, but also in our own internal world in which we are each alone with ourselves, there are curious events that challenge our understanding of our lives and hint that there is something we don't know about. All of us experience eerie moments of déjà vu or of clairvoyance. Sometimes it seems we remember something from the future instead of from the past. Sometimes we meet someone who seems like an angel or a messenger from heaven, too magical to be real, who says just what we need to hear at that moment to restore direction to our lives. We all occasionally experience moments when we feel we know all the answers, when the barriers that had seemed to cloud our vision drop away and our lives suddenly make sense.

These are the moments when, probably more than at other times, we are most open to direct experience, when the categories of rationality, common sense, and collective consensus are left behind. These are moments when the mythopoetic consciousness is closest to us, for it was from such moments, cultivated and savored, that the the metaphors of the great mythological systems were constructed in the first place. These are the moments when we perceive the presence of a Great Secret and when we see that our lives, at least on this level of consciousness, are intelligible only in terms of the myths. For these are times when our lives are manifesting indications to us, when it almost seems as though the gods are speaking directly to us through the agency of the world, when our sights are raised above the triviality of the everyday, and we feel ourselves connected with the greater reality that surrounds us.

The experience of the mystics is really not very far from each of us, though because we don't have language with which to talk about it, we usually remain silent and secretive about such experiences of the fringes.

∾

Most of us find these high experiences interesting, but also a little suspect. We certainly think that we should not put too much credence in them or talk too freely about them. We feel that, as sensible, rational, modern individuals, we should dismiss such feelings as superstitious nonsense—perhaps even fearing that they are precursors of madness—for these experiences are clearly beyond the scientific requirements of replicability and sensory verification.

Unfortunately the decision to focus our attention, not on the world of the gods, but on the commonplace world may be the choice of a world, governed by blind chance, that threatens to humiliate us, maim us, or destroy us, a world in which control over our lives has been lost and we feel almost as though we are automatons within a self-perpetuating system beyond the control even of its designers. Then our lives seem doomed to triviality, unable to rise above the immediate and the practical. Yet, even in that flat and pallid world of everyday consciousness, over which we feel no control, we discover that each of us is still held ultimately responsible for his or her own life, in the sense that no one else has to accept the consequences, the joys and sufferings, of that life.

What the intimations of a higher order of significance and meaning can suggest to us is that we can willingly assume that responsibility by gaining control of how we interpret and understand our lives—who we are and what our existence means. We can choose to use metaphors and symbols that have roots deeper than everyday reality, that reach out into the greater reality that is forever veiled in secrecy. We can choose to escape the trivial by intentionally connecting our lives with the great themes and carriers of meaning that have provided sustenance for the multitude of human lives preceding ours.

We can value, as a call to an adventure in consciousness, the experiences that evade sensible explanation. We can see that our predecessors had long perceived such phenomena and developed systems of interpretation so that these experiences became guideposts pointing out a direction to life. We can understand that, in great part, what have come down to us as the explanations of cosmology, the dynamics of salvation, the dramatizations of the lives of heroic figures, have all been schemata for interpreting such bizarre phenomena and such transcendent feelings. We can understand these experiences as providing clues to us about our lives that are explicable only according to the patterns of fairy tale, legend, tradition, and religion. We can choose to mythologize our lives in ways that reverence the sense of significance, or even just unusualness, that satisfies our need for rootedness in greater reality. And yet we can avoid positing any specific qualities or attributes—including existence—to that reality, for we can understand that its nature is shrouded in secrecy.

Thus the sense that there is something we think we ought to know but don't, that there is a Great Secret, calls us to leave the trivial and venture into a world of greater significance. This call to adventure is the beginning of the hero's journey toward discovery. We can all look for this call within our own lives, seeing that this quest is the drive of consciousness to expand and enhance and encompass itself.

The young Prince Gautama had been satisfied with the pleasures of his father's palace until one day the gods decided it was the propitious time to set him on the path to Buddhahood. While he was riding in his chariot, there appeared one day on the side of the road an old man, then on another day a diseased man, then on another a dead body, and finally a monk. Each of these apparitions was a manifestation of the call to retire from the world and to seek beneath its surface the hidden wisdom that would make sense of the conditions of suffering and death in which human beings live.

While King Arthur's knights were gathered about the table feasting— we are told in the great mythic cycle of the Arthurian legends, which manifest fundamentally Western perceptions about the nature of the spirit—there appeared to them a vision of the Grail, the cup that Jesus had drunk from during the Last Supper. It signified the fount of grace and justification, the achievement of which was the goal of the Christian life. Yet as quickly as it was recognized, it was gone. The knights agreed that what could give meaning and satisfaction to their lives would be a quest to recover the Grail.

Moses was herding his flocks when Yahweh spoke to him out of the burning bush. Paul was thrown from his horse on the Damascus road when Jesus called him to announce the Christian Gospel. Saint Joan was watching over her sheep when she heard the voices of saints. Martin Luther was sitting in a privy when he realized that he must preach the nature of justification by faith alone. However symbolized, in historical or legendary images, the call to adventure begins with a remarkable event or an insight that reveals to the hero that he or she has discovered something about life, destiny, the universe, the will of God, and must seek further to discover more to give meaning to life. The hero's journey begins with the intimation that there is a Great Secret.

The sense that there is, hidden somehow within our world, a reality that if we could find it would bring us satisfaction and joy, causes us to feel a sense of wonder and awe at the possibilities of life. And that wonder will, in fact, begin to transform our consciousness so that virtue will flower in and transform our world. The seers of old looked upon the Secret and felt awe—which they expressed in metaphorical forms—and it so transformed their lives that they were respected and remembered as good men and women who were loved by those around them and whose lives were worthy of imitation.

What the mystics and visionaries experienced as emptiness was the sense that life is fluid and open. They saw how belief was like a ladder that leads upward, not toward Truth, but toward virtue. We too can climb the ladder of the myths to that same sense of wonder at the multidimensionality and splendor of life. We too can allow that wonder to change our lives and to transform, with us, the world in which we live. We do that by opening ourselves up to the healing power of the archetypal symbols, allowing the myths to work on us and feed us with varying senses of meaning in our world which can lead us to appreciate our lives, to love our lives, to cherish our experience.

What saves us from believing in our own mythical pretensions and keeps us detached from the symbols so that they do not pull us down into literal dogmatism, is the realization—made possible for us today by the widespread sense of the emptiness of Truth—that all these beliefs are but clues to a secret that has no ultimate meaning, that they are exercises of mind, techniques which when properly utilized can produce wonder and open us to transformation, so that we expand and enlarge our consciousness.

What lures us deeper into the myths is the sense of the Secret, the sense that the myths lead somewhere, that there is something we ought to know but don't that yet has the power to save us. This is the primary intuition of religion. It is the call to the adventure by which the hero is transformed on his or her journey. We too can feel the lure of the Great Secret, and we can look into our lives as though they were puzzles, labyrinths through which we are led by signposts toward something wonderful.

When we become conscious of our own lives as the life of God, manifesting the qualities that are metaphorized in the myths, we are restored to innocence and born into freedom. When we begin to see the gods active in our lives—their influences made visible through the interpretation of their activities according to the mythic patterns—our attitudes change and life begins to buoy us up and support us, carrying us into the emptiness which is our realization that nothing really matters and that everything is okay, that we can rejoice fully in our lives because we can approach the world with divine disinterest, accepting what comes to us and what we bring about in our lives as clues to a Great Secret.

Indeed, the very function of religion itself is most fundamentally to suggest to us that life is bigger than we think, to stretch our imaginations, to spark our sense of wonder, to proclaim the call to adventure by hinting at the existence of alternate realities that undermine a naive and simple understanding of the world. In this light the knowledge explosion, the complexity, pluralism, and relativism of modern times seem not at all inimical to religious consciousness. For they can, in fact, be understood as the particular forms by which modern men and women are called to question their interpretation of reality and to experience at the core of their perception of themselves the presence of the Secret.

℘

Not only religion but, as we have seen, science and popular thinking, contain clear manifestations of how consciousness seems to reveal to itself its own insubstantiality. But so often these challenges to the everyday world are not perceived as such; people take these manifestations of the transcendent reality so literally that they result in nonsense. Understanding the role of myth in revealing the Secret permits us the critical distance from which to make sense of what seems otherwise merely silly, incomprehensible, or abstruse, and to find clues that point us in the direction of our search.

A prime example of such silliness is purportedly scientific explanation of religious and mythic sensibilities. Scientific literalism, we saw as we began this discussion, is partly responsible for the modern predicament. In the minds of many people, science seems the only source of Truth. As a result of this, and yet also almost in reaction to the scientific monopoly of truth, a whole rash of pseudoscientific ideas have flourished that claim scientific ratiocination for occult and mythical phenomena: the Bermuda Triangle, pyramidology, so-called scientific astrology, Atlantis, and more—even demonic possession as a cause of mental illness.

Prototypical of this kind of thinking was the series of books and articles in the supermarket tabloids that appeared during the 1970s that pursued the hypothesis of Erich Von Daniken that the stories of the gods are, in fact, distortions by primitive minds of accounts of visitations to earth by "ancient astronauts." The evidence Von Daniken marshaled was certainly remarkable, although further investigation showed that at least some of it was contrived. His description of phenomena that he claimed could not be explained scientifically pushed open the horizons of the mind. And his explanation of ancient astronauts certainly seemed original.

Like other original thinkers, he argued that objection to his ideas came from narrow-mindedness. But, in fact, it was Von Daniken who had narrow horizons. In his effort to debunk the myths of the gods he was constructing new myths, but without knowing he was doing so. His myths, like most of those of the newly developed religions and quasi-religions and of resurrected occultist thinking, assumed a realistic and scientific tone. Like all myths, they provided alternatives to the commonplace history and science, but they were not radical enough in questioning their own assumptions.

Von Daniken's lists of unexplainable phenomena are, indeed, wondrous, but his explanations tended to confirm, rather than challenge, the literalist world view so characteristic of modern-day culture. The theories of space visitors take the parameters of technological society as absolutes and project them back onto the past. In believing he had reduced the myths of religion to primitive descriptions of technological feats, he missed the point of the myths. Von Daniken's epistemology was naive. But then, so is that of most of his scientific critics.

What Von Daniken's unexplainable phenomena indicate is that, like the birth of the world saviors, the birth of humankind was attended by signs and wonders. That is, that we really don't understand—and, from our limited viewpoint, probably can't—what consciousness is or where it came from. Mystery lies at the depth of human history as it does in the depths of the psyche, individual and collective. That they are mysterious and inspire wonder, and not that they are scientifically logical, is, after all, why Von Daniken's ideas sold.

During the 1980s this same phenomenon appeared in the fascination with so-called alien abductions. One of the major champions of these ideas was a friend and high school classmate of mine, Whitley Strieber. In his bestselling *Communion,* Whitley described how he'd had the experience of being carried off in the night by alien visitors, taken to a room in a spaceship, examined, and then returned to his bed. His memories of the event were suppressed so that they only became available under hypnosis. What was most remarkable about his experiences was that he was not alone in having them. Indeed, a whole multitude of people have responded to his book declaring that they too had been abducted, examined, and then returned with their memories shrouded and confused.

Some of these stories of alien abduction have appeared in the tabloids, perhaps in the same issue with a story about a woman who, say, gave birth to an ancient Egyptian mummy. Whitley Strieber, however, is far more intelligent and less sensational than the *National Enquirer.* In his book *Communion,* and its follow-up *Transformation,* he seriously questioned what it was that happened to him—and to the others—that he could explain to himself only as an encounter with space aliens. He investigated the roots of such experiences, finding a whole history of fringe phenomena that often involved appearances of lights, ships, or other things in the sky. Whitley concluded he really didn't know what had happened to him, but that something had, something wonderful, something frightening—something that needs to be understood, but that eludes understanding.

The great popularity these ideas achieved indicates the desire of the public to have something to believe in that will inspire them with wonder. It also reveals how modern-day mythic images appear more in the guise of science than religion. C. G. Jung recognized that myth has taken on the figures of science. Jung proposed that "flying saucers" are a modern example of mythical experience. He thought that they represent manifestations of the collective psyche, that they are mandalas (religious symbols of wholeness and of divinity) projected outward into the heavens.

The flying saucer, then, and the alien visitor is a direct descendant of the angel that was experienced by medieval visionaries. In times past, when the focus of wonder was humankind's place in the cosmos, "man was the measure"; therefore the mystery of life, which inspired wonder, was manifested from the psyche in human form.

Today, the focus of wonder, at least for the populace, is science and technology. The great feats that were once believed to be the powers of magic or *siddhis* that came from extended meditation are now the common experience of technological consumers. Instantaneous travel, flight, clairvoyance, clairaudience, and healing are today made commonplace by supersonic transports, television, telephone, and wonder drugs. Thus, the mystery of life is manifested from the psyche in technological forms.

So far the Blessed Virgin Mary has yet to appear in a rocket ship (that would, after all, be mixing metaphors), though in the apparitions at Fatima the sign she offered was an astronomical event with "scientifically verifiable" effects. To the masses that had assembled for the last apparition, she showed the sun dance in the sky and then plummet toward the earth. It had been raining that day and the crowds were soaked, yet after the "miracle" their clothes were all dried, just as though the sun's intensity had increased during the time it appeared to come closer to earth.

Astronomers, of course, did not observe the earth move out of its orbit or the sun change its place in the solar system. (Either event would, in fact, have destroyed all life on the planet.) But the crowds saw something, something wonderful, something frightening—something that needs to be understood, but that eludes understanding. (Whitley Strieber, by the way, joked with me informally during the heyday of his books' popularity that it seemed like he'd ended up in competition with the B. V. M.)

☙

That traditional mystical notions are beginning to assume scientific forms is perhaps most visible in the "mythology" of science fiction. *Star Trek, 2001: A Space Odyssey, Close Encounters of the Third Kind,* and the *Star Wars* series, with its mystical notion of "the Force," have captured the popular imagination and presented age-old themes of religious traditions. These movies, as well as the kindred genre of horror and supernatural films, make available to all of us the kind of magical, mystical experience that only a few had in ages past. In *Hellraiser,* for instance, we can all see a vision of hell not unlike that revealed in meditations to Saint Theresa of Lisieux. Special effects technology has transformed reality and manifested imagination.

It is telling that in one of the Star Trek movies, *Star Trek V: The Final Frontier,* Captain Kirk and his crew travel to the center of the universe to find God. And there, indeed, they do. An apparently omnipotent being manifests itself to them, reveals the variety of forms by which it is known, settling on God the Father as the right apparition for the earth-based crew. The benevolent old man with a long white beard then asks the Captain's assistance in the loan of a starship. When Kirk concludes that a real God shouldn't need a starship he, rather peremptorially, blows Him up.* Is that, perhaps, a comment that science—and the technology that can accomplish the wonders that in the past only a god could do—has now discredited God and, indeed, destroyed Him?

Science fiction has developed as a literary genre in response to the growth of technological influences. It can be a truly mythical form, for it deals with the categories of imagination and possibility. And like all myth it speaks in the vernacular. That is, it begins with the familiar and accepted world view of technology and then alters it in ways that seem consistent with that view projected into the future. It layers new realities upon the present one, in order to arrive at conclusions that may be altogether new and different.

Of course, as in any popular genre, there are vast numbers of science fiction films and novels that make no real statement about anything. On the other hand, there are some that speak very pointedly to the deepest questions of human life.

Arthur C. Clarke's *Childhood's End* (or his better known *2001: A Space Odyssey* and its sequels *2010* and *2040*) is an excellent example of science fiction as myth. *Childhood's End* begins in the prosaic world of rocketship technology and world politics and, while remaining true to the realistic qualities of these, comes to proclaim the occult and extrasensory as elements of humankind's contact with the cosmic "Overmind," and finally depicts an apocalyptic apotheosis of the race. The rather mysterious disclaimer that appears on the verso of the title page—"The opinions in this book are not those of the author"—may have meant, of course, that Clarke was feuding with his editor about some point of politics, but without knowing what it really means, it certainly may suggest to the reader that Clarke was taking the wisdom expressed in the novel from a deep archetypal source beyond himself.

---

* In the movie this flaw in God almost makes sense. Though, in fact, isn't the notion that God needs human beings to carry out God's will the basis of religious morality? Perhaps the flaw in the Star Trek god wasn't that he needed a starship but that he just didn't *command* the crew of the Enterprise to obey his will. If the god had been less accommodating and more demanding, perhaps, Captain Kirk wouldn't have been so skeptical.

Curiously, *Childhood's End* beautifully dramatizes the cosmology and mysticism of the Jesuit paleontologist Pierre Teilhard de Chardin, though, since *Childhood's End* was published before Teilhard's books became generally available, Clarke probably had no knowledge of Teilhard's thought.

Clarke's *The City and the Stars* describes the process by which history is confused with myth. It recounts earth's history from a cosmological perspective that clearly rises above triviality, speaking of millennia as we usually speak of hours. The novel's city of the distant future is run by a vast computer that recycles its citizens through lifetime after lifetime in a technological version of the Hindu notion of reincarnation.

The age-old themes recur in science fiction in what may be acceptable form today. Ursula K. LeGuin's *The Left Hand of Darkness* portrays the myth of the androgyne. Samuel R. Delany's *The Einstein Intersection* deals with the nature of myth and the journey of the Orpheus-hero; Frank Herbert's *Dune* and Robert Heinlein's *Stranger in a Strange Land,* with the theme of messianism.

Sometimes the novels make no pretense and speak directly about the elements of myth and religion. Walter M. Miller, Jr.'s classic, *A Canticle for Leibowitz* (whence I learned the word "peregrination"), records a possible future of humankind as it affects a Roman Catholic monastic order. The noted Christian theologian C. S. Lewis, in his "Space Trilogy," consciously used the fantasy medium of science fiction to present in relatively fresh language the Christian cosmology, the myth of the original Fall, the battle between Good and Evil, and the medieval myths of the Grail and the reign of Arthur Pendragon.

Science fiction has, of course, dealt with the experience of emptiness. Paddy Chayefsky's *Altered States* describes a rather pessimistic encounter with emptiness. The movie which gave actor William Hurt his start established a familiar image in the public mind of the protagonist nearly reduced to a formless mass of protoplasm because he could not deal with either the personal, emotional, or the epistemological problems posed by the experience of the Void.

Robert Sheckley's short story *Ask a Foolish Question* offers a sentimental and more epistemological metaphor for dealing with the problem of rational understanding trying to cope with the transcendence of Ultimate Knowledge. Sheckley's story tells of a memory bank, a vast computer mind that knows everything there is to know about the universe. It knows beyond time and space. It knows beyond every category or linguistic limitation. And it is called Answerer, because its function is to answer proper questions addressed to it. It has but one limitation, which is a limitation of the nature of knowledge: It can only answer proper, meaningful questions.

On a planet that is neither large nor small but exactly the right size, Answerer sits, repeating the answers to itself and seeing that all things are as they should be. It was built to last as long as time—which for some races in the universe is very long, and for others very short. For Answerer, it is just enough. Answerer is very large to some and very small to others. It can be thought of as very complex, although it can also be thought of as very simple. For Answerer, it is just as it should be.

To this omniscient being come three questioners, each from a different intelligent life-form, each so different in its perception of time and space that it is totally inexplicable in terms of the others' reality. For Answerer, of course, each is perfect and perfectly understandable just as it is, because Answerer knows. Each questioner in turn puts to the computer its most basic query: What is life? What is death? What is real? What is it all about? But to none of them can Answerer give an answer because none of the pilgrims to its shrine can ask a meaningful question.

One of the characters compares Answerer's difficulty to that of a scientist trying to explain to an aborigine, in a way that will satisfy the aspiring archer and still not sacrifice any scientific rigor, why he can't shoot his arrow into the sun. For, as the story concludes, in order to ask a sensible question, one must already know most of the answer.

☙

We modern Americans are not so different from the pilgrims to Answerer's planet. Some of the most contemporary models of nuclear physics are counter-intuitive, that is, they cannot be imagined or made sense of in terms of familiar experience. When we listen to the explanations of modern physics we are as confounded as the aborigine. And yet, in our inability to understand we can find a clue to the Ultimate Secret. A dramatic example is Geoffrey Chew's "bootstrap hypothesis," which was discussed in Fritjof Capra's influential book of the late 1970s, *The Tao of Physics,* which championed and popularized the paradigm-shifting notion that concepts in modern high-energy, post-atomic age physics parallel ideas of ancient Eastern mysticism.

The bootstrap hypothesis is an extrapolation of "S-matrix theory," which describes subnuclear particle interactions. S-matrix theory suggests that all the properties and interactions of the strong-interacting particles called hadrons can be determined from three general principles.

The first, called relativity, specifies that the probabilities of hadron interactions must be independent of their orientation in space and of the motion of the observer, that is, they are not artifacts of the experiment. The second, unitarity, holds that the outcome of an interaction must be predictable in terms of probabilities whose sum is equal to one, that is, the observer can be certain that the particles have either interacted or not. The third, causality, demands that energy and momentum be transferred through space only by particles and in such a way that a particle can come into existence in one reaction and be destroyed in another only if the former precedes the latter, that is, cause and effect must follow one another in ordinary temporal sequence.

The implications are profound according to Chew. For if these general principles, which are the bases of the scientific method, are sufficient to determine *all* the properties of hadrons, then apparently the basic structures of the physical world are ultimately determined by the methods of observation. Thus, as suggested by the Uncertainty Principle and the Copenhagen Interpretation of Quantum Mechanics, the phenomena that are observed in nature are creations of the measuring and categorizing mind that observes them. Consciousness creates the universe and not, as in the classical realist world view, the reverse.

Chew's bootstrap hypothesis suggests that the universe can only be seen as a dynamic web of interrelated events, not as an assemblage of individual entities with specific properties. The entire web is determined by the overall consistency of the mutual interrelations of all the parts. (This, of course, sounds very much like the principle of "mutual co-origination" taught by Najarguna.) The model can be summed up in the phrase, "Every particle consists of all other particles." Hadrons are composite structures composed of other hadrons, none of which is any more elementary than another, and the binding force that holds the composite structures together is the exchange of hadrons. Chew explained: "Each particle helps to generate other particles which in turn generate it." Hence the derivation of the name "bootstrap," for the whole set of hadrons generates itself and "pulls itself up by its own bootstraps."

The implication, of course, is that the whole universe is held together by its mutual consistency, in which each event interpenetrates each other event. Consciousness, then, is not an epiphenomenon that has accidentally come about in the universe. It is a necessary element for the self-consistency by which the universe generates itself. This is a mystical teaching expressed in modern, mathematical formulation. And the fact that scientists are thinking these kinds of ideas, even if the particular hypothesis does not prove to be verifiable, demonstrates that real science proposes no naive realism.

Indeed, today's science demands that consciousness be pushed farther and farther beyond the boundaries of everyday perception as it faces the utter unintelligibility of the bootstraps of its own origins. This is a science that produces its best discoveries through an enhancement and enrichment of the capacity of consciousness to conceive of itself in novel forms as an essential element of the universe. And this has, in the past, been the work of the creators of myth.

Curiously, after having seemingly devastated the religious, mythical world view by its rational skepticism, science has come round to creating its own "mystical" world view. Indeed, for all that it flattens and reduces reality, science has given us a new language for the invisible reality and a new supernatural order. Science has replaced the medieval three-level world of hell, earth, and heaven with the microcosm, mesocosm, and macrocosm. Most of us, even with all our scientific sophistication, cannot conceive completely the blurry lines around the middle level in which we live. And there are cosmologists who believe that the number of such orders of size is infinite; that our entire universe may be but an electron in the next universe up, and concomitantly, every electron in our universe is itself a universe in the next level down. It is difficult to say that kind of idea is realistic. It has long since become mythological in character because reason cannot contain it. It cannot "mean" anything because it has no correlates in common experience.

Science has gone beyond the ability of the mind to contain it, and not only in speculation but in practice. The power unleashed by science is unimaginable. The energy of the microcosm when released, as it was above Hiroshima and Nagasaki, rends the fabric of space itself. To few gods have been attributed such strength. Understanding that the function of the mind is to create metaphors for its experience allows us to see beyond the surface of this science, not to repudiate it, but to include it, and with its help to find in personal, mystical experience the metaphorand which has given rise to the universe. That metaphorand is the multidimensional cosmos. And the expanse of the physical universe is the most powerful clue we have to the depth and vastness of that reality of which our individual consciousnesses are momentary manifestations. For our world is, of course, the projection onto three-dimensional space of that multidimensional cosmos.

Technology has allowed us to look out into space, beyond the planets, beyond the stars, into the emptiness between the galaxies. In the near-space astronomers can see with optical and radiowave telescopes there are something like a hundred billion galaxies. Recently so-called blue galaxies have been discovered beyond that near-space. These are so far away that only the highest energy (blue) light manages to survive the time and space to get to us. These virtually infinitely distant galaxies appear to form a packed-solid backdrop behind the heavens. (At last, perhaps, science has discovered the fixed stars.) And there must be more blue galaxies out there than there are grains of sand on the whole planet Earth.

Each galaxy contains hundreds of millions of stars, each star a sun. The world on which we live, and think our concerns of great importance, is dwarfed beyond comprehension. Yet our minds can reach out and encompass that vastness. All of that universe exists within our consciousness and still is not diminished. The vision of the night sky—including, of course, the appearance of the great astrological figures—is the obvious clue to who we really are: bright spots of energy swirling in emptiness. Joseph Campbell succinctly stated this point in the title of one of his last books, published in 1986, a year before his death: *The Inner Reaches of Outer Space: Myth as Metaphor and Religion.*

In that universe each star may well host a family of planets, and some of the planets may host life not unlike the life on our own. We have yet to meet such extraterrestrials, yet already our mythology speaks eloquently of them. They are the manifestations in physical space of the alien orders of consciousness, spoken of as the gods, demigods, angels, demons, and the like. There are orders of consciousness, we can imagine, so different from what we know that we cannot envision them. Yet the mind of God, God beyond God, includes and is them all. That is the

message, much more than a naive explanation of archaeological mysteries, that the ideas of an Erich von Daniken suggest.

In 1900 we barely knew any of that was out there. When I was growing up in the fifties, galaxies were called nebulas and imagined to be relatively close clouds of glowing dust. There's a familiar story about
scientists at the turn of the century expressing sympathy for their suc-
cessors who would have nothing else to do but refine *their* measure-
ments because, it seemed to them, everything was already known. Only
a few years later Einstein published the Special Theory of Relativity.
And everything changed. As the year 2000 is approaching, why should
we think things are any different? Why should we think that now *we*
know everything? Shouldn't we learn the lessons of history and presume
that virtually everything we now think to be true—including the notion
of truth itself—will be supplanted? Given history, why would we even
consider thinking that the current scientific worldview exhausts all descriptions of the universe?

Religion clearly fails when it takes on the trappings of science, when
it claims to explain a supernatural, non-visible universe in the same way
that science describes the natural, visible universe. Doesn't it seem that
science would fail when it takes on the trappings of religion, when it
claims to explain everything and to deny existence to the things it
doesn't explain?

The cosmologies of Buddhism and Hinduism describe countless systems of worlds emanating from this one. The present world system is
but this moment of consciousness which we perceive as our egos. In today's science that universe of worlds is perceived not only as levels of
dream within dream, but as the stars and planets, galaxies and galactic
clusters that we look up at night to see; to lift our heads in prayer; to
feel wonder.

౷

What we see to be the "first" myth, which piques our curiosity, inspires wonder, and announces the call to adventure, and also the "last"
myth, which cuts through our naive dependence on all the others and
proves to be the discovery of the god behind the myths, is the myth of
the Great Secret.

The theme of the Secret, which runs through all the religious traditions, reveals that a quality of consciousness itself is its unknowability and yet its tendency everywhere to reveal itself. That is to say that the nature of consciousness—the source of our experience of being alive—is revealed throughout the world in all the metaphors that men and women use to describe their experience of life to themselves, and yet can never quite be pinned down and made explicit. This is because the nature of consciousness, as Eckhart said about the Godhead, is the foundation of all knowledge and so can never become an item in the content of knowledge. That is, there exists no Archimedian point from which consciousness itself can be known.

A teacher of mine at Saint Louis University, a Jesuit existentialist, Walter J. Ong, S.J., illustrated this point, saying that the inside of a blazing furnace does not look like anything, since no eyes can exist inside the furnace to look at it. A 1975 cartoon in *The New Yorker* illustrated it also, depicting two fish swimming in a pool, one of them saying to the other: "I've been swimming in it all my life, but all I know about it is it's water."

⛭

The myth of the Great Secret, as a theme in all myth, indicates that myth is metaphor that points to something beyond itself. It is the clue to the understanding of the mythologization process. The realization of it was for me like a bolt of lightning suddenly cutting through the confusion I had felt in facing the emptiness of Truth.

In Tibetan Buddhist iconography, that insight that cuts through illusion is depicted by the *dorje*. This stylized four-pronged trident was originally the familiar scepter of power with which the gods hurled thunderbolts. The symbol was adopted by the Buddhists for the experience of enlightenment, which seems to illumine the mind and pierce the illusion just as lightning illumines the night and pierces the darkness. The dorje (often depicted in the quatrefoil mandala above) also symbolizes diamond, the adamantine substance that resists scarring just as enlightenment transcends ignorance. These two diverse images derive from the charming folk belief that diamonds are formed by lightning congealing when it strikes the earth.

A dorje is also a small dumbbell-shaped implement used by the Tibetan Vajrayana Buddhists in meditation (a three-dimensional version of one of the axes of the mandala). The dorje is held in the masculine right hand; a four-pronged trident-tipped bell, symbolizing the goddess, is held in the feminine left (Cf. *Hero,* p. 171). A few years ago, my partner, Kip Dollar, bought me an actual brass dorje at an Oriental antiquities shop in Washington, D.C. It is three hundred and fifty years old. It has been held in the hands of adept meditators, enlightened beings, and bodhisattvas for twenty generations. If only because of my knowledge of this history, the object is charged with power.

Since I have been meditating with the dorje, I have come in touch with what I experience as memory traces—and which, in reincarnation mythology, might be called karmic resonances or past life recollections—of the Bodhisattva consciousness that chose to be reborn, as me, in the difficult and fretful, but oh so promising, time of the Atomic Age, the Age of AIDS, and the New Age. I sometimes think, mythologically (as I thought about the imaginary protective guardian Grendel at the Mann Ranch), that some lama managed to project his meditation implement down through time and space so that it would end up in the hands of a being who would inherit his karma.

I think, more practically and realistically, that that dorje was handed down to me—not the actual object which Kip gave me, but the meaning behind it which it manifests and which made it such an appropriate gift for me—by Joe Campbell. For the dorje is the manifestation in time and space of the intuition of the Great Secret and that is what Campbell's vision and style fomented in my spiritual life.

The diamond that is the myth of the Great Secret can be for modern humankind a wonder-inspiring image of transcendent experience. And it is the basis for our seeing that our lives are filled with clues to our own nature. For the Great Secret is everywhere hinted at in our experience, since it is the basis of that experience. In the paradoxical meaning of the phrase "the myth of the Great Secret," is the essential wisdom. In the technical sense of religious studies, "the myth of the Great Secret" refers to the pattern of clues to ineffable Divine Truth that constitute religion and spiritual practice. In the commonplace sense of the word "myth" as falsehood, the phrase reveals the mirror image of that Divine Truth which is simply that none of it's true and there's no secret at all.

"This is it," Campbell told Bill Moyers in the second of the interview programs, "and if you don't get it here, you won't get it anywhere. And the experience of eternity right here and now is the function of life." (*Power of Myth*, p. 67)

CHAPTER FIVE

Synchronicity and the Story of Your Life

The apprehension of the source *of this undifferentiated yet everywhere particularized substratum of being [which is the power known to science as energy, to the Melanesians as* MANA, *to the Sioux Indians as* WAKONDA, *the Hindus as* SHAKTI, *and the Christians as the power of God] is rendered frustrate by the very organs through which the apprehension must be accomplished. The forms of sensibility and the categories of human thought, which are themselves manifestations of this power, so confine the mind that it is normally impossible not only to see, but even to conceive, beyond the colorful, fluid, infinitely various and bewildering phenomenal spectacle. (Hero, p. 258)*

In the life of one open to experience, one who pays attention to the patterns that weave through life, signs abound that give direction to his or her wandering. Partly as an example of how we can find such signs, in the previous chapter I wove together several expressions of mythic themes that appear in the religious traditions and in popular culture. In this chapter I will again weave together such themes, some of which have been especially important in my own life.

Part of what was so intriguing about Joseph Campbell's style of presentation, but also sometimes annoying and baffling, was that in weaving his message he seemed to jump from one subject to another. In his great synthesis, of course, this was justifiable because all the various subjects he touched on and stories he told were interlinked. One of the most impressive things about his lectures was that no matter how far afield a particular point might lead him into telling other stories from other traditions to shore up or exemplify the argument at hand, he almost always worked his way back, through the layers of association, to the point he started from. One could see the skilled wordsmith at work in those feats. Unfortunately, on television, that skill is hidden by the work of the video editors. People who've seen Campbell only on the heavily edited Bill Moyers shows—or who weren't paying close enough attention during an actual lecture—might get quite exasperated with him for never managing to stick to, or ever get to, the point. Like the knights out hunting the Grail, he sometimes seemed forever off on a tangent.

This, of course, is the way of mythological thinking. The points are always made indirectly through stories and symbols. As a trainee in psychiatric mental health, I sometimes wondered if all this were just what the doctors in the white suits call "loose associations" and consider a major symptom of schizophrenia. Though when I was first learning this kind of thinking for myself, psychiatrist R. D. Laing was popularizing the notion that schizophrenia represents a kind of shamanic ordeal or passage rite and not a brain malfunction. (Though, because there's so little understanding of this process, in the modern scientific world in which the ordeal is not supported by the proper mythological framework to explain it, it often goes awry.)

Psychoanalysis champions the practice of free association. Mythology stimulates intuition by opening the mind's associations. The easygoing, loose associating style that captivated so many people who heard Campbell seems to create a ground for modern day insight. The style is catching. And readers of this book will see—and some be annoyed and baffled by it too—that I've adopted a similar style.

One of the richest, and most difficult, passages in *The Hero With a Thousand Faces* appears as the epigraph of this chapter. In these densely packed words, Campbell explained the fundamental truth of his vision and the fundamental truth of religion. He also explained the style of his loose association. The paragraph quoted above continues:

> The function of ritual and myth is to make possible, and then to facilitate, the jump—by analogy. Forms and conceptions that the mind and its senses can comprehend are presented and arranged in such a way as to suggest a truth or openness beyond. And then, the conditions for meditation having been provided, the individual is left alone. Myth is but the penultimate; the ultimate is openness—that void, or being, beyond the categories—into which the mind must plunge alone and be dissolved. Therefore, God and the gods are only convenient means—themselves of the nature of the world of names and forms, though eloquent of, and

ultimately conducive to, the ineffable. They are mere symbols to move and
awaken the mind, and call it past themselves. (*Hero,* p. 258)

Myth and religion provide the framework for understanding the clues
to the ineffable. They provide the language for the signposts which
guide us beyond the village compound into the wilderness of God. We,
of course, place these signs in our lives ourselves: by our intention to
perceive them and by the selective perception through which our minds
filter experience. They do not necessarily come from outside influences.
That from across the room we hear our own name spoken during a
cocktail party, for instance, suggests less that we are being called by
God to pay attention to divine instructions than that our senses are simply keyed to bring certain information to immediate notice. Though if
it occurs to one of us that the calling of the name *is* a sign of divine election, then this person might rightly decide to examine how well religious obligations are being acquitted because perhaps his or her
unconscious is trying to tell them something.

This person should probably not, however, begin to listen for the
voice of God speaking direct instructions. Except in a very few instances, that is merely an invitation to madness. The gods may once
have spoken so directly, as Julian Jaynes hypothesized in the fascinating
*The Origins of Consciousness in the Breakdown of the Bicameral
Mind,* but the structures in the brain that provided those experiences
are now vestigial. Today the gods are silent; their voices seem to im-
portune only when the brain is toxic from excess production of its own
neurotransmitters or from ingestion of hallucinogens.

On the other hand, the unconscious that is trying to tell us something
seems sometimes to be much bigger than just our personal psyche.
There is, apparently, something like what C. G. Jung called the "collective unconscious." There are apparently connections we all share with
what I've been calling a "greater reality." This greater reality reveals itself as strange things that make you think there's something you ought
to know, but don't. Sometimes this greater reality may actually impinge
into your everyday reality and give you a sign.

Such an experience can be stunning. It can cause the world of everyday reality suddenly to appear like a stage set. Then, it seems, someone
opens a door for you, a door you've always known was there but which
you've known you weren't supposed to open. And through that door,
to your surprise, you see the scaffolding that holds up the sets and

painted surfaces that you have been taking for granted and have been taking for reality. To your surprise, perhaps you even see the stagehands waiting distractedly, sipping coffee and smoking cigarettes, waiting to change the sets, and behind them the supernumeraries awaiting their cues to come onstage to keep alive for you the illusion of the world. To your surprise, you see through that door and the universe changes. And you must change your attitude toward it. For suddenly, to your surprise, you discover that the whole thing is going on for your entertainment.

Occasionally, perhaps after a fine dinner with a glass or two of wine in the company of good friends, during conversation over coffee, when the feelings at the table are very jovial and you are most comfortable and at home, there will be a lull in the conversation, a quieting of laughter after a particularly well appreciated joke. And one of the guests will lean across the table and say softly to you, "Listen, let me tell you a secret . . ."

And he will tell you what you have known all along, but never dared to believe. He will open that door you've known was there. He will tell you that, after all, you are the only one here; you are the reason for it all. He will tell you that the rest of them are actors who have been hired to entertain you and to play out your life before you. He will tell you that you are different from all the others, for they are only surfaces, projections of your own thoughts and feelings; that they conspire to be the universe for you; and that they seldom, very seldom, ever let you in on the secret. And he will tell you, with a conspiratorial tone in his voice, that he is taking a liberty with you and, for a moment, stepping out of character to tell you who you really are.

And then he will smile and toast you with his glass or pour you another cup of coffee. And the conversation will suddenly resume, and the room will ring with laughter again, and your friend will seem as he has always seemed to you, but you will feel a chill. And you will wonder what just happened. You will wonder if it really happened at all. You will wonder.

The next morning, when in a more sober and skeptical state of mind, you might doubt the significance of such an event. You might think your friend was playing a joke on you. But you might also realize the bald truth of it. And you might realize that that revelation of centrality can be made to each and every person. And *that* realization might, indeed, be more a source of wonder than the previous evening's curious intermission.

This realization of centrality is familiar in mystical literature. It founds Gerard Manley Hopkins' notion of inscape. It culminates C. S. Lewis's mystical message in his wonderful novel *Perelandra* in which the protagonist discovers that, in what he call the Great Dance, all events are intricately interwoven so that each thing is at the center and for it all else was made. This same image appears in Hindu myth as the Net of Indra (a favorite of Joseph Campbell's, by the way). It is what we just saw Geoffrey Chew describe as the interpenetration of hadrons in the dynamic web of the bootstrap universe. And it is what we'll see later the holographic model of the universe suggests is the real character of the universe outside the perceptual categories of the human mind.

To each of us it can be said that we are at the center of the universe and for us it was all made. We, in turn, have created one another and have created God as the dispenser of clues to remind us, now and then, of who we really are. But of course, even when we are reminded—as you were just now, dear Reader—the reminders remain always imprecise and indefinite metaphors. Still, they have the power to evoke wonder and they can call us to change our lives.

Hindu tradition affirms *Tat tvam asi* (Thou art that). All that is around one, all that one experiences, all that is joyful or painful—that thou art. There is nothing from which one stands apart.

Sufism, the mystical tradition in Islam, interprets the fundamental Islamic credo, "There is no God but God," to mean "There is no reality but God." In the reality of Allah, in all human and spiritual relationships, Allah is the love, the lover, and the beloved.

Rastafarianism, the political, revolutionary, newly arising folk religion of Jamaica, the themes of which pervade popular reggae music, teaches that the personal name of God is "I"; therefore each person, when he or she speaks of self, speaks of God by name.

Judaism, for all that its unnameable god has become concretized in the historical, realistic Jehovah, had seen something analogous to Rasta, for YHWH speaking from the burning bush, was to have revealed his name as "I am."

The Mahayana myth of the bodhisattva declares that there is but one being who lives in all, who has vowed to be everybody, and who is the one being who lives in the universe.

Such myths suggest that we cannot know directly our own nature, that who we are is elusive and slips off into the emptiness as we begin to pursue it, so that finally it can be spoken of only in such tantalizing metaphors. And that is the point of the notion of emptiness: that we cannot know the true nature of the universe. Though we may know that we exist, we won't know what that means in relation to anything else, and so cannot know what that "we" is that exists. Descartes thought he had reached a basic truth: "I think, therefore I am." But he still could not say what the thinking subject, which he had discovered existed, really was.

We human beings could, after all, be disembodied spirits, floating in space, interacting with one another; or, perhaps, bottled brains, preserved in sophisticated life-support systems, interconnected with intricate neuroelectronic hookups, hallucinating an embodied world through consensual agreement. These images appear in human thought from Parmenides and his *Poem* to popular science fiction and its portrayal of so-called advanced races. Perhaps such an advanced race is not so much further evolved in time as more basic in essence, and this portrayal is a mythical way of expressing a truth about who we really are.

A Zen story tells of the Taoist sage Chuang-Tse who dreamed he was a butterfly. When he awoke he realized that he did not know if he were Chuang-Tse dreaming he had been a butterfly or if, indeed, he were a butterfly dreaming he was Chuang-Tse.

The image of the dream is a familiar metaphor for the state of human consciousness. The common experience of the dreamer is that he or she is always the focus of everything that happens. Perhaps that, too, is the common experience of all of us in waking consciousness, and what we yet carefully deny lest we be charged with narcissism and solipsism. But solipsism is the logical implication of emptiness and of the effort to live the wandering life open to signs of life's direction. And solipsism is the logical implication of the everyday reality that we never experience ourself as an other. We are always different from the other and curiously mysterious even to ourselves.

When the Buddha was born, having passed from the side of his mother, Queen Maya, as she leaned against a tree, he took seven steps, pointed up, pointed down, and said in a voice of thunder: "Worlds above, worlds below, there is no one in the world like me."

Joseph Campbell informally appended to his telling of that tale of the Buddha's wondrous birth the remark by D. T. Suzuki that that same thing is said by each human child when at its birth it cries out for the first time. "I am here," the child is saying, "Worlds above, worlds below, there is no one in the world like me."

In *The Hierarchy of Heaven and Earth: A New Diagram of Man in the Universe,* Douglas E. Harding provided a charming example of this sentiment. He said something to the effect that I see that I am not like others because, whereas all the other people I see have hands, arms, legs, and a trunk like mine, atop their shoulders is a head. Atop my shoulders, however, is mounted not a head but a world. I do not experience myself crammed into an eight-inch ball, peering out through portholes. I am free and at large in a world that seems to surround me and yet that obviously comes into being within that part of me that on other people looks like a head.

The same spiritual traditions that teach, as we saw, that the "I" is central also teach that ego must be overcome, perhaps because ego is an impediment to the centrality. In descriptions of today's modern predicament we hear that ours has become a culture of narcissism. Can it be that the experience of emptiness is both the source of the solipsism and the anodyne of the narcissism?

☙

Under the rubric "multiple solipsism," Alan Watts proposed a myth that deals with these issues. His myth anthropomorphically portrays God before creation as aware only of himself, basking in his own consciousness of existence. After countless and timeless aeons of meditating on his own excellence, he grows bored with the whole thing and begins to dream that he is other than God. He dreams first of pleasures and delights, but soon finds them boring and insipid. Then he dreams of adventures and excitement, until he wearies of being heroic and daring. Then he dreams of great and terrible tragedies, though these, too, become banal and jejune. For so long as he maintains the awareness that he is God, the illusions of pleasure, of adventure, and of suffering do not hold his attention. He realizes it is only by forgetting he is God that his dreams can satisfy the goal of filling eternity with countless experiences.

Thus the universe comes into being by God's choice to forget he is God, to fall out of eternity into time, to dream the individual lives of individual human persons, made up of the intermingling of delight, adventure, and tragedy. Each human being is God entertaining himself. Each individual is an illusion, but the illusion in which each one is at the center is so complex and so interwoven that all are at the center.

There is a multitude of centers, all working together to perform the dance of the Lord in emptiness—a multiple solipsism.

The point of Watts's cosmogonic fairy tale is that the reality of God is so total that not even God is able to know himself, for he is never able to step outside himself to assume a perspective. Since no overview is possible, because there is no way for God to get outside himself, he is able to achieve self-knowledge only from within, from the countless points of view that are experienced as the universe by human beings who are the sensory organs of the universe sensing itself.

The point of life, then, as Watts declared, is never to break out of life or to become self-conscious of being God, for that would put an end to the entertainment. The point is to enjoy the performance, to make life as full and as intense and as aesthetically pleasing as possible. It is to this end that one can deal with one's life experience as one deals with the experience in a dream.

When people are quiet unto themselves or asleep and in the dream-time, they are most immediately conscious simply of being. Being plays itself before them as the symbolic contents of the meditation or the dream. When they are awake and active, their dreams interact with the dreams of all the others. And that consensual dream is the world of waking consciousness. It, too, manifests itself symbolically and richly. It is the mirror in which the individuals perceive themselves.

Myths are of the nature of dreams. We cannot decide tonight's dream. But we can intend to remember our dreams; we can set pen and paper by our bedside and resolve to recall our dreams upon awakening; we can make space in our lives to pay attention to our dreams. Just so, we can make space to recognize our myths; we can open our minds to learning the patterns of myth; we can read about them; we can look for reverberations of them in modern literature, movies, and television; and we can allow them to influence the way we interpret our lives. We can seek in them ways to follow our bliss, to use the phrase Campbell was so fond of.

We can let mythical patterns arise in our lives just as dreams arise in our sleep. Psychiatry asserts that recalling and working with dreams is therapeutic. Likewise, discovering and working with myths can be therapeutic. It can provide the sense of rootedness so needed in the face of insecurity. It can provide a sense of expansiveness in the face of reductionism. And it can undo the triviality of the prosaic world and stimulate insight and vision.

In fact, the patterns will be present in our lives whether we are aware of them or not, just as we dream whether we recall the dreams or not. They surface when we allow ourselves to reflect upon our lives. We all carry with us the history of our life experiences. It is precisely that which makes us who we are, which makes each one of us different from each other. We are each ourselves, and not our brothers or sisters or our friends, because we have had different sets of life experiences and, therefore, perspectives different from all the others. And, within our lives, we are each a multitude of possible persons.

For when we engage in reflection—in reverie, or perhaps in conversation with a friend, late on an afternoon in winter when just the two of us are snowed inside the house and the warmth from the fireplace is calming and soporific—we highlight some experiences and neglect others. We construct patterns.

If in the recounting we tend to emphasize amorous adventures, we may seem socially and sexually self-confident, a little promiscuous, sensuous, maybe even a little profligate. If instead we emphasize spiritual experiences, we may seem holy, virtuous, and well-motivated, perhaps even slightly enlightened (or maybe slightly crazy). If we recount our lives as the history of our work experience, we may seem diligent, industrious, devoted, or else lackadaisical and improvident; if the history of our work experience is the amount of money we made, then successful or greedy. If, by chance, we seem to emphasize the trips to the grocery store and the laundromat, we may seem very practical, though perhaps unimaginative and dull.

Thus, by highlighting some experiences and discounting others, we shape our history. It is this intentionality that structures experience from chaos. By an investigation and interpretation of the patterns in our lives, we can invent who we are and who we will become.

Sigmund Freud, who revolutionized human thought by calling attention to the power of the psychological factors that shape lives, termed this investigation and interpretation "psychoanalysis." Freud believed the patterns of a person's life were determined and controlled by sexual and neurological drives that participated in, and were explained by, the Darwinist scenario of human evolution. These drives and their effects were revealed, he thought, in dreams, free associations, slips of the tongue, and the like. Freud had little sense of the mythological figures. His student and one-time protégé, C. G. Jung, however, did.

಴

Jung noticed that dream content seemed to manifest certain common figures also found in myth and legend. He came to believe that conscious life is affected by an interplay of forces in the unconscious—which he called archetypes—revealed by symbols that have been inherited by generation after generation in a "collective unconscious." Thus Jung's thought became an important foundation in psychological theory for discussion of myth and its effects on the psyche.

As I've said, my own introduction to Jung was through Joseph Campbell. Thus I'd already learned the poetical approach that Campbell took in his writing before I discovered the more scientific, psychiatric approach of Jung himself. Campbell was fascinated by American Indian lore even as a child. He apprenticed in the study of comparative religions by posthumously editing the papers of Heinrich Zimmer. And he became a young colleague of "Old Man" Jung when he edited the *Eranos Yearbooks* which were the proceedings of a meeting at Eranos of Jung and his disciples from the Jung Institute in Zurich. But Campbell was never quite a Jungian, and orthodox Jungians have tended to be skeptical of Campbell. Nonetheless, the attitude toward myth and symbol that one finds in Campbell is certainly a kind of flower of the awareness of religion as a psychological phenomenon championed by Jung.

The Jungian archetypes are constellations of thought, associations of experiences that occur at a preconscious level and reveal something like a filing system, according to which the psyche sorts and values its experience. The archetypes are the effective categories by which the self structures experience into the commonly agreed-upon forms that are the everyday world. In this respect, Jung's thought shows the influence of the *Critiques* of Immanuel Kant (and thus back to Meister Eckhart), for in effect Jung was redefining the categories of reason as the patterns of psychological phenomena.

Jung believed that archetypal associations constitute the framework of the psyche and that the archetypes manifest self-regulatory mechanisms in the psyche. He hypothesized that since psychopathology arises from distortions of the archetypal patterns, the suffering mind is healed by activating these patterns and bringing them into consciousness. When life gets out of kilter with its organizing patterns, one exhibits symptoms of emotional and psychological distress. The deliberate effort to find these patterns in dreams and in conscious symbolizing activity (called the "transcendent function of the psyche") can provide clues to what is causing and what will correct the distortion. Jung said that a fundamental discovery in his own life, one that was the basis of his psychological theory, was that each person lives out a myth. It is only by finding out what that myth is that life can be lived fully. A major assumption in Jungian thought is that the good life is the full life, that a person should have a richness of experience, blending opposites and comprising polarities.

Part of the investigation and interpretation of life can be to draw together and make sense of all events in life; to uncover connecting themes that manifest archetypal influences. For the "meaning" of one's life is the interplay of associations within one's experience. In one of the most notable sequences in the Bill Moyers conversations with Joseph Campbell, Moyers asked if the purpose of myth is to give meaning to life. Campbell answered:

> People say that what we're all seeking is a meaning for life. I don't think that's what we're really seeking. I think that what we're seeking is an experience of being alive, so that our life experiences on the purely physical plane will have some resonances within our own innermost being and reality, so that we actually feel the rapture of being alive. That's what it's all finally about . . . (*Power of Myth*, p. 5)

I think what Campbell was struggling to convey is that the function of myth isn't just an intellectual exercise. The associations that the myths and metaphors provide are not just in the mind, but in the vital spirit. They connect us with something beyond ourselves. That's what Jung was hinting at in his notion of a collective unconscious. In fact, of course, when we use the word "meaning" in a phrase like "the meaning of life" we are seldom talking about an intellectual exercise. When a person experiences a mid-life crisis over the meaning of their life, that meaning is not in the mind, but precisely in that vital spirit seeking to feel the rapture of being alive.

We use the word "meaning" in these two senses all the time. To cite an example, the meaning—in the intellecual sense—of, say, the Incarnation of Christ is that the second person of the Blessed Trinity took on human nature and was born as the human being Jesus. "Yes, but," one might reply, "what does *that* mean?" And now the answer to that question is another kind of meaning—meaning in the vital spiritual sense. And what it means, if it means anything for the individual, is a nonverbal and non-verbalizable experience of rapture (which, perhaps, comes from sensing that one's individual life is somehow connected with something so much bigger because God chose to take on such a life, and, indeed, thereby transform human nature).

Joe's repudiation then of meaning was really a positing of the non-verbal spiritual experience. And that is exemplified in the poetical way he handled myths, metaphors, and stories. Because he was not so concerned about the meaning of a myth, the way a biblical exegete might, for instance, be concerned with the "real meaning" of a Scripture text, Joe was able to interweave a variety of myths and metaphors to tell a good story; i.e., one that resonated with his listeners innermost being.

Meaning—in both senses—can be introduced to what might otherwise appear only random and disjointed by the way one interprets one's life. And order will arise out of chaos. For that is, after all, the creative work: to create meaning and order out of confusion; to structure a universe, by intentionality, out of emptiness; to construct the story of one's life.

The structure of that story—and the meaning that comes out of it—is to a great extent determined by the context in which the structuring is done. This process, for instance, is the basis of Twelve Step programs, where the context is recovery from an experience of powerlessness, due to addiction, and the technique is the accomplishment of the twelve steps. The steps include doing a searching and fearless moral inventory of one's life, recognizing where one has caused harm, and then making direct amends wherever possible. This process brings one into touch with a Higher Power, which is to say, with one's spiritual life, wherein one no longer feels powerless.

☙

Jung recognized the human need to find meaning—again in both senses—in even coincidental experiences. He found that meaning is not connected only to simple causal relations within experience. For, while causality seems to describe the material, physical world, it cannot contain the experiential world. Jung postulated, therefore, the existence of an "acausal connecting principle," of the same stature as causality, which includes consciousness in its description of the interconnected patterns of experience. This principle he called "synchronicity."

The notion was not unique to Jung. It can be found in the early Buddhist atomic theory of the *Abhidharma* and in the *Monadology* of Leibnitz. As "seriality," biologist Paul Kammerer, Jung's contemporary, saw it as a factor in biological evolution. And the physicist Wolfgang Pauli, with whom Jung developed his understanding of the notion, used it to explain nuclear decay.

Uranium and the other radioactive elements decay into nonradioactive elements. The decay is "caused" by the inherent instability of the radioactive atom, which is simply too big to be held by the atomic forces that bind atoms together. The nucleus contains too many particles, and so splits apart to form two smaller, stable nuclei, each of which carries with it the proper number of electrons to form a complete atom. In the process some particles are lost and energy is released; this is radiation. When the process of nuclear decay, or fission, is sped up so that what would in nature take millennia occurs instead in microseconds, a high-energy, high-radiation explosion occurs.

What is curious about nuclear decay is that it ordinarily spreads itself over a vast period of time. Simple causality would suggest that all the inherently unstable nuclei should have fissioned simultaneously soon after their formation in the explosion of stars. Causality does not explain how some of the nuclei are able to hold together so that the decay follows a slow and orderly sequence. Pauli, one of the fathers of atomic theory, thought that perhaps there was another principle at work which connected events in an orderly sequence but which obeyed different rules. He remembered that Leibnitz, one of the creators of calculus and a major influence on scientific thinking, had suggested that two clocks sitting side by side always display the same time and so, by a principle Leibnitz had called synchronicity, are connected meaningfully in the mind of an observer, even though there is no causal connection between the clocks that keeps them synchronized. Perhaps, Pauli thought, the orderly sequence of radioactive decay is explained by a similar kind of connection.

What's especially interesting about Pauli's idea is that it seems to collapse the actual breakdown of atoms and the sense of an orderly sequence in the mind of observers. This is, of course, but one example of the direction modern physics has taken in which conscious observation is recognized to be part of the external phenomena being observed.

Jung borrowed this idea to explain how events that are causally unconnected can yet seem to an observer meaningfully associated. His development of the notion of synchronicity was directly linked to his study of oracular techniques, most specifically of the Chinese oracle book, the *I Ching* or *Book of Changes*. The presuppositions upon which the *I Ching* is based hold that all events are in some way connected simply by the fact that they happen in temporal sequence in relation to one another. (Time, then, is not an independent flow of activity in the universe, but is the matrix in which experience is placed.) This suggests that there are no unique, separate events in the life of the universe. All is an organic whole, a single great event that, when spread out across the mandala of time and space, only appears to be made up of many singular, discrete events, some of which appear connected by causality but many of which do not appear connected at all. With effort, however, noncausal connections can be found. The primary characteristic of such connections is that they appear meaningful to the human observer. "Coincidence" then takes on a much more respectable appearance, describing, rather than denying, connection.

✺

Psychic and occult phenomena, which under causality seem inexplicable, become partly intelligible under the rubric of synchronicity. Causal explanations are neither necessary nor suitable. Synchronicity is as valid a connecting principle as causality. (Indeed, causality can be understood as a particular instance of synchronicity.) Telepathy is explained not by subtle, undetectable waves that pass between two persons but by the notice of the simultaneity of the same experience in both of them. These experiences occur more frequently for some people, who are called telepathic because, more often than most, they *are* thinking the same thing as another. Astrological correlations between personality and the location of the stars at the time of one's birth are explained by the unity of all parts of the universe.

Indeed, the application of scientific principles to a non-causal system like astrology results in nonsense, no matter who is doing it. There are no rays from Jupiter or minute gravitational influences that affect the personality of a child born on a certain date in relation to the position of Jupiter in its orbit. The astrologer who purports to be scientific by discussing gravitational tides and their effect on brain chemistry in the newborn infant is mixing metaphors. So too is the rational scientist who claims to explain away astrology by declaring that, because different ancient civilizations pictured stellar constellations differently, no symbolic interpretation of them is possible; or debunks astrology by calculating the strength of the gravitational tides to demonstrate that they are too weak to influence brain chemistry.

Like other myths, astrology can offer not an explanation that will dovetail with astronomy, but an entirely alternative explanation of human experience. The symbols of astrology can offer us data which we deliberately seek out and interpret in our quest for meaning, because they shift our perspective away from the trivial and one-dimensional and instill in us the sense of the universal organic ecology that is the basis of synchronicity. In this view, astrology is only tangentially related to the actual positions of the stars and planets. What we can be interested in astrologically is how we personally respond, say, to the horoscopes in the daily paper. What is potentially synchronized is less the astronomical universe than the personal, that is, the series of events that unfold and are noticed in our consciousness.

If the universe is a single "organism," then no events are truly unconnected and the appearance of randomness derives only from the observer's inability to perceive all the connections. From above a layer of cloud, individual peaks appear to stand majestically isolated and alone. From below the clouds, they can be seen as rocky prominences of the same mountain range. Because our minds can never stand outside of themselves to know themselves, we can never perceive the substratum of our knowledge. And so things and events appear only occasionally connected. An awareness of synchronicity allows one to look below the clouds. It allows one to connect all the details of life. Thus it can play a major role in the construction of one's life story.

In constructing one's life as a work of art, one can observe how coincidental details reveal ironies, symmetries, and foreshadowings of major life experiences. Even accidents can seem to reflect the patterns of the life. And as one looks back, or looks out at the present, to find coherences, details that reveal intentionality and direction in life can seem to coalesce out of the background. Indeed, just like a good novel, an integrated piece of art that tells an interesting and significant story and has no superfluous details and no "red herrings," so an integrated life has no totally extraneous events or random happenings.

In the collection of conversations with New Dimensions Radio interviewer Michael Toms, published as *An Open Life,* Joseph Campbell cites "a wonderful paper by Schopenhauer, called 'An Apparent Intention of the Fate of the Individual,' in which he points out that when you . . . look back over your life, it seems to be almost as orderly as a composed novel. And just as in Dickens' novels, little accidental meetings and so forth turn out to be main features in the plot, so in your life. And what seem to have been mistakes at the time, turn out to be direc-

tive crises. And then [Schopenhauer] asks: 'Who wrote this novel?'"
(*Open Life*, p. 24)
This is, of course, the clue to who you really are.

☜

One can generate interpretations for circumstances that seem unconnected to one's life but that nevertheless make themselves noticed. Such
interpretations need be no more complex or meaningful than just that
one is moving along with the flow of life. Astrological and oracular
techniques, like the *I Ching* or the Tarot, were developed precisely to
provide these indications. But less structured events, something said on
a television show or the song playing on the radio in the next room, can
also be sources of coincidental patterns.

One can ask oneself "why" questions about the course of one's life.
There is virtually an infinite number of "why" questions and one cannot
ask them all. But one can ask those that seem to stand out—as they do
especially at those crisis times when one seeks to find meaning in one's
life. Some of these involve the major, but often uncontrollable, events
that form the backdrop of life; some, personal feelings, desires, and decisions; some, curious details that seem interwoven into larger themes.
My life and the lives of people I've known offer examples:

Why am I who I am and not someone else?

Why was I born in early August of 1945?

Why did my grandmother die the day after I played with her so long?

Why am I heterosexual? And why did I fall in love with the woman
to whom I am married?

Why am I homosexual? Why is the world I live in so homophobic?
And why did a terrible disease appear to afflict us?

Why did I go to college at Harvard?

Why was my name in monastic life Peregrine?

Why am I black?

Why am I white?

Why was there a song called 'Wanderer' popular during the days
when I first wrote this book?

Why was I born in Switzerland in the wake of the Holocaust, on November 2, when the Catholics were celebrating the feast of the souls in
Purgatory?

Why did I develop testicular cancer?

Why did I play the lead in *Funny Girl* when I was in college?

Why did the fall of the coins result in hexagram thirty-six when I threw the *I Ching* before going to the airport to board a jet airplane?

Why does The Magician come up so often when I deal the Tarot?

Why did the bus I was riding break down this morning?

Why am I reading *The Myth of the Great Secret* at this time in my life?

And why am I asking crazy questions like these?

Such questions do not necessarily have rational answers, and even when they do, the rational answer is usually not what is being sought. The rational reason, for instance, that I was born in August 1945 is that my parents related sexually some nine months earlier. Perhaps it had been cold that November night, perhaps they had gone to the theater and were feeling especially romantic. Whatever the circumstances surrounding my conception, they do not answer the mythic question: Why was I born in early August 1945?

Such questions have mythological and symbolic answers that are meaningful, not because they relate to any external reality, but because they color and influence the understanding of one's life. August 1945 was a change in the history of humankind. My birth virtually coincided with the detonation of the atomic bomb at Hiroshima when a fireball, like Shiva "brighter than a thousand suns," descended on the feast of the Transfiguration of Jesus Christ, during the month of Leo when the sun is in its native house. This thought affects my life story. Because of it I feel a devotional affinity to Amida, the Japanese Sun Buddha; because of it I've worked and demonstrated and written about the overarching threat of nuclear arms.

Such an answer, of course, cannot be taken literally. It makes no sense at all in the rational world of mundane discourse. It does not tell about "reality," but it does tell me about patterns in my life that can be articulated and enhanced. It reminds me that the birth of heroes in myth is accompanied by signs and wonders, and so I can remember that I too am called to be a hero. More specifically, I can remember that in me was incarnated the hero-Self that incarnates in everybody. It does not make me special, it only reminds me that life itself is special. But it makes sense only within a symbolic interpretation of my life. It could drive me crazy if I took it too seriously.

I've recounted how the coincidence of the word "peregrine" has woven through my life. In another incidence of this leitmotif two other of the examples I offered above came together. You may recall that Saint Peregrine himself joined the Servite Order following the seemingly miraculous healing of a cancerous lesion on his leg. Saint Peregrine is, therefore, honored as a patron of cancer cures.

When in an intimate conversation some years ago, I pushed my friend Bill to acknowledge that there had been a physical change happening in his body he had been denying for months, I proved almost inadvertantly a healer myself. At my insistence, and with my assistance, Bill went to see a doctor the next morning. The doctor referred him *stat* to a urologist, who called in an oncologist, who had him admitted to the hospital by that evening and in surgery the next morning. Bill had one testicle removed that had developed an encapsulated tumor. The testicle could have ruptured at any moment, and would have eventually, spewing malignant cells throughout his body.

But the surgery was in time and was effective. Bill's life was saved and he was cured of cancer. The surgeon, of course, was the immediate cause of the cure, but I was certainly a necessary link in the chain of causality. In that sense, my presence in Bill's life was the occasion for the cure. In that sense, I again was Peregrine.

Saint Peregrine's feast day is May 2. "Coincidentally" Bill's emergency surgery took place on the morning of May 2.

☙

Truly, life is a work of art to be appreciated for more than just its scientifically verifiable factuality. But finding obscure meanings and patterns in unrelated events is a pathology that is termed in psychiatry "magical thinking" or "paranoia." And so the "why" questions must be asked only with a very clear awareness that their answers are metaphorical and that mythical answers must not be taken seriously. For this process of mythologization is intended to tie together the details of the life and find pleasing, life-affirming connections and associations by patterning experience on the great myths in order to reveal the intentionality that structures the world of experience and to direct that power toward integrating the life. It should not encourage madness.

Thus the criterion for observing synchronicity must be that the significance imputed is, first, metaphorical, and second, affirming and supportive. The work of interpretation must allay fears, not stimulate them. We live enough of the time in a paranoid world. Indeed, "paranoia" is no longer an esoteric term of psychoanalytic theory; it has become a part of ordinary discourse because it describes the common and widespread feeling today that we are in danger all the time. The world that we have created is hostile in great part. Our machines threaten to maim or kill us; the pollution of our industries poisons our air and water; the politics of our world could at any moment plunge us into nuclear holocaust; crime in the cities is rampant; nowhere are we safe.

Our only refuge is the meaning we can find for ourselves and share with one another. In *The Natural Mind,* avant-garde psychiatrist Andrew Weil spoke of "benign paranoia," which takes its name from the application of psychiatric nomenclature to the experience that in religion has been called Divine Providence. This is the faith that God, almost as puppet master, coordinates and intervenes in the affairs of the world. Benign paranoia is the realization that human beings are indeed taken care of by life. In marked contradistinction, paranoia, as a pathological indicator, refers most often to the very opposite sense: that the universe is inimical and threatening, that all the given clues and coincidences seem to point toward doom. (Even when paranoia presents as grandiosity, it seems to be but a fierce defense against feelings of threat and doom.) Perhaps the "pathology" of the condition is not, in fact, the awareness of coincidental patterns, but the serious and malign interpretation. In *The Road Less Traveled,* perennially best-selling psychiatrist M. Scott Peck speaks of this phenomenon under the rubric "grace": the fact is most coincidences seem to happen in our favor.

The great traditions indeed declare that life is benign, and even supportive. Not a hair falls from one's head, Jesus said, but the Father knows and intends it with a loving concern. The bodhisattva embraces all suffering, for he observes that it is but illusion, and life here and now is nirvana and there is nothing to fear. All the things that seem to threaten and destroy, *The Tibetan Book* of *the Dead* assures us, are only manifestations of our own thought-forms that can harm us in no real way. All that happens reveals the presence of love and caring at the heart of the universe.

Identifying benign and affirming coincidences in our lives balances the threat of mass society by reminding us of a wisdom that was once dearly believed: that the universe is ultimately benign and all things work together for good.

Some of my friends, especially those who think of themselves as either very sophisticated or very spiritual, have made fun of me for one of the major sources of my "meaningful coincidences." I sometimes agree with them and belittle myself for taking seriously anything quite so silly. Nonetheless, I have for years observed a curious correlation between the patterns in my life and the themes in popular music. From the time I was very young and pious I sought to find religious significance in the music I heard around me. It wasn't always easy to find religious sentiment in rock and roll. I never liked Elvis Presley because his songs were particularly resistive to such interpretation. The middle-period Beatles, on the other hand, and the whole genre of metaphysical music of the late sixties provided me a heyday.

The reason, of course, that we feel silly about paying attention to phenomena like popular music is that we have been told it is profane. Yet in a world in which everything can be an instrument of revelation, nothing is profane. In much the way that of old the data of nature—the patterns of stars in the night sky, the omens of weather, the results of oracles—were incorporated into human life and given meaning, so today we can and must sort through and find meaning in the mass of data we are exposed to. We truly live at a unique time in human history. Never before have human beings experienced such massive barrages of information. Everywhere we find words to read, advertising announcements to consider, television and radio messages to listen to. The silence is filled with meaning.

In fact, most of us do find meaning in the barrage, and especially in music. For music is extraordinarily powerful in shaping and altering consciousness; we can often change our mood at will by choosing to listen to one kind of music over another. We all have favorite songs, the words or rhythm of which seem to stimulate us. When we are in love we routinely discover "our song" that speaks perfectly of mutual feelings. Rather than dismiss as profane the elements of popular culture—like AM radio or television or even the horoscopes that appear in the daily papers—we can incorporate them into our overall perception of our lives. We can invent meaning for them.

⁂

The world is full of signs and omens. Most of us are at least occasionally aware of them. They often tend to surface like the patterns in a Rorschach inkblot. In that sense they reveal patterns in our own minds.

From these patterns we can create meaning and impose that meaning upon the world. We can take responsibility for investing our experience with meaning. We can put order into the vast barrage of data. We can choose to interpret it in ways that foster our spirituality instead of those that merely drive us to buy products or participate in popular fads.

Human beings have always looked for "signs." God has always been beseeched to make known his will. He is notoriously obstinate in this regard, though now and then an omen is verified. An important step in my own maturation—one that I still struggle with—has been to see that the real sign is not outside me but is in my openness to find meaning in my experience. Each of us, sometime in our lives, looks for a great and marvelous star-signal to bless us with a sign, and yet as we stand watching for this sign of encouragement, we fail to see a sign in the seeking of it. The signs that do appear are important less for what they indicate than for the fact that we perceive them as signs. They do indeed point out the way for us to follow, precisely because we have given them significance by noticing them.

We human beings create our life stories as we wander through our experience. Despite a cultural commitment to rationality, we all ask irrational questions of our lives all the time. And this "magical thinking" has a real basis and positive side. It is the source of much of the joy and intensity of childhood, when life is still fresh and new. Rather than deny that foundation upon which our adult experience is built, let us take responsibility for it. And let us begin to feel free to admit to one another that we often think "crazy, magical thoughts." Then we can begin to come out of frightened, paranoid shells and include one another in our creation of the better world we fantasize and hope for. Then we can begin to experience wonder.

❧

Wonder calls us to ask incisive questions: What is it I need to know in order to live my life fully and to come to terms with this great reality that I can never grasp directly, that is always elusive, rainbow-running from my comprehension, but that draws me into my future? How can I allow myself to be drawn by it and simultaneously maintain dignity and responsibility for my own life? How can I let it speak to me, saying: You must change your life? If the presence of secrecy undoes all the explanations of reality I have learned, then who am I and what must I do in my life?

Certainly one of the lessons in the myths of afterlife is that at the end of life one ought to be able to look back and feel no regrets, because one's life has been a work of art, a fine and beautiful creation that can stand on its own merits, possessing its own loveliness, without needing to be done over again. According to the great afterlife metaphor of the West, the work created by the individual and presented to God may be found worthy to be placed in some heavenly gallery where the best examples of God's creation are preserved for his joy and appreciation, or it may be found ungainly, poorly designed and executed, flawed, or even ugly, worthy only to be tossed into the furnace. In the great competing metaphor of the East, the work may, by its own maker, be judged complete and ready to be left at rest, or it may be found to need further work and be taken back to the bench.

Even when we attempt diligently to mold our lives according to the most aesthetic patterns, we have only limited vision. We cannot see the future or even all the influences of the present. We may have flaws in our creation. But even so, we must strive to create our lives so that in the end, in the last moments as life is flickering away, as the Clear Light is blanching out our individuality and time is stretching toward eternity, we can say: I have no regrets.

"God made man," said Elie Wiesel, "because he loves stories." The stories of the multiplicity of human lives constitute the basis of the religious traditions. What religion is about is how individuals live their lives. The great myths are distillations of the experiences of the multitudes. The stories that men and women live out are the food and drink, the entertainment, and the lifeblood of God. For God is the ultimate story. The life story of God is the stories that human beings have lived. And one's autobiography is one's point of contact with God.

The work of creating that autobiography is to ride the patterns of the clues to one's story, as a bird rides the patterns of the winds or as a navigator guides his ship along the patterns of the oceans' currents. Then life is enhanced and made more wonderful, more alive, easier, and spontaneous. The work of myth is to call one's consciousness beyond the surface of life so that these larger patterns can be perceived and followed. Myth is not about something outside life, but about how life is lived most intensely. The problem of Truth falls away; it is the problem of living abundantly that confronts men and women, of becoming more intensely conscious of the play of life.

We are not here as judges, but as witnesses. For the judgment that we make on life is always the same. It is the judgment God made in the Garden when he rested from all the work that he had done: Behold, it is good.

☙

I have been arguing that the mystical, religious function of myth (perhaps different from the sociological and even cosmological functions) is to induce a state of consciousness that is characterized by a sense of wonder, openness to experience, love of life, and a keen curiosity and impetus to delve deep for clues to the meaning of life. This has been my experience.

What seems to be a flaw in my argument, however, is that, even in my own experience, religious people do not seem to be primarily characterizable by the qualities I've identified. Instead, so many who declare themselves to be true-believing Christians, for example—like those who arose as a political force in the 1980s, calling themselves the "moral majority"—seem to be characterized by qualities of conservatism, self-righteousness, acquisitiveness, obsession with economic security, antagonism toward sexuality, and narrow-minded anti-intellectualism. That is not to say, of course, that actual individuals in the moral majority are not virtuous and well-motivated, but that as a group their ideas of living the good Christian life seem on the whole inimical to the kind of openness and freethinking that I've portrayed as the goals of the spiritual life.

It is certainly a commonplace that the Church has been guilty of more crimes against humanity than any other institution in Western culture and that religion has blocked social progress at every turn. But these are partly naive accusations that neglect facts of history. For even as it has been a drag on its acceleration, the Church has been an enormous force behind progress. The Christian notion of life as a test of moral accomplishment, even as it has stunted the maturation of personal and sexual emotions, has been a tremendous source of our striving for excellence and achievement and has civilized us and taught us to live together in relative harmony. The Christian view that humanity is the culmination and glory of nature has been responsible for the development of the scientific approach. For every Galileo whose contribution to scientific knowledge was challenged or suppressed by the Church, there was a Gregor Mendel making significant scientific discoveries within the Church. For every Giordano Bruno burned at the stake for unorthodox ideas, there was a Nicholas Cusanus revered for incisive and profound speculations.

But for all that, religion within historical times has not often been the source of mystical expansiveness that I argue it should and can be. I think this is because the symbols and figures that stir wonder, inspire openness, and drive the mind beyond its trivial vision evolve more rapidly than the institutions that exist to promulgate them. Religious institutions (in part because of their additional sociological function of providing stability and of keeping tradition alive in culture and in part because of their penchant for taking the metaphors literally and seriously) have tended to fall behind the advance of consciousness. The content of religious transformation hasn't kept up with what's really going on in the collective psyche.

Religion, very importantly, took on as one of its areas of responsibility in the building of culture the maintenance of sexual and reproductive arrangements. This meant regulating the passions and controlling the passage of property, title, class status and the like from one generation to another. In a male-dominated society, it was important, for instance, that the patriarch's mantle pass to his firstborn son. While it was relatively easy to determine who a child's mother was, it was not so easy to determine who its father was. The only way was to regulate women's sexual behavior.

Modern genetic anthropology—under phraseology like "the selfish gene"—has shown us that males have a drive to promote their own genetic offspring and to kill the offspring of other males in order to assure the success of their own. Sexual taboos, communicated through religious myths, civilized that drive. Through much of human history, as the population was growing in spite of the great odds against survival, the control of reproduction was a social, cultural imperative. Thus religion came to focus on sexual ethics—in spite of the curious fact that very little in the myths or the words of the founders had anything to do with sex.

Within recent times the issues have changed. Medical science and civil authority have taken over responsibilities for tracking genetic transmission. The religious concerns could have then shifted back toward something that *was* generally part of the founders' teachings: responsibility for the quality of other people's lives.

The big issue today is the survival of the planet, not the survival of a particular gene line. This is a big shift. It changes the way we see certain ethical questions.

The old, sex taboo-oriented ethics was focused specifically on individual acts. It was sinful to have sex with a woman to whom a man was not bound in a way that made him responsible for her children because she might get pregnant and the child would have no birthright. Today contraception takes care of the chance factors. It was sinful to steal; it was sinful to murder. These were important ethical issues that in extreme example can be handled by police authority, but in more subtle examples must be handled by ethics.

Ironically, the shift toward survival of the planet over survival of individual gene lines seems to slacken up on sex, but tightens restrictions on, say, theft and murder. When individuals acts are viewed in their systems context, it becomes clear that perfectly legal and socially acceptable acts may result in the same kinds of hardships that theft and murder do. A bank's foreclosing on the house of an out-of-work steel worker is a form of theft. And everybody who has money in the bank in some way participates in the guilt for the sin. Even worse are perfectly legal and socially acceptable actions that result in hardships to the planetary ecology. Investing in a firm that manufactures parts for nuclear weapons, for instance, is participating in pollution and the potential murder of the planet.

A modern day ethics, based in an awareness of ecological systems, is far more subtle and for that reason more difficult to pin down to specifics. What's happened, unfortunately, in our contemporary world is that we've rejected the outmoded traditional ethics of individual acts, but have not replaced it with an ethics of systems. We end up with no ethics at all. This is a serious failing of religion.

The religions have also failed to keep up with the growth of human consciousness because they have misunderstood the nature of their truth in relation to scientific truth. This was a point that Campbell made over and over again.

When science came along, with its notions of an objective, external universe of knowable facts, Christian religion leapt on that as the kind of facts it wanted to have in order to be right. It took the scientific notion as a verification of its mythic theme of historical incarnation. In doing so, in fact, it chose the lesser kind of authority. Metaphor and spiritual significance are far more moving and life-changing, than facts.

The Middle Ages knew about allegory and, indeed, much of Christian Scripture was understood to be allegorical—meaning it was about something besides what it seemed to be on the surface. Current-day Biblical literalism, on the other hand, dismisses such allegorical and metaphorical significance and thus sacrifices the power of the symbols beneath the surface.

Indeed, the symbols that inspire wonder and that have given rise to the gods have been changing. Consciousness itself is now a more apt image of transcendental reality than, perhaps, the personality of an ancient Semitic Father God. Yet the Christian churches have not been able to keep up with the radical changes of the symbolic material and are still preaching the will of that anachronistic God.

Curiously, the Church has not even been able to keep up with its own founder's reformation of the image of the Father God. Jesus's mission was to reorient the vision of God from an angry, vengeful lawgiver to a gentle, compassionate parent who had entered history as a human being in order to portray godliness as totally human. Jesus ridiculed the legalism of religion in his day. He taught compassion and forgiveness and proclaimed that the spirit of God resided in all people. Yet the Christian churches generally failed to recognize his teaching and very quickly raised him to the stature of the Almighty Father, thereby distancing the Christ figure from human experience, and preserving the authority of the narrow-minded Jehovah. (Ironically the Jews, whose god Yahweh was first and whose religion Jesus set out to reform, have done better than the Christians at getting over legalism.)

The failure of religion to keep up with the active and vital symbols that communicate spiritual consciousness has distorted the effectiveness of the symbols. Jehovah is out of date. The inspiration that could come from, and the need for, the image of a jealous, racially protective, bellicose desert storm god is not present in modern, urbanized, technologized society. Indeed, the qualities that belief in that God engender too often reflect only his rather petulant personality.

The image of the divine coming into reality—which is the symbol of birth into consciousness—including even the not coincidental sexual entendre, conveys the significant message: The world saviors are always coming. That is, they are always in the present moment moving into the future. They are not stagnant, they have not been left behind in history.

That is why their history is of little account. Jesus is coming again, and to the Buddha is given the title *Tathagata*, "the one who has come," or "the one thus come."

Indeed, in Buddhism all reality is said to be *tathata*, "thus come," which is also translated as "suchness." Tathata means that the world of experience is just what it is; it does not refer to anything outside itself. It is considered a marvel of Buddhist thought that suchness and emptiness, tathata and sunyata, are the same. Since reality does not "mean" anything, it is empty: It has no content, no reality outside of reality. The Buddha's discovery was that it all just is, and that he too was just part of what was happening. "It just keeps on keeping on" and there is no antecedent for "it." Tathagata is then well translated "Here I am," where "I" has no antecedent (*anatman*); and "here" is constantly in flux (*anitya*) so that it too can never be pinned down. "Here I am" conveys no information outside itself; thus the universe is tathata, "just here." The teaching of the Buddha is that we begin with life; the spiritual, philosophical, and ethical life quest begins here and there is nowhere to go. For wherever one goes, it's "here." Suffering (*duhkha*) arises from the false conception that there is something to reality other than just being here.

This is, of course, the point that Joe Campbell was making when he said that the function of myth is not to provide meaning but an experience of the rapture of being alive.

☙

Religion has come to seem antagonistic to life because it has not been allowed to evolve fast enough. Today, however, whether we like it or not, we are forced to reexamine the epistemological assumptions of our religions because they have become so outdated that they no longer function and, instead of hinting at a marvelous and multidimensional world, seem only to confirm (though in a confused way) the one-dimensional world that is the modern predicament.

We must escape that one-dimensional world. It is incapable of supporting us today. We can see that simpleminded biblical Fundamentalism is not obviously salvific and mystically transforming (though, of course, individual Fundamentalists may be mystically transformed) because it is simpleminded. And, for the same reason, simpleminded science cannot be salvific or transforming.

What can save science from simplemindedness is that its subject matter always proves more ingenious than scientists. Under scientific investigation the universe, instead of just lying down and revealing all its secrets, has become ever more complex. What can save religion from simplemindedness is the realization that its subject matter, too, is forever shifting and eluding specification. God as secret allows both a reasonable and practical interpretation of religious images to fit social and personal needs and a continual openness to new meanings and new senses of complexity. Then, in fact, religion and science can—as they did of old—work together to keep pushing outward the boundaries of consciousness, so that life gets bigger and bigger.

It is essential that today we begin to understand more carefully the function of the metaphor of God. Then we can determine criteria for evaluating the use of the metaphor, so that it does push open our horizons. A society might rightly choose to go to war, or choose to exclude certain alien peoples, or choose to legislate child-rearing practices in favor of the nuclear family arrangement. But, though the God metaphor is often used to justify or explain the choices, such issues do not have much to do with God.

When we begin to look at God as the experience that connects us with greater reality, then we can begin to look more carefully at how we use the metaphor. We can see that its major effect must be to open people's horizons, to help them love life and affirm their experience, to raise them above space and time, and hint at the multiple levels of existence that surround them. Then we can see why God must not be blamed for everything that has been done in God's name. And only as we begin to do that, can we save a place for religion in an intelligent, thinking world and resolve the foolish conflict between our various symbolic systems. Then we can begin to ask the important question: "What will be the new myth?"

CHAPTER SIX

Techniques of the
World Saviors

*Perhaps the most eloquent possible symbol of this
mystery is that of the god crucified, the god offered,
"himself to himself." Read in one direction, the
meaning is the passage of the phenomenal hero into
superconsciousness. . . . But also, God has descended
voluntarily and taken upon himself this phenomenal
agony. God assumes the life of man and man releases
the God within himself at the mid-point of the cross-
arms of the same "coincidence of opposites," the same
sun door through which God descends and Man
ascends—each as the other's food. (Hero, p. 260)*

Joseph Campbell's approach to myth was exemplified in his style of
weaving together stories, images, and metaphors from different traditions. That the myths can be intermixed in order to clarify their deeper
meaning, as Campbell did in *The Hero With a Thousand Faces* in order
to extract what he called the mono-myth of the hero's journey, presumes
that the various traditions arise from a common source "which [has] remained as constant throughout the course of human history as the form
and nervous structure of the human physique itself." (*Hero*, p. 257)

This is a presumption that the individual religions—especially those
in the West—would disagree with, each claiming hegemony over the
others, each maintaining that it alone has truth. That kind of exclusivism has resulted in the history of wars, persecutions, and *autos-da-fé*
("acts of faith," as religious executions were ironically called)—from
pre-Biblical times to the present day, from Ireland to Iraq—that make
many modern individuals understandably cynical about religion. It just
doesn't make sense.

Joe's facility and willingness to intermix the tales simply dismisses the objectionable exclusivism and, in passing, demonstrates a whole different epistemology of religious truth. It certainly spoke to me and transformed my understanding, simultaneously saving my religious impulses while satisfying my modern sensibilities.

In my account of my work with Harvard sociologist-researcher Toby Marotta, *In Search of God in the Sexual Underworld,* I presented such a weaving together of myth themes to demonstrate the major point of that book: that the social problems of the sexual underworld—prostitution, pornography, drugs, violence, even molestation—derive more from the condemnations of sexuality in our culture than from the inherent disorderedness of bodily urges. The discovery of our research, in mystical terms, was that how we look at the world determines what we see and that spiritual vision is supposed to transform what we see in order to save it, not to condemn it.

There's a Buddhist aphorism to that effect: Fools live in a foolish world; bodhisattvas live in a bodhisattva world, buddhas live in a buddha world. It's no wonder then that men like Jerry Falwell or the Reverend Wildmon, founder of the American Family Association, see sin and debauchery all around them, even in a holy—if, admittedly, erotically charged—parable about Jesus like Nikos Katzanzaki's *Last Temptation of Christ;* or that some of their ilk, like Jimmy Swaggart, end up falling into the muck they generate all around them.

Using some notions straight out of Campbell and some out of my own insights, I want to demonstrate how we can find the wisdom of saving the world and the flesh in surprising places. After all, in a Buddha world, even the grass is enlightened and every story is a lesson in enlightenment. In Joel Chandler Harris's story of Brer Rabbit and the Tar-baby, for instance, we find a classic description of the hero's confrontation with the world and a hint at the wisdom by which the hero saves himself and the world.

Brer Fox tried time and time again to catch Brer Rabbit, but time and time again Brer Rabbit got away. Then one day, Brer Fox got him some tar, and made himself a Tar-baby. Then he took this here Tar-baby and sat her in the road and then he lay off in the bushes. By-and-by along came Brer Rabbit—lippity, chippity, chippity, lippity—just as sassy as a jaybird.

Brer Fox, he lay low.

This story of Brer Rabbit parallels an Indian folk story of the Buddha. Long before he was incarnated as the wise teacher who would enter nirvana in his lifetime, his spirit lived as an heroic, young adventurer called

Prince Five-weapons. On the journey back to his father's kingdom, following completion of his martial training, he came to a dark and forbidding forest in which lived a fierce ogre called Sticky Hair. He was warned to go another way, but he was confident and fearless and set forth straight into the ogre's domain.

Brer Rabbit's confrontation with the Tar-baby was a little less intentional, but soon no less militant. For when the Tar-baby did not respond to his salutation, even after hollerin', in case the Tar-baby was deaf, Brer Rabbit took it upon himself to teach the Tar-baby a lesson in civility. So he threatened to whack her upside the head if she didn't take off her hat and say howdy.

Brer Fox, he lay low, and the Tar-baby just stayed still, saying nothing. Brer Rabbit drew back his fist and took her a whack on the side of the head. His fist went right into the tar and stuck there. After threatening to hit her again if she didn't let him loose, Brer Rabbit fetched her a whack with his other hand. And that stuck too.

Brer Rabbit kicked the Tar-baby with first one foot, then the other, and finally, in desperation, butted her with his head 'til he was stuck firm to the Tar-baby in five places. Just then Brer Fox sauntered forth from his hiding place and, just as innocent as a mockingbird, greeted Brer Rabbit. This time it was Brer Rabbit that ain't sayin' nothing. Well, Brer Fox was pretty pleased with himself. He'd caught Brer Rabbit fair and square. Ain't nobody made Brer Rabbit try to strike up an acquaintance with the Tar-baby. And nobody invited him to stick his hands, his feet, or his head in the tar. He did that all on his own. And now he'd be stuck 'til Brer Fox went and lit a brush fire, pulled him out of the tar, and barbecued him for lunch.

Brer Rabbit saw he'd been caught dead to rights and he talked mighty humble. "I don't care what you do with me, Brer Fox, so long as you don't fling me in that there briar patch."

Seeing as how it was going to be a lot of work to make a fire and apparently not caring whether lunch was cooked or raw, Brer Fox reckoned he could just hang the rabbit. "Hang me just as high as you please, Brer Fox, but for the Lawd's sake, don't fling me in that briar patch," said Brer Rabbit.

Seeing as how he had no rope, Brer Fox decided to drown the rabbit. "Drown me just as deep as you please, Brer Fox, but don't fling me in that briar patch," said Brer Rabbit.

Seeing as how there was no water around, the Fox said he'd just skin the rabbit. "Skin me, Brer Fox, snatch out my eyeballs, pull out my hair, tear out my ears by the roots and cut off my legs," said Brer Rabbit, "but please, please, Brer Fox, don't fling me in the briar patch."

Well, Brer Fox was pretty fed up with Brer Rabbit's whining. He really didn't care about eating him so much as he did hurting him as bad as he could. So he caught him up by the hind legs, pulled him out of the Tar-baby, slung him around in the air, and flung him right into the middle of that there briar patch.

There was a considerable flutter where the rabbit struck and Brer Fox hung around to see what was going to happen. By and by he heard someone calling to him, and way up the hill he saw Brer Rabbit sitting on a log combing the tar out of his fur. "Bred and born in the briar patch, Brer Fox, bred and born in the briar patch. Briars can't hurt me," sang Brer Rabbit as he skipped off just as lively as a cricket in the embers.

To become a hero, the Buddha had to overcome fear and trick death. When he was seated beneath the Bo Tree on the Immovable Spot, where he would soon attain his enlightenment, he was assailed by Kama-Mara, the Lord of Desire and Death. To put an end to the temptation he touched his hand to the earth, proclaiming his right to be there. And the earth mother-goddess roared in a voice of thunder that terrified Kama-Mara and all his minions, so that they fled, leaving the Buddha in peace. He had seen that so long as he stayed grounded, firm in his resolve, unfrightened by the illusions of fear and desire, he was unstuck.

But the confrontation with Kama-Mara over the right to be on the Immovable Spot was not to come for several incarnations after Prince Five-weapons' battle with Sticky Hair. He had another adventure to deal with first.

The Prince took his name from the five weapons he bore: poisoned arrows, sword, spear, and club, and his own body trained in martial arts. With these he expected to slay the ogre who, in turn, took his name, as one might imagine, from the thick hair all over his body into which stuck any weapon used against him.

Five-weapons, upon finding the ogre, smote him with his arrows. They stuck in the hair. Then he tried his fabulous sword. It too stuck. One by one the weapons, including, of course, the Prince's hands, feet, and head, got stuck fast in the ogre's hair. But the Prince was undaunted.

Hesitating before eating him up, the ogre asked the youth, "Why are you not afraid?"

"Why should I be afraid? Death is certain in every life," declared the

Prince. "Besides I carry in my belly a thunderbolt for a weapon you cannot withstand. If you eat me up, the thunderbolt will blow you to pieces. And, in that case, we'll both perish."

Sticky Hair, not quite as difficult to convince, but just as credulous as Brer Fox, submitted to the wisdom of the future Buddha, was converted, practiced self-denial, and became a divine spirit dwelling in the forest.

❧

Each of us is equipped with five weapons. For, as Campbell points out (following A. K. Coomaraswamy and others), the five weapons are the five external senses with which we contact the world. Sticky Hair and the Tar-baby represent that world. In his enlightenment the Buddha discovered that the world that threatens to eat us up, tear out our ears by the roots, and cut off our legs is but the physical manifestation of our thoughts and experiences, like a dream or mirage. But when we engage the world through our senses we become stuck in it. We take it seriously. We become imprisoned in our own creation, caught in the form we give to our experience of self, valuing one thing over another, succumbing to fear and desire, resisting life. We get stuck in the world because we fail to look beyond it, understand it in a greater context, or take responsibility for our participation in its creation.

The hero is wiser than the world. Oh, Brer Rabbit had got himself stuck all right, but when he saw the nature of the Tarbaby and the grinning face of Brer Fox, he very quickly got wise. What he knew—that Brer Fox didn't—is that rabbits are different from foxes: that people live in different universes with different assumptions, expectations, aims, and values based on their upbringing and experience. Because the fox was so full of hate and lived in such a one-dimensional world, he assumed because he himself wouldn't want to fall into a briar patch Brer Rabbit was telling the truth when he pleaded with him not to throw him into them there briars. The fox fell for the ruse and the hero got away.

Young Five-weapons revealed to Sticky Hair that besides the physical world in which swords cut and clubs crush and mangle, there is an etheric world in which Sticky Hair's defenses could not protect him. In Indian thought, there were not five senses but six, for mind was considered a sense. It was through the power of mind to observe the other senses, and to discover the wisdom that death need not be feared, that the Prince was armed with the lightning bolt in his belly.

This bolt, by the way, is the power that transforms Billy Batson into Captain Marvel in the modern comic book myth. Invocation of the mantra "Shazam" (an acronym for the heroic qualities of Solomon's wisdom, Hercules' strength, Atlas' stamina, Zeus' power, Achilles' courage, and Mercury's speed) reminds the hero trapped in the illusion of human personality of who he really is and releases super powers.

If even comic books and Saturday morning television reveal the essential wisdom, why do we fail to possess the powers? The Buddha answered that, of course, we do possess them: Behold the universe we have created. But we are so mesmerized by that creation that we do not remember our ego-transcendent identity and we do not realize that we are creating it just the way we want to.

Our modern vantage point allows us to observe ourselves (though it is precisely this ability which is responsible for our loss of belief). We are conscious of the operation of our minds. Just as our minds are responsible for the advances we have achieved, so are they for the problems that have resulted. And yet only our ability to observe ourselves can solve these problems which, like Tar-baby and Sticky Hair, seem to trap us more deeply the more we grapple with them. Only a change in consciousness, in how we perceive the world, can save us from being trapped in it.

The wisdom of the mythological teachings is always, in part, concerned with how to get unstuck from the world, how to see with the spiritual eye beyond the senses to who we really are. This wisdom is what is conveyed in the stories of the heroes' journeys, for the heroes are always seeking their true identity.

๛

The heroes of Mahayana Buddhism are Siddhartha Gautama, who entered nirvana and became the Lord Buddha, and the bodhisattva Avalokitesvara, who renounced nirvana to save all sentient beings. Compared to early Buddhism, which taught that life was all suffering and that each individual had to work to escape from life into a nirvana that was simply extinction, as we have observed earlier, the Mahayanist reinterpretation of the Buddha's teachings several hundred years after his death was relatively life-affirming.

Mahayana sages, like Nagarjuna, taught that the world arises through a process of "mutual coorigination" in which nothing is known individually or independently but only relatively in its interacting with everything else in a great cosmic unity. Since nothing is absolute, nothing can be known of Absolute Truth. All knowledge is empty. Even the teachings of the Buddha are not absolute, but only hints at a greater, unknowable, ineffable Truth. The denial of all absolute distinctions implies that there is no ascertainable difference between samsara, the world of change and apparent suffering, and nirvana, the state beyond change and suffering. Samsara is nirvana. The world is no different from heaven. They taught a radical monism in which all beings are manifestations of the One Being. The illusion from which all must be saved is that individual existence is real. The Mahayanists recommended compassion for others as the "skillful means" of attaining enlightenment and escaping rebirth. They accepted life in the world, not just in the monastery, as an exercise in gaining enlightenment.

To communicate the emptiness of Absolute Truth, radical monism, and compassion as the means to salvation, the Mahayanists told the story of the bodhisattva Avalokitesvara. The myth tells that the lovely, androgynous saint, Avalokitesvara, was on the verge of entering into nirvana, thus leaving behind forever the world of samsara. Just as his meditation was deepening and his insight into the transience of all phenomena growing, he was distracted by a great groaning, rising up all about him in the world. He came out of his trance and, looking around him, asked: What is this groaning I hear? All the birds and trees and grass and all sentient beings replied to him: O Avalokitesvara, our lives are times of suffering and pain; we live in a delusion from which we cannot seem to escape. You are so beautiful and so kind. Your presence here among us has given us joy and a reason for living. We all love you so, and we are saddened by the prospect of your leaving us. And so we groan.

At that the young saint was filled with compassion and chose not to enter nirvana, but to remain in the cycle of birth and death so that the others would not have to suffer. And he vowed to renounce nirvana until all sentient beings were equally enlightened. He saw that it was better that one should suffer than that all should. And he took upon himself their suffering, so that he alone would wander the cycles of karma, far from the homeland.

Avalokitesvara, whose name means "The Lord Looking Down in Pity," agreed to take upon himself the suffering of the world. And he willed that the merit for this selfless act should go out from him to all beings, so that all should be saved. I will not enter nirvana, he vowed, until all beings have entered nirvana. By the generosity of Avalokitesvara all the rest have already gone home.

The bodhisattva's vow is expressed ritually in a litany all Mahayanists are urged to repeat:

> *However innumerable beings are, I vow to save them;*
> *however inexhaustible the passions are, I vow to extinguish them;*
> *however immeasurable the Dharmas are, I vow to master them;*
> *however incomparable the Buddha-truth is, I vow to attain it.*

His name also means "The Lord Who Is Seen Within." For, of course, what the myth means is that at the essence of every person is the Lord Savior. Salvation comes from recognizing who we really are. And from that perspective then everything that happens to us is but an experience of our true essence.

In the Japanese story of the bodhisattva Amida there is a variation on Avalokitesvara's vow. As Amida was about to enter nirvana, he too felt compassion for all beings. He declared that he would not complete his entry into nirvana unless it were guaranteed that all beings who had called upon his help, saying his name as few as ten times in their lives, would at death gain immediate admission to the Pure Land. He subsequently entered nirvana, becoming Amida, the Sun Buddha.

To followers of Shin Buddhism, called the Pure Land Sect, his departure was a sure sign that salvation awaits those who honor the name of Amida and reverently chant his mantra: *Namo Amida Butsu* (Honor to the Buddha Amida). Perhaps soon after dawn on the sixth of August 1945, when citizens of Hiroshima observed the noonday sun descending upon them several hours early, some of them saw not the wrath of America annihilating them in an act of war but the face of Amida the Sun Buddha welcoming them into the Pure Land, making them one with the sun.

At any rate, in spite of the horrors—or, indeed, because of them—Avalokitesvara alone remains, though he soon will follow. And when he does, when, after experiencing all the suffering in every world system whatsoever, he turns to enter the gates of nirvana, he will discover that there is no nirvana and no samsara, that there have never been sentient beings, and there has never been a bodhisattva who has suffered, and that all is empty and has been so from the beginning.

☙

Avalokitesvara is portrayed as bisexual, both male and female, uniting the opposites. In this androgyny he personifies the principle of emptiness: samsara is nirvana, nirvana is samsara: there are no exclusive categories. Today "bisexual" has also come to mean being both heterosexual and homosexual, uniting the opposites.

When I first learned about Avalokitesvara, I was not worldly enough to distinguish between these two meanings of bisexual. Learning of bisexual gods (of which Avalokitesvara is but one in a crowded pantheon) helped me to reevaluate deeply ingrained—and personally destructive—prejudices about homosexuality. For the myths tell us that from the mystical perspective the distinctions between male and female and between homosexual and heterosexual—as between time and eternity, pluralism and monism—are meaningless.

Even Saint Paul declared that in Christ there is neither male nor female. And the Jesus of the Gnostic Gospel of Thomas declared that until one had made the male as female and the female as male, one could not enter the kingdom. Like the myth of the androgynous bodhisattva, this suggests that one has to overcome the tendency of the mind to differentiate and value before one can perceive the unity of life. For what Jesus called the Kingdom was probably not an afterlife, but a mystical realization of the ultimate unity of all beings. In the canonical, but only slightly less gnostic, Gospel of John, Jesus prayed that all may be one, even as he had realized he was one with the Father. In Buddhist terms, Jesus was a bodhisattva, for he took upon himself the sin—the pain, the brokenness, the blindness, the stupidity and apparent failure—of the world.

☙

Jesus—a world savior like the Buddha or the bodhisattva and a battler with the world and its suffering like Brer Rabbit and Prince Five-weapons—discovered that the way to overcome the world and the flesh was to embrace it; the way to overcome death was to die. Jesus was

nailed to a cross. The cross, extending in the four directions of the com-
pass, represented the physical world. Jesus suffered five wounds by
which his senses were crucified on the tree of the knowledge of good and
evil. The fruit of that tree, when eaten by Adam, resulted in the vision
of the polarities which trapped him and all his offspring in the world of
suffering. Crucifixion on that tree resulted for Jesus in the vision beyond
the polarities.

The story of the confirmation to Thomas the Apostle, who said he
would not believe in Jesus' return until he had placed his own hands in
Jesus' wounds, is the only indication in Scripture that Jesus had been
nailed to his cross. Elsewhere it is simply reported he was crucified. As
almost every depiction of the scene shows of the two thieves, victims of
crucifixion were ordinarily tied by the arms to a horizontal beam and
left to die, usually of asphixiation when the weight of the hanging body
caused the muscles in the chest and diaphragm to go into spasm.

But Jesus is said to have suffered five wounds: in the hands and feet,
caused by nails with which he was affixed to the cross, and in the heart,
caused by a spear with which he was stabbed by the Roman Centurion,
who seems to have been a believer, to make certain he was dead (and,
incidentally, to drain the blood from his body as required in the preparation of the Passover lamb). The crucifixion was cut short and the
men killed because it was necessary to dispose of their bodies. The feast
of Passover was beginning and Jews would be forbidden to prepare
graves.

The five wounds were significant of the opening of the senses by
which the vision of the Kingdom could be regained. Five "wounds" appear similarly on the body of Tara, the goddess of compassion, born of
a tear of the bodhisattva Avalokitesvara. She bears openings in her
hands and feet and in her forehead; from within Tara's wounds eyes
look out to see the mystically transformed world.

On the cross, Jesus said, at least partially in the ritual language of Hebrew, words that have perplexed many Christians: *Eli, eli, lema sabac-
thani.* And (according to the two Gospels that record this story) he then
gave up his spirit to God. These are the opening words of the Twenty-
second Psalm, a prayer that is part of a cycle of texts that refer to the
"suffering servant," the just man who, though innocent, takes upon
himself the sins of the people, becoming the scapegoat to suffer for
them, once for all. Jesus' intonation of the words, "My God, my God,
why have you forsaken me?" was not a sign of his despair. It was very

truly his recitation of what in a different context we know as the bo-dhisattva's vow.

By the merit of his act he became more than just a man trapped in space and time. He became, as he prayed in the priestly prayer in the Saint John Gospel, one with all humanity. And he was crowned, with a crown of thorns and briars, King of the Universe, Savior of the World.

To Dismas, the good thief, Jesus declared: "This day you are with me in Paradise." The word in Scripture is paradise, not heaven; it was the word for the Garden in Genesis. Jesus seems to have been declaring not that Dismas would enter some ethereal afterlife, but that, because he had recognized he was responsible for his own acts and deserved cru-cifixion and, unlike the other thief, did not taunt Jesus to free him, Dis-mas' cross had also become the tree of life and to him also was restored the vision of the Garden.

Jesus' words to Dismas that the willingness to accept responsibility for one's own acts restored one to Paradise, and Jesus' own willingness to go beyond that to accept responsibility for the acts of the whole world, reveal an essential meaning of the myth of the crucifixion. The Christian message, similar to yet differently inflected from the Bud-dhist, is at least on one level that, while the suffering of the world may not be escaped, it can be transcended. In the Gnostic Acts of John, lead-ing the Apostles in a kind of mystic dance, Jesus instructed them: "Learn how to suffer and you shall be able not to suffer." And that is accomplished by taking responsibility for the world in all its manifes-tations, by embracing it in oneself and in others as the means by which the senses can be opened, by accepting things just as they are without resistance, by practicing compassion not condemnation. This is more consistent with Jesus' practical admonitions to forgive sinners and love even one's enemies than with the later tendency of Christians to judge righteously as sinful certain lifestyles and to persecute those who did not adhere to a rigid standard of orthodoxy.

Jesus, unlike many of his followers, saw what Brer Rabbit saw: dif-ferent people live in different universes and one person's briar patch is another's home; one person's hell is another's heaven; and to be one with the Ultimate, to be one with God, one has to embrace all the heav-ens and all the hells equally. And so from his perspective as the Christ—the ultimate Self—he was willing to fling himself into the briars. For the road of adventure, the road back to the Garden, leads right into the middle of the briar patch. The briars of Brer Rabbit's escape and the briars of Jesus' crown are one and the same: the occasion to change the way we look at the world.

႟

"In a twinkle we shall all be changed," said Saint Paul.

Not in a twinkle, but in the agony of three hours on the cross and the emptiness of three days in the tomb, Jesus Christ was changed from man to god. His body was transformed, the myth tells, from a body of flesh, which, trapped in individuality by the perspective of the senses, could suffer and die, to a body of light and glory, which, freed from the limitations of perspective, could pass through walls and cover distance in an instant.

The Resurrection is considered the central mystery of Christianity. In it are clues for how to live in the world and in the flesh. That is what the mystery is about. Too frequently, however, the Resurrection is presented not about life in the flesh, but about some sort of disembodied afterlife.

Just as the bodhisattva, in one version of the vow, offers himself as "the food and drink in the famine of the ages' end," so Jesus said his physical body would be meat and his blood drink for his followers so they could enter his Kingdom. He offered himself as the lamb of the Passover sacrifice. The blood of this lamb, smeared on the doorposts, alerted the Angel of Death to pass over the homes of the chosen people; its flesh fed them during their pilgrimage to the Promised Land. And of his body that would be sacrificed, Jesus said, "If you destroy this temple, I shall build it up again in three days."

The disciples perhaps took his metaphor of reconstruction too literally—an error they made often. They consistently misunderstood his message, expecting in the Kingdom not mystical vision but political accession. And so it was that on the third day after Jesus' death, when they went to the place where his remains had been laid, to their dismay they found only an empty tomb, not a reconstituted Jesus. It must have seemed to them that their Lord had failed to rebuild the temple that had been destroyed or resurrect the victim who had been ritually sacrificed for the new Passover.

But then one by one they began to experience strange events. At unexpected times they felt Jesus' presence. In the gardener on Joseph Arimathea's land, Mary recognized him. In a stranger two of the disciples met on the way to the little town of Emmaus outside Jerusalem, when they sat down to eat together, they experienced him. In a shadowy figure cooking breakfast over a fire by the edge of the sea, to which as sailors they'd returned after Jesus' death, they recognized him. In the upper room in which they'd hidden in fear, the Apostles saw him in a mystical body.

John Dominic Crossan, a biblical theologian under whom I studied as a Servite in Chicago, argued that the notable differences between the narratives in the four Gospels suggest that the simple physical resuscitation of Jesus was not the real sense of the Resurrection intended by the Evangelists. If, as so many have maintained afterwards, the historicity of such a resuscitation were the central fact of Christianity upon which all else rises or falls, Crossan argued, the accounts should agree in their report of the historical events. After all, the essence of historicity is consistency among witnesses' accounts. But the accounts are not consistent: the Evangelists treated the Resurrection just as they did other events in Jesus' life—not as historical facts—but as symbolic carriers of spiritual and mystical meaning. What the Gospels do agree on is that on the third day the tomb was empty and soon afterwards the disciples experienced mystical phenomena that are variously depicted as apparitions of Jesus, their ability to work wonders, and the descent of the Holy Spirit.

What actually happened to Jesus' body remains a mystery. Perhaps the corpse was reanimated, as most Christians believe. Perhaps it was stolen, as suggested in the Matthew Gospel, by entrepreneurs, hoping it might still possess some healing power or at least bring a small fee from pilgrims. Perhaps it simply disappeared.*

---

* The bodies of yogis have occasionally been reported to dissolve into light or flame at their deaths. Scientific analysis of the mysterious shroud of Turin suggested that the image of the body was formed by some form of scorching radiation. The shroud was believed to have been the burial cloth of Jesus and the radiation would have occurred at the time his body was transformed to light. Further analysis, however, has questioned this explanation because the fibers of the shroud do not appear to date back to Jesus' time. Still, there is no viable explanation of how the image was formed.

The shroud of Turin is a curiosity of religious history. Could it be that what

Or perhaps the disciples literally consumed the body of Jesus. After all, at the Last Supper Jesus had taken bread and blessed it and given it to his disciples, showing them "This is my body" and instructing them "take and eat." And he had taken a cup of wine and blessed it and given it to them, showing them also "This is the cup of my blood, take and drink." Thus he would be physically present in the disciples' own bodies.

What the Resurrection seems to indicate is that Christ has remained mystically, yet also physically, present. This is, of course, what is meant by the sacrament of the Eucharist. For two millennia the Roman Church has insisted that the eucharistic bread and wine are not merely symbols but are in fact, transsubstantially, the body and blood of Jesus. The revulsion we feel when we consider the cannibalism inherent in this image or in Jesus' rather straightforward instructions at the Last Supper only reveals how little we appreciate sacramentality or understand the meaning of the historicity of the Incarnation. For the historicity of Christianity is itself mythological. The myth of historicity means that spiritual reality is embodied in time and in the flesh. The historical events do not need to have "actually" happened for the notion of their historicity to be meaningful.

≈

In the ancient Roman liturgy of the Easter Vigil, grains of incense were enfixed with stylized wax nails into the five cardinal points of a cross inscribed on the Paschal Candle. The candle represented Christ as the "light of the world." The grains of incense represented the sweetness of the wounds by which the world was transformed. To the right and left of the cross were inscribed the numerals for the current year; above and below, the Greek letters alpha and omega: the cross, which is the acceptance of things just as they are, is formed by the intersection of the temporal and the eternal.

---

formed the image was the belief of all those who came to see it and worship at its shrine? Which is to ask, I suppose, can hoaxes become "real" if they're believed long enough? The scientific answer, of course, is "no." The mystical answer, on the other hand, seems to be "of course." That's where *all* the myths come from, after all.

With consciously sexual symbolism recognized by the Church, the priest who prepared the Paschal Candle then plunged it three times, each time deeper, into a pool of water. As he did this, he prayed that the Spirit descend into the water—which, representing the material world transformed, would be used throughout the coming year for baptism—making it fruitful for regeneration so that those who partook of its sacrament would be "born again new children in true innocence."

This ceremony manifests the tradition that Jesus' death fecundated a new earth. This image, in turn, manifests the even older tradition of the slaughtered king or corn god, who sacrificed himself at the end of his reign in order to bring life to the soil upon which his people depended for food.

Some years ago I wandered into the chapel of the Catholic ministry at the University of California at Santa Barbara. Behind the altar hung a huge mural of the crucifixion in stark black and white, like a photo collage. I was stunned by it. The corpus was surrounded by chromosomal and genetic structures on one side and interplanetary and galactic images on the other. Jesus' body was formed of vascular and striated muscle tissue. It stood before and grew into a cross that was a stylization of the female reproductive organs. The arms of the cross were like fallopian tubes. Within an ovarian form on the left crossarm, a skeletal fetus reached out its hand to insert its fingers into the print of the nail in the savior's palm. Above Jesus' face, bowed in life-bestowing death, the spectral hands of the Father blessing his Son formed the head of the phallus by which the Christ was fructifying the material organic world. The painting, by Michael Dvortcsak, was titled in Teilhardian fashion: Christ Invests Himself Organically with the Very Majesty of His Universe.

The sacrifice of the incarnated Self accepting biological and mortal manifestation engenders new life in foetal humankind who reach out, like twin brother Thomas to test the validity of the Resurrection. (In Gnostic Christianity, such as that presented in the non-canonical Gospel of Thomas, the image of the twin signified mystical identity with Jesus the Christ. The confirmation to Thomas signified the Apostle's realization that Jesus was flesh, and not a ghost, in Thomas' own body.) The blessed belief even of those who have not yet seen, but who have believed, transforms the nature of organic existence. Christ died not to enter into a new life by which he could escape the world, but to give us new life by which to experience that world, in the very flesh in which the Christ Self remains forever incarnate.

⟡

In promising to "master the immeasurable dharmas," the bodhisattva Avalokitesvara identified himself with all beings. In realizing the radical oneness of all consciousness, he became the one being incarnated in all, the one able to perceive the world from all possible perspectives, the one "divine spark," as Eckhart called it, and the Holy Ghost, as mainstream Christians call it, by which the Godhead is present in every being. Hence Avalokitesvara became savior of the world because he is the only being in the world and he has saved himself, and everyone else, by his realization that none are saved till all are saved, and by his choice to save himself by saving all of us—the ultimate act of enlightened, radical self-interest.

Joseph Campbell wrote of the bodhisattva:

> Peace is at the heart of all because Avalokitesvara-Kwannon, the mighty Bodhisattva, Boundless Love, includes, regards, and dwells within (without exception) every sentient being. The perfection of the delicate wings of an insect, broken in the passage of time, he regards—and he himself is both their perfection and their disintegration. The perennial agony of man, self-torturing, deluded, tangled in the net of his own tenuous delirium, frustrated, yet having within himself, undiscovered, absolutely unutilized, the secret of release: this too he regards—and is. Serene above man, the angels; below man, the demons and unhappy dead: these all are drawn to the Bodhisattva by the rays of his jewel hands, and they are he, as he is they. The bounded, shackled centers of consciousness, myriadfold, on every plane of existence (not only in this present universe, limited by the Milky Way, but beyond, into the reaches of space), galaxy beyond galaxy, world beyond world of universes, coming into being out of the timeless pool of the void, bursting into life, and like a bubble therewith vanishing: time and time again: lives by the multitude: all suffering: each bounded in the tenuous, tight circle of itself—lashing, killing, hating, and desiring peace beyond victory: these are all the children, the mad figures of the transitory yet inexhaustible, long world dream of the All-Regarding, whose essence is the essence of Emptiness: "The Lord Looking Down in Pity."
>
> But the name means also: "The Lord Who is Seen Within." We are all reflexes of the image of the Bodhisattva. The sufferer within us is that divine being. We and that protecting father are one. This is the redeeming

insight. And so it must be known that, though this ignorant, limited, self-defending, suffering body may regard itself as threatened by some other—the enemy—that one too is the God . . . we live not in this physique only, but in all bodies, all physiques of the world, as the Bodhisattva. (*The Hero With a Thousand Faces*, pp. 160–62)

That is why all Mahayanists ritually recite the vows. For the vows are clues to one's own truest identity and to the ultimate redeeming insight.

Jesus' mystical vision had shown him that his individuality too was evanescent. He had seen that in the destruction of his body, sacrificed and devoured, surrendering form back into emptiness—as ego consciousness surrenders to unconsciousness—he would be transformed: he would dissolve back into the collective. In being subsumed he would become one with his followers, incorporated into them, seeing through their eyes, hearing with their ears, touching them with their hands—free of individual perspective.

In entering death, proclaiming the bodhisattva-savior's vow to suffer for us all, Jesus is reborn in each person. He has become one with the consciousness that perceives all experience and founds all existence. Each of us is Jesus reborn—not so much, of course, in our bodies of matter (born of mother) which exist in different places in space and time from the body of Jesus—but in our pure awareness (born of virgin) of life simply as it is in the present moment. In Christ (that is, in the pure awareness that is the consciousness in each of us) we all rise from the dead, for we are reborn in children over and over again, not necessarily as reincarnating individuals but as the life itself that causes our children to grow into adults and then to die to make space for more children and more life.

The myth of the Resurrection gives physical reality to Jesus' spiritual discovery of life beyond death—not simply of continuous living, but of an abundant, transpersonal vitality beyond space and time. The Resurrection reveals how rooted is the temporal in the eternal, the individual in the collective, and the physical in the spiritual.

The myth of the resurrection of the body (Jesus' in history and ours at the Second Coming) signifies that life keeps coming back in the flesh. To see that is to see that death need not be feared, that embodied life is good, that we are all manifestations of the same life. To see that is to be born again of the water (of the ocean out of which life first grew and of the amniotic water of our birth) and of the spirit (which is the breath respiring through all of us, and which, as William James saw, is modulated into consciousness in each of us). It is to see that we are all risen from the dead because of God's act of creation of space and time.

In time the creative will is our experience of tense. For the future into which we are being born is always being created in time out of the past from which we have been reborn. Indeed, being reborn means seeing that we are that creative will knowing itself and choosing out of infinite compassion and interest to be all beings.

In space that will is seen as light. For all life grows up from the earth driven by the power pouring down from the sun. In his resurrection Jesus became light, one with the sun. Thus the bread and the wine really *are* the body and blood of Jesus because the wheat growing out of rich soil, nourished by the deterioration of organic matter in the dark humus, is the embodiment of the light, and the wine, pressed from the grapes, invigorated by the propagation of yeasts in the rich red juices, is the blood of the sun.

The point of sacrament is to give physical reality to spiritual truth. Jesus' conquest of death is his presence in the flesh of his followers. And the point of transforming our vision is to find in the flesh, with all its sexual immediacy, the sacrament of our experience of God. True innocence, Christ invested organically, a new way to see the world, vision transformed, the fecundation of a new heaven and a new earth—this is what the spiritual teachings promise. Such vision will, in fact, transform the world of history.

Joseph Campbell frequently quoted a line from the Thomas Gospel: In answer to the disciples' question: When will the kingdom come? Jesus said: The kingdom will not come by *expectation.* The kingdom of the Father *is* spread over the earth and men do not see it. "In other words," Joe said, "bring it about in your hearts. And that is precisely the sense of Nirvanic realization. This is it. All you have to do is see it." (*An Open Life*, p. 57.)

That is what the Second Coming refers to: when our sights have all changed we will see that Christ comes again because, of course, he's never left. Like Avalokitesvara he has remained in our bodies as us.

☙

One of many current attempts to articulate this wisdom is the amazingly popular *A Course in Miracles.* The Course is a three-volume set of books that was "dictated" to an anonymous, and previously agnostic, psychology professor at Columbia University. Her name was Helen Schucman. The "speaker" in the books, most of the time, seems to be Jesus. The message, however, is only occasionally like orthodox Christianity.

I came by the Course in a curious (miraculous?) way. I had been in New York City with my friend and one-time collaborator Toby Marotta, talking with people in the publishing business. We had been given the name of an editor at a Christian Fundamentalist press. Since one of the manuscripts we were marketing was Toby's Harvard dissertation analyzing the history of the homosexual rights movement in America, we didn't think he would be of much assistance to us, but as a courtesy to the person who had given us his name we called him. Yes, he said, he'd like to meet us, if only socially. We made a date to meet in Central Park.

He turned out to be a delightful man, not at all what I had been expecting from a Christian Fundamentalist. He talked with us superficially about New York, about the publishing business, about our lives. I talked a little about Buddhism and comparative religion. He said something that caught me off guard. He made an offhand remark about "those of us who have made the vow." What had he meant by that? "Bodhisattva?" I said quizzically and cryptically. If he didn't pick up on it, I'd know he had not meant what I'd thought.

"Well, yes," he said. I hadn't expected to meet a bodhisattva that day or to have him recognize that I too was drawn to that spirituality. Later, over drinks in one of the fancy hotels that face the park on Fifty-ninth Street, he asked me if I had heard of *A Course in Miracles*. I hadn't.

One day a month or two later, back home in San Francisco, I was feeling a bit glum, uncertain of the direction my life was moving. All day I'd been singing under my breath a song by The Moody Blues. Though I really couldn't understand all the lyrics, the refrain seemed to catch what I was feeling: "I'm looking for someone to change my life. I'm looking for a miracle in my life."

I came home in the afternoon to find a package waiting for me. Inside it were three books titled *A Course in Miracles*. My bodhisattva friend had gotten them to me right on time.

The next day I began studying the Course, which the book—assuming a pattern of reincarnations—tells "is a required course. Only the time you take it is voluntary. Free will does not mean you can establish the curriculum. It only means that you can elect what you want to take at a given time."

The Course consists, in part, of practicing a 365-day series of short meditations. The starting meditations center on the experience of emptiness: "Nothing I see means anything"; "I have given everything all the meaning that it has for me." A mythology is gradually introduced which says that God, of whom each of us is a "Son" like Jesus, wills happiness and health for each of us. But because we "see only the past," living in memories that are fraught with anxiety and dissatisfaction, we tend to create around ourselves an illusion full of disease and ignorance. The Course promises to teach us to work "miracles," which are natural consequences of grace in our lives. "When they do not occur something has gone wrong." And the Course warns that "miracles are habits, and should be involuntary. They should not be under conscious control. Consciously selected miracles can be misguided."

The secret to working miracles is forgiveness. And forgiveness consists in seeing that disease and suffering are illusions that only seem to exist because of memories of the past. The method of the Course is to forgive all that seems to have wronged us, to rise above fear and desire, and to see that life is indeed giving us all that we need, since clearly, God wills our good fortune and what we have is exactly what we need and everything is working out just the way it should.

That same wisdom, expressed without the Christian mythology, appears in a concise and wise little book that grew out of the psychedelic Age-of-Aquarius, Summer-of-Love mysticism of San Francisco's Haight-Ashbury culture. This is Thaddeus Golas's *The Lazy Man's Guide to Enlightenment*. The metaphysics is simple and as vague as the emptiness it alludes to would require: "We are equal beings and the universe is our relations with each other." We cannot know what kind of beings we are; we can only know that we are in relationship with one another.

The spirituality is simple and phrased in short mantra-like epigrams: "No resistance." "Love it the way it is." "Love as much as you can from wherever you are." "I wouldn't deny this experience to the One Mind." The spiritual method of *The Lazy Man's Guide* is to "raise the level of one's vibrations" by loving and affirming life, remembering the epigrams as aids to lowering resistance and generating love.

Perhaps the most effective spiritual method of all is to believe in life.

We cannot fight it. We can only pay attention, resisting as little as possible, investing it with meaning and significance that allow us to say yes to our experience. For in that experience and nowhere else can we find a God that is capable of satisfying and supporting us.

The verification almost every belief system claims for its doctrine is that "it works." For believers in every system—especially as new converts—begin to experience miracles, find meaning and significance in their lives, discover joy and delight. Coincidences abound; the universe seems full of the sweet touch of God. For it is, after all, not the content of belief that matters, but the fact of belief. True believers find that life supports them because their faith, and their contact with the deep stratum of consciousness from which faith arises, activates and vivifies them.

We don't need miracles—though we may get them—nor do we need intentionally to manipulate our destiny. We need simply to accept our lives attentively, to be aware of being alive in a benign universe. Then our lives can be seen to be full of miracles.

CHAPTER SEVEN

The Path of the Wanderer

Eternity isn't some later time. Eternity isn't a long time.
Eternity has nothing to do with time. Eternity is that
dimension of here and now which thinking and time
cuts out. This is it. And if you don't get it here, you
won't get it anywhere. And the experience of eternity
right here and now is the function of life.

There's a wonderful formula that the Buddhists have for
the Bodhisattva, the one whose being (sattva) *is*
enlightenment (bodhi), *who realizes his identity with*
eternity and at the same time his participation in time.
And the attitude is not to withdraw from the world
when you realize how horrible it is, but to realize that
this horror is simply the foreground of a wonder and to
come back and participate in it.

(Power of Myth video, II)

We are each a self—and the Self—searching through our store of experiences, past and present (which is the world), to find a path and to create a future. Each of us is constructing a life story. We are all wanderers, seeking the face of God. It is our heritage. Adam was a wanderer, walking with God in the cool of the evening, beholding God face to face, living open to every new experience as a further revelation of the divine presence. That weary afternoon at the castle, I experienced an enlightened moment and beheld the face behind the veil of my time-and-space reality. I have beheld God face to face.

Indeed, in each face into which I have looked I have beheld God. That was the revelation of that day. Likewise, early twentieth-century English mystic Caryll Houselander described a period of a few days in her life during which she saw the face of Christ behind that of every person on the street. I have come to understand this Truth, but most of the time my sense of it is only very intellectual and distant. But now and then, behind certain faces the divine presence becomes especially real, and a person who might otherwise have been just another person on the street becomes a manifestation of transcendent mythical reality.

One night, I was with friends in front of a theater in the San Francisco's North Beach area. A friend and fellow former Servite was acting in Ken Kesey's *One Flew Over the Cuckoo's Nest*. A young man engaged me in conversation. I was at first a little put off. He was disheveled, his clothes crumpled and worn, his face and hands dirty. But his eyes were bright and alive and his smile captivating. I ended up standing there in the street for an hour or more while he told me about himself.

He said his name was Monty. He was in his early thirties. He'd been an executive in an advertising firm, he said, successful according to American standards. He had, however, come to feel that the security and success of his career were an impediment to his spiritual growth. He felt that there was no challenge left to his soul. And so one day—I imagine in the fervor of conviction—he quit his job, sold or gave away his belongings, gave up his apartment, and went to live on the streets. He was surviving by living simply and frugally, foraging food, occasionally accepting an invitation to stay at someone's house (in those days before the explosion of homelessness in America, it wasn't hard to get an invitation to crash some place in San Francisco), depending on Providence, and overcoming desire. Overcoming desire, he said, was the most necessary thing if the spiritual life were to prosper.

He never asked me for money, but I did give him my address and invited him to visit. A couple of days later, just after supper, Monty came to the house. He had been at the beach to watch the sunset. I was living then with four others in a house near the ocean. I invited him in and fixed some food for him. He was grateful.

I spent a long time talking with him. I was deeply affected by his decision to be a wanderer. He seemed to be living the mendicant life in a way that put to shame my safe, protected, and institutionalized attempts. I wondered if I should try to follow his example. I was frightened by that thought.

It got late. I invited him to sleep over. He accepted. But when I offered to prepare a bed for him, he declined. Fighting the temptation to need comfort, he said, was the hardest part of his life choice. The luxury of the bed would only make that temptation worse. He preferred to sleep on the floor in the living room. The next morning he left and I have never seen him again.

Late that night, as I wrestled with the example of mendicancy he presented me, he took on a magical aura. He held me loosely in his arms to comfort me and told me that my life—like the lives of all of us, I suppose—would be full of suffering and that, even so, I would make it through. He said I'd been right to choose the bodhisattva's path. He said it was not the suffering I had to fear, but the fear of it. Most any suffering we can survive; few hardships are so terrible that they destroy the soul. But what will destroy the soul, cause it to wither up and die unnoticed, he said, is the fear of suffering that builds up walls around the heart and keeps out the life. The sources of that fear are anger that things are the way they are and not as we'd like them to be and desire that they be different from the way they are.

The message of Monty's appearance in my life was, perhaps, that what mendicancy really means is not so much destitution—though it probably does demand basic simplicity—or lack of security, but the willingness to accept life as it comes. There's nothing in itself wrong with making plans for the future or keeping a savings account. But there probably is something damaging to the spiritual life in trying to make sure that every possible future is foreseen and every exigency accounted for. Such an attitude restricts the life and limits experience. Fear and desire must be overcome, because until they are one can never enjoy what is actual.

The cynicism that my training in psychiatry has taught me argues that Monty was schizophrenic, compensated enough to survive on his own, but living in a dreamworld. I wonder if his dreamworld wasn't a better place than the collective dreamworld the rest of us live in.

Despite the madness that might have characterized Monty's psychology, he was for me an "incarnation" of the Buddha. In my interpretation of my life, I can see how he had passed beyond the polarities and awakened from the dream of the world. I can understand how he presented me with a clue to the meaning of my own life-dream. The day Monty came to visit, he brought me a present. It was a small glass bottle, encrusted inside with sea sand and smelling faintly of spearmint. He'd found it on the beach. Perhaps it came from far away. I still have it, a souvenir of my wandering, my present from the Buddha.

Like the myth of the dreamer that describes humankind trapped in world-deluding sleep, the myth of the wanderer describes us lost from our true homeland, seeking to recapture some glimpse of it. According to the myth in the West, the exile originated with Adam and Eve.

Once we lived, it is told, in a state of bliss and oneness with God. Through daring to want to be like God, we ate of the fruit of the tree of knowledge of good and evil, and by that act did, in fact, become like God. Yet we were blinded. For the knowledge of good and evil results in the vision of polarities. The world is split down the middle: male and female, light and dark, true and false, good and evil. We experience the world not as whole but only as changing and conflicting. The "coincidence of opposites," Nicholas of Cusa declared, is what makes up the "Wall of Paradise." We still live in the Garden, and yet it is hidden from us by this wall because we cannot see past the polarities. We are forced to see things linearly, one at a time, step by step. We can never achieve a vantage point beyond the immediate moment. We are trapped in time, which is the matrix of linearity and contradiction. And we are trapped in the limited perspective of ego.

What we did not eat of is the fruit of the tree of eternal life. That fruit would allow vision free of the limitations of perspective. If we could eat of it, our eyes would be opened, the "doors of perception" cleansed, and we would see things as they really are, as infinite; we would see from eternity, unstuck in time.

The God of Genesis was a jealous and miserly God. He drove human beings from the Garden lest they put forth their hands and take from the tree of life. And he set a cherub with a swift and flaming two-edged sword to guard the path to the tree. That two-edged sword is, of course, the appearance of contradiction, of good and evil. It flashes in our eyes, making us believe that some things are desirable and others repugnant, making us fear life and wish things to be other than they are.

In the East, too, the myths describe humankind blinded by the appearances of the world. But in these myths the exile was not so final. The tree of life is only protected by the cherub, not made inaccessible. Buddhist temples are often guarded by statues of demons. They represent the poles of linearity. One pronounces the first letter of the Sanskrit alphabet, the other the last. These guardians are Fear and Desire. Between them the devotee must walk in order to enter the sacred space within. There sits in calm repose the image of the Buddha or bodhisattva who has passed beyond the opposites. The Buddha has eaten of the fruit of the tree of life. He sits beneath the tree meditating on the truth that the world of suffering is an illusion generated by ignorance and hankering.

The path the Buddha trod is still guarded by the cherub with the flashing sword. The way is arduous. For Jesus the road to the tree of life led to Calvary and a bloody crucifixion on the tree. It is a path of adventure. The journeyer must trick the cherub or dash past faster than the sword can flash. That "active door" is symbolized elsewhere as the pair of clashing rocks and as the maelstrom and the monster between which Odysseus had to pass.

The secret to making it through is to accept things as they are, to see that fear and desire are illusions. Yet that vision is thwarted by the clashing of the active door. The wanderer sets out to discover the way. He or she is continually beset by the appearance of good and evil. Contradictions rise up everywhere. Thus the wanderer must remain ever vigilant to the clues that reveal the movements of the door. When the time is right, when the omens indicate that the path lies clear, he or she can move. Thus the wandering life must be lived conscious of the patterns that provide clues.

The myth describes a character, like the wanderer in Hermann Hesse's novel *Narcissus and Goldmund,* who lives on the road, dependent on nature, almost like the animals, concerned only with the simplest issues of survival, free of the cares of houseowners, with no attachment to property or to plans or to belief in progress and security. The wanderer lives acutely aware of transitoriness and death, knowing that nothing can be saved forever and that every construction crumbles finally into dust. Only the grave yawns ominously, a fine and private place that all will one day enter, the only future human beings can ever be sure of.

To the wanderer, individual men and women are like flowers—beautiful but delicate and wilting—that blossom in their season, decorate the wayside for a moment, then wither and blow away in the winds of time. Even the wanderer's own life seems but a gleam in the darkness, a rose in the desert illuminated by individual vision for a moment before the rose withers and the light winks out.

There have always been wanderers. Some were the wandering monks who left one abbey to look for another when political tides changed. Some were the mendicants who chose to live with no purse and no house in order to find the Christ who called himself a wanderer and an outcast with no place to lay his head. Some were simply beggars and bandits who kept one day ahead of the law, looking for new benefactors or new booty. Some, more recently in America, have been, first, the explorers and mountaineers who looked for adventure just beyond the frontiers of civilization, and then the tramps and hobos who set out on the road after economic depressions demonstrated the fickleness of fortune, and recently the beatniks and hippies, who rebelled against the values of mainstream society and sought some higher truth or adventure on their own.

Today the dharma bums, easy riders, and flower children seem to have settled down and built homes and even fortunes. Not all have stayed true to the wandering life, but some have. Their success has not necessarily abrogated their wandering. For to be a wanderer only tangentially requires that one live on the road. What makes one a wanderer is the acceptance of change as part of life, detachment from expectations and demands, and an innocent faith that whatever happens will be okay, that all experience teaches a lesson, that glimmering faintly behind the surface of world, Paradise still waits to reveal itself in radiant splendor.

❧

The willingness to change is an essential requirement for the spiritual life. It was behind Jesus' praise of the poor—for the poor who have nothing to lose are most open to change. And it was behind the teaching of emptiness. After all, the reason for observing the emptiness of all doctrine and the formlessness of all truth is to learn openness to that experience which is beyond knowledge. The God who is clung to as security and certainty is a stultifying idol. The God who provides all that one wants, and asks for nothing more than obedience to rules of social propriety, offers no challenge. The God, on the other hand, who thwarts plans and answers requests in only the most obtuse ways, yet who remains alluring and beckoning, who himself is a wanderer and has learned the lesson of the road, is a God big enough to draw us beyond fear and desire into that still place where even that God is nothing at all and eternity waits in the hand outstretched, a fruit for us to eat and thus to see beyond the opposites to who we really are.

The myth of the bodhisattva Avalokitesvara describes a wanderer so detached from his limited perspective and so open to whatever befell him that when his sense of compassion suggested it to him, he was willing to take upon himself the karma of the whole world. He was so open to experience that he could comprise the experience of all beings.

As we've seen, the bodhisattva manifests under the image of androgyny what Nagarjuna's complex argument for emptiness concluded: There is no ascertainable difference between nirvana and samsara, between heaven and the world. The bodhisattva is able to take upon himself the suffering of the world because he sees through the suffering, knowing that it is just illusion. For he knows that it is just experience. It too is part of life, no better, no worse than anything else, no cause for fear and no occasion for desire.

The attitude of the wanderer grows immediately out of the apprehension of emptiness. For as one sees that everything is meaningless, that there's too much ever to know, that God is just a story that people made up, then one sees that no explanation will ever be right, and so long as one doesn't take them too seriously, one is free to choose for entertainment between the explanations of life.

Obviously, the best explanation is that this present experience is heaven (there is no ascertainable difference between samsara and nirvana; the kingdom of God is within you). Though, of course, to choose that explanation requires giving up any notion of what heaven is. And that is just what the realization of emptiness forces on one. Then whatever happens is acceptable. And there is no reason not to choose it deliberately. Indeed, the choice even of suffering, even of all the suffering in every world system whatsoever, the choice that Jesus made to suffer for the sin of the world, is possible. And that choice, the myths of these saviors reveal, is the instrument by which suffering is transformed. What makes certain experience suffering is the dread and refusal of it. When one sees it just as experience and can choose it, then it isn't suffering anymore.

To be a wanderer means to be empty of opinions and unchangeable views. It means to see that nothing really matters, for things are just the way they are, yet for that very reason wonderful, for that is just how we choose them. And it means to be looking everywhere for signs to guide one's path, since the only right path is the one consistent with itself; and it is the one that reveals to us our affirmation of life even in the face of suffering and evil.

The role of humankind, Alan Watts said, is to be God's "sense organs," to experience all that it is possible to experience. I've already cited science fiction novelist Arthur C. Clarke as a spokesman of mythological wisdom. This idea too can be found in the metaphor of one of his best-known stories, "The Nine Billion Names of God."

Clarke's story opens in the Manhattan offices of a major data processing company. Several representatives of a Himalayan monastery have come to lease a computer. They explain that it was the intuition of the founder of their community that the purpose of human life is to uncover and record the names of God. Over years of theological consideration, the monks have developed an alphabet; all possible combinations and permutations of the characters, according to certain simple principles of grammar, will spell out all of God's names. There are, it seems, about nine billion.

The Order has been laboring scrupulously over three centuries to figure out and copy the combinations of letters and file them reverently in tomes in their great library. Recently they've realized that modern technology could assist their spiritual work. They have, therefore, come to arrange for the use of a computer and printer that will quickly figure and print out the required arrangement of characters. Well, the job seemed somewhat unusual, but the computer firm prided itself on the adaptability of its equipment.

The story shifts to a steep path down the side of a Himalayan mountain. The two technicians who accompanied the computer have decided that, since the machine was nearing completion of its task, they ought to leave. After all, they reasoned, the monks were expecting something to come of all this. When the machine had finished and nothing happened, the monks were likely to get angry, destroy the machine, and perhaps attack them. As they were halfway down the path, the electrical lighting in the monastery went out, signifying that the printer had completed its run and been shut down. The job was done. The last printouts were being taken to their place in the library.

One of the technicians remarked on the narrowness of their escape, but there was no answer from the other. When he looked over, he saw that his friend was silently staring into space. He, too, looked up: "(there is always a last time for everything.) Overhead, without any fuss, the stars were going out."

The discovery of the nine billion names can represent the accumulation of experience. Each of us, and within each life each experience, is one of the "names of God." To contribute to the discovery and cataloguing of the nine billion names, we must open ourselves to experience, resisting nothing, refusing no experience to the One Mind, flowing easily and gently with life.

Birth is our entry into that life. Gradually we come to share our awareness of life through a twofold process of altering ourselves to fit the world and altering the world to suit ourselves. The great developmental psychologist Piaget called these two processes "assimilation" and "accommodation." They are not simple. The world is constantly evading our efforts to bring it under control and our personal sensibilities resist adjusting to reality.

We seem always at least a little at odds with life. Things don't happen quite as smoothly as we'd expect or like. We can't quite figure out how it is all supposed to work. The world does not divide easily into true and false, right and wrong, good and evil. That this is so must occur to an individual as he or she grows from the naïveté of childhood, when mother and father seemed to know all the answers, to the sophistication of adulthood, when moral and philosophical dilemmas seem everywhere. And it must occur to the race itself as it grows, similarly, from naive realism toward a more and more complex understanding of what is meant by truth. The ethics of mass society are incredibly difficult. As good a case can be made for war or abortion or nuclear energy proliferation or governmental secrecy as can be made against them. There are no simple answers to the questions that face individuals and the race.

Truth is elusive. We cannot understand why life has happened the way it has. Clifford Simak, another science fiction mythopoet, designed for one of his characters in a novel called A *Choice of Gods* a mystical experience that conveys the elusiveness of truth: "The world had opened out and so had the universe, or what she since thought must have been the universe, laying all spread out before her, with every nook revealed, with all the knowledge, all the reasons there—a universe in which time and space had been ruled out because time and space were only put there in the first place to make it impossible for anyone to grasp the universe."

That precisely describes the intuition I had at the castle. It likely describes experiences many of us have had mystically or psychedelically. But what are time and space? Who or what put them there? Who is the trickster who keeps the Self from realizing its true nature in us and as us?

Joseph Campbell seemed to love the stories about trickster gods. He frequently recounted a story about a Nigerian trickster god named Edshu who walked down the road wearing a hat colored differently on each side so that when one farmer working in the fields might ask his neighbor, for instance, "Who was that man who came by in the red hat?" the other farmer would answer, "What man in a red hat? The only man I saw walk by was wearing a blue hat." And they'd get into a god-incited fight. Yahweh was a trickster god when he struck the builders of the Tower of Babel with the variety of languages. Trickster gods love to create confusion. But why?

In "The Mysterious Stranger," Mark Twain told the story of a trickster who appears to a young boy in Austria. The stranger proves to have magical powers and plays havoc in the print shop where the boy is apprenticed. He is able to take the boy backward and forward in time to educate him about the ways of humankind. He shows him the folly and pettiness that humans so easily fall into and the complexity of human motivation. Finally, the stranger reveals to the boy, as his last lesson, an experience of emptiness:

> Life itself is only a vision, a dream . . . *Nothing* exists: all is a dream. God—man—the world—the sun, the moon, the wilderness of stars—a dream, all a dream; they have no existence. *Nothing exists save empty space—and you!*
>
> And you are not you—you have no body, no blood, no bones, you are but a *thought*. . . . —a vagrant thought, a useless thought, a homeless thought, wandering forlorn among the empty eternities!
>
> I myself have no existence; I am but a dream—your dream, creature of your imagination. In a moment you will realize this, then you will banish me from your visions and I shall dissolve into the nothingness out of which you made me . . .

Then the stranger disappears, leaving the boy to realize that all he had said was true, that the notion of the reality that all people have taken for granted is preposterous and full of inconsistencies, and that seeing that it is all a dream and that each person is at the center of this grand illusion, enjoins him to dream not more dreams but *better* dreams. The tricksters, like jesters, remind us not to take our selves and our reality too seriously, that the distinctions we make between good and evil, right and wrong are in the mind and must, in fact, be transcended.

Twain's mysterious stranger identifies himself as Satan—a fact that is, in part, a sign of Twain's familiar irreverent cynicism. But it exemplifies an insight into the nature of evil. For evil is that which betrays the illusion. That is to say, the human need for an objective, solid reality is so strong that it names as "evil" and "forbidden" that which makes apparent the unstructured quality of the universe. Evil is that which reveals the chaos at one's feet which one had been taking for solid ground.

A Zen aphorism describing emptiness declares: "Nothing above, nothing below, nothing to right or left, not one square inch on which to stand!" It is the nature of knowledge and our inability to achieve an Archimedian perspective that is responsible for the conspiracy to keep us from knowing the truth.

The biblical Satan of the Book of Job, in fact, was no enemy of God. He was a member of the Heavenly Court. His role was that of an attorney general. It was Satan who kept God on his toes lest he fall under the spell of his own illusion. That is why in the Roman process of canonization the Defender of the Faith, who asks, in the interests of the Church, the hard and the insinuating and embarrassing questions about the candidate for sainthood, is called the Devil's Advocate.

Satan made insinuations about Job's goodness to prevent God from making a fool of himself and to challenge Job's self-righteousness. And self-righteousness is just the belief that one has all the answers and knows the truth. In fact, Job's correct answer to God was finally to accept the emptiness: "I have dealt with great things that I do not understand; things too wonderful for me, which I cannot know. I had heard of you by word of mouth, but now my eye has seen you."

The role of Satan is, not to lead us astray, but to keep us also on our toes lest we become complacent and cease to attend to the emptiness beneath our feet. Curiously, modern Christians seem to have misread totally the myth of the devil. In their zeal to do God's work against the devil, they have often become mightily self-righteous. But God's work, administered through the devil, is precisely to keep them from such self-righteousness.

☙

We face that devil in two directions: internally and externally. Internally we confront our own moral evil, and externally we confront both the evil in nature and, what is a particularly difficult instance of external evil, the moral evil in others.

In facing our own moral evil, we must recognize that religion has tended to obscure morality by confusing the violence wrought against people with violence wrought against institutions. For institutions tend to maintain themselves by condemning that which threatens their authority and by preserving for themselves rights and privileges by which they define themselves. The institutionalization of social relationships, of religious sentiments, and of mystical wisdom has resulted far less often in condemnations of violence against human persons—violence roused by the passions of hate and fear—than in the condemnation of violations of social codes—violations motivated by the passions of love and adventurousness.

Often what is condemned as moral evil is that which was once sacralized. Experiences that were fraught with transcendent significance were once reserved for initiates who had been instructed in their use. Among these were sex and drugs, both of which can bring about transpersonal states of consciousness. These may well have been restricted in order to impress upon non-initiates just how powerful these really were. But as the mystical roots of religion were forgotten and there ceased to be initiates trained in the use of powerful techniques, all that was left were the restrictions and condemnations. The fact that folk religions, like witchcraft and some of the native American and Indian religions and more recently modern Tantric-based meditation practices, use both sexual and drug-induced states religiously, confirms the power of such experiences.

"Sex, Drugs and Rock 'n Roll" have been the tricksters that have brought down Western Civilization, which is to say, revealed and manifested the immense cultural confusion of the modern predicament. Oddly, for many of us who lived our youths through the 1960s, these were often the source of experiences of transcendence, but that is never how the mainstream culture perceived what was happening. And the institutions of culture have warred against the tricksters in a way that made them into monsters that have laid waste our cities with disease and violence. Yet even these, terrible as they are, are still reminders of the emptiness.

Etymologically, our word "profane" means "for, or in front of, the temple." We may read that as what was outside the temple. But we may also read it as what was left at the temple door. What the people sacrificed, the priests consumed; between the profane and the holy there is no ascertainable difference. We can understand then that sometimes apparent condemnations actually reveal power and significance. In investigating the mythic dimensions of our lives, we must look carefully at everything we have been told is forbidden, in order to understand whether it was forbidden because it is life-denying or because it is too powerfully vital.

The life-affirming obligation we all share is to expand and enhance our experience of the variety and grandeur of creation, to contribute to the collection of the nine billion names. In the past, religious teaching often seemed to disparage human experience. The world of the senses was condemned and people were urged to live for the hereafter. By and large, the spiritual enterprise was to escape from the world. For those in the past, the call of the spirit was to rise above the physical world that was so much with them, because, as Protestant theologian Harvey Cox has astutely pointed out, men and women then lived a much more earthy existence than most of us. They lived with disease and vermin, household and bodily waste, decay and death all around them. Life often demanded strenuous labor. The smell of the soil and the hardworking body was everywhere.

Today, however, our stance toward the world has changed. We value sensory experience—from a scientific, depersonalized point of view—in a way different from that of our ancestors. The modern world, for all our sophisticated and deadly pollution, is enormously more sanitary and etherealized than theirs. We defecate in white porcelain bowls and flush away the waste without ever looking. We shower daily and deodorize our bodies. Most diseases have been overcome; the old are put away in meticulously clean convalescent hospitals; death by violence is sensationally publicized, but death by the slow decay of nature is hidden away. Our food comes sterilely wrapped in plastic. Many of us have never seen a maggot.

The call of the wanderer is to change his or her life, to make a radical conversion. In the modern world, shot through with disdain for the material world, for the body and its natural processes, the conversion may be to reengage the world on multiple levels, not to flee from it. The spirit of mendicancy calls us again to challenge the middle-class values of security, domesticity, and moral and social propriety. The experiences we garner for God must be not only bodiless and intellectualized, but also earthy and natural. Then we are adding something to God, balancing the tendency of modern thought and middle-class technocracy to repudiate the material, unpredictable, passionate natural world.

The meaning of passion and human interaction has become obfuscated. Despite—or perhaps because of—the presence everywhere of almost pornographic advertising, which, since it is more concerned with consumption of goods than with erotic sensuality, is hardly really sexual at all, our culture is essentially desexualized. Our conversion demands that we invent meaning for our experience of sexuality and attraction.

We find clues in basic mythological patterns that describe sexuality, for sex has always been one of the major areas of interest to the mythopoetic mind. Sexual arousal, whether experienced with the participation of another person or enjoyed alone in the presence only of oneself and one's fantasies, alters consciousness. The state of arousal itself manifests God's pleasuring himself in the creative act whereby the universe came to be—full of beauty and full of embodiment for each of us. The desires of the flesh, the myths warn, can lead us away from God, but they can also be divinized by understanding them as promptings of life seeking its own vibrant enjoyment. And as Saint Paul—of all people—recognized, attraction metaphorizes the relation between God and the world, between spirit and matter.

Attraction, sexual and nonsexual, between a woman and a man witnesses to the interplay of opposites which generates the world. Chinese philosophy calls these primal forces the yin and the yang, dark and light, receptive and creative, passive and active, feminine and masculine. Female and male are special cases of these polarities. The attraction between male and female manifests the duality that stirs creation.

In the same way, attraction, nonsexual and sexual, between two men or between two women witnesses to the ultimate unity of the world beyond duality. Monistic philosophies have seen that beneath the apparent swirl of polarities, ever growing, ever changing, clashing in conflict and cooperating in love, lies a deeper stratum in which all is at rest in a self-mirroring perception that all is one and that the opposites are illusory. The attraction between same-sex individuals manifests the identity that precedes the duality.

Modern psychology, especially bodywork-oriented psychotherapy, has discovered that sexuality has other functions in human beings besides reproduction. Paradoxically, engaging in sex outside the reproductive context has been called indulging our animal nature. It is precisely the opposite. Animal nature is to copulate instinctively only to produce progeny. As Jacob Bronowski observed, what is natural for human beings is certainly not behavior that is found also in animals, but what is different and unique to humans. Human beings, of course, feel the instinct to produce progeny, but that is only part of our sexual experience. (Our overpopulated world proves we needn't fear that condoning nonprocreative sex will threaten racial survival.) Precisely the way we differ from animals that have rigid sexual cycles and less involving and less orgasmic intercourse is that human sexual contact involves consciousness and volition.

According to Reichian and neo-Reichian bodywork therapists, the whole body is involved in psychological processes; consciousness and intelligence are not merely in the brain. They have discovered that traumas, fears, negative conditioning, and the like result in tightness and restrictions in the body that distort both psychological and purely physical processes. These can result not only in neurosis and mental illness, but also in psychosomatic disorders, cardiovascular disease, and perhaps even cancer.

Reichian therapy consists of practicing better and more complete releases of tension through crying, screaming, vomiting, and coming to orgasm. Learning to allow spasmodic release and emotional catharsis helps prevent deformation of the nervous system. The surge of energy during orgasm can break open the blocks and keep the system clear of restrictions to the vital flow. The role of orgasm in the human being then is more than just ejaculation or reception of genetic material. The aim of "total orgasm" is not simply to get a narcissistic satisfaction, as suggested by many critics of the California-based fascination during the seventies with bigger and better orgasms, but to activate an important self-regulating mechanism in the mind-body system.

Orgasm is protrayed mythologically—*kundalini* in Tantrism, for instance—as a conscious experience of cosmic energy. Orgasm is certainly an experience of neurological dynamics. It has no content. Like a dream it is forgotten almost as soon as it is over.

Perhaps the function of sex and orgasm in human beings has been not only to clear the individual nervous system but—and consequently—to affect the way the nervous system itself has evolved. Human beings are sexually motivated differently from almost every other species on our planet. Because women's sexual interest is not restricted by an estrus cycle, human beings are sexually and psychologically available and motivated all the time. We engage in sexual foreplay beyond instinctual seduction rituals. We experience orgasm more completely, it appears, than other animals. Indeed, our females *have* orgasms, something not particularly needed for the continuation of the species (as, sadly, generations of women suffering religion-induced frigidity can attest). And, at least among land animals, we alone have developed sophisticated language and complex brain functions. Perhaps our sexuality is in some ways responsible for, or at least intrinsic to, our evolution of intelligence and conscious thought.

In discussing the role of the spiritual aspects of consciousness, I've been suggesting that perhaps the ability to experience wonder, to feel curiosity, to develop myth, and to ask questions forced open the neural pathways that directed the path of survival up toward consciousness and humanity. Similarly, sexuality can be understood as the experience in the flesh of what in the mind is wonder and curiosity. Sexual attraction is the desire to know another's body, to feel the flesh, to experience the rhythms of the other's movement. It is the drive to enter into relationship with the other, to try to see from the other's perspective, and so to add complexity to one's own experience of life. And within the act of lovemaking itself, sex is the experience of joy in being embodied and of the body being caught up by a deeply primal, transpersonal force. It is not surprising that one consequence of such an experience of wonder should be genetic transfer and reproduction of life through time and through evolutionary advance. Sex as experience of the life force perhaps precedes sex as a tool for reproduction. Our sexuality, far from being a distraction from God, can be understood as the instrument by which God created us and continues to manifest Godself to us.

Particularly in the sense that all of us are manifestations of the One Self, our experience of loving another person is our participation in the divine love for creation. And our experience of being loved is our perception of God's love for us. Indeed God has no way to demonstrate love for creatures except through the creatures' love for one another. This love for creation is not some curious will that creatures overcome their corporality. The flesh is the mode of creation. God's love for us and our love for God is experienced in our flesh.

We are blinded to the holiness of the flesh by fear and desire, by the tendency of the senses to get stuck, to delude us into believing we are just egos, by our failure to see the whole, to see life in context, by our failure "to see the forest for the trees." Of course the importance of sex can be exaggerated and desire can get out of hand. But we will not develop vision by fleeing the flesh, by condemning our sexuality, by making other people wrong for enjoying sex, by refusing to love God's manifestation in the flesh. A positive attitude toward sex can help bring us into touch with the resurrected body we carry, so unconsciously, along with us all our lives.

Isn't this positive attitude, this affirmation of incarnated human life, what is meant by the saviors' embrace of the human condition—even of sin and suffering? "God so loved the world . . ."

Especially in dealing with the tradition-violating styles of sexual behavior that modern society seems to be moving toward and that the churches have long condemned, we must seek to understand the signs that guide our wandering. The condemnations may provide signs for some, but not for others. The signs can never be taken only at face value. Choosing one's own sexual style—deciding not to get married or to pursue a variety of partners or to come out as gay—breaks with tradition. In such a life the position of the tradition may assist growth, because it forces deep personal retrenchment and self-evaluation in which the individual grows ever more conscious. The dilemma posed by the old morality that must be overthrown can drive the mind beyond the superficial rules into a state in which one sees that one must take responsibility for one's own experience and so let go of morality as an outside force and integrate it into one's own personal code of behavior. Violating taboos, the Tantrics of both Buddhism and Hinduism have discovered, can be spiritually compelling and enriching.

Of course, it is not necessary that taboos be violated, but it probably *is* necessary that the sometimes confusing and disturbing, yet always alluring and compelling, sexual feelings be placed in a context which divinizes them. The universe can be seen as dual; it can be seen as unitary. God is the lover seeking his complementary opposite in the world, and the lover beholding the goodness in his/her own reflection. God is the solitary pleasuring self, the adventurer playing joyfully in the world, and the mother giving birth. All of the styles of sexuality can be divinized.

Drugs, too, have often been taboo. Yet evidence points to extensive use of psychedelic potions by primitive seers. And even Christianity uses alcohol sacramentally. Indeed, Gordon Wasson and others have hypothesized that Christianity was originally a drug-based cult. Drugs do alter consciousness and suggest that reality is not as fixed as we often assume. Just as drug experience can sometimes seem to divinize the world, we can divinize the use of drugs. The divinization changes the attitude toward drug experimentation, just as it changes the experience of sexual relationship. A grace and virtue enters in that prevents violence and urges prudence and good sense in dealing with taboos. For taboos must not be thrown off as though they meant nothing. Indeed, taboos exist precisely because what they guard, and what can be divinized, is very powerful and must be handled carefully and consciously.

&

What constitutes true moral evil is violence against persons. Such violence (and we will come back to this point later) is all too often motivated by the idea that some things matter. Thus we feel compelled to act to protect our own survival and those things that symbolize survival for us—like possessions, reputation, future prospects—even when such actions violate the survival of other persons and their survival symbols. We steal from our employers or cheat on our tax returns and we invest money in a bank because it pays good interest even though we know the bank is using its money to finance genocide on the other side of the world. The real evil we fall into is not in taking home the ballpoint pens and paper clips, making up deductions, or investing capital, but in closing our eyes and not paying attention to the ramifications of our actions. Even more than such conniving with ourselves, the evil we commit is allowing to come into existence the systems of economic and social life that compel and reward all of us for filching the paper clips, creating the tax shelters, and investing our money without ever really taking responsibility for our actions.

As we begin to open our eyes and take responsibility for how other human lives are affected by the way we live ours, we will begin to live differently. We will begin to divinize our perceptions of our sexuality, our sociability, even the payment of our taxes.

&

Harder to divinize, however, is our perception of the apparent natural evil of the external world. The world is full of events that stun the mind. French philosopher Paul Ricoeur saw as signs of true evil events that violate our sense of the natural order of life: a frog hops to the edge of a fire, gazes into the flames, and then leaps in. Events far more stunning than this appear in the news every day. Much more than the frog's hypnosis by the flame, they are, in the jargon of legal fiction, acts of God. An electrical circuit shorts out, the arc sets fire to a grand hotel, and two hundred people die. A leak in a furnace causes an explosion in an elementary school and innocent children, engulfed in the expanding, searing gases, burn to death.

Evil of this sort is as much a part of the fabric of the world as gravity. That there is such evil does not prove there is no God, but only that the God who ministers over earthquakes, hurricanes, freak accidents, and the rest is beyond any of our anthropomorphic concepts.

Indeed, the existence of such evil calls out for a God, calls out for a perspective from which the evil makes sense. A totally good universe needs no God; one in which there is terrible evil requires a God to justify the evil as part of a greater vision. And that is why, in the face of an incomprehensible universe, human beings have invented gods who could somehow understand and justify the behavior of the world.

But still more difficult to deal with is the evil that comes from fellow human beings. People are incredibly cruel to one another. Though we cannot understand why there need be such moral evil, why people can't just behave more kindly, we can, I think, understand a lesson in their behavior: When human beings deny the emptiness and begin to believe that things matter, when we fall victim to fear and desire, we also fall victim to an urge to violence that is no less than astonishing, that today is so empowered that it can annihilate the planet.

Of course, we must stop that. We must disarm the nuclear weapons. Paradoxically, we can only do that when we've realized that it really doesn't matter to emptiness if we blow ourselves to hell or not. The clue behind those bombs poised atop fiery missiles is just that emptiness is all around us. Within the context of emptiness, we must each in our own lives become responsible for our own conduct, our own participation in the systems that corrupt us, our own moral evil of violence sparked by fear and desire.

Even though we cannot explain evil, we can interpret its appearances in our lives. We can fit the misfortunes that befall us from nature or from other persons into the stories we are constructing of our lives, so that the signs that at first glance seem to point away from the direction of our lives can instead point toward it. We can take responsibility, if not for the evil, at least for our interpretation of it.

When misfortune befalls us, rather than focusing on our dissatisfaction, we can—while feeling the grief, anger, and pain, of course—move beyond it to incorporate the event into the greater story of our lives. Perhaps we can see how this event has protected us from some even more disturbing alternative—one we can imagine and describe. We can interpret the misfortune within the myths that speak of God's loving care as chastising, even as it purifies and prepares us for greater joy. We can see that the experience seems a misfortune only because we do not understand the larger implications of it in our lives. Perhaps, then, we can see that what is experienced as pain and suffering is our lack of understanding and control.

In recent times, one of the most difficult of such issues to deal with has been the appearance of AIDS. This disease has been not merely a medical emergency of the greatest proportions, it has been the occasion of immense bigotry and cruelty. It has, in many ways, been a test case for religious virtue—the leprosy of our day. Sadly, in most every instance—with, of course, a few notable exceptions—the religious institutions failed the test. The Christian churches preached fire and brimstone instead of compassion.

How we will eventually understand the impact of AIDS—good and bad—we can only guess. It is certainly forcing religious questions on secular society. I fervently hope AIDS will turn out to have major beneficial consequences. The most practical of which I think we can expect is that it will have turned the focus of medicine toward immunology in the years just before a wave of apocalyptic plagues befall the planet.

One of the predictions of medical environmentalists has been that the widespread—and cavalier—use of antibiotics will produce virulent strains of household bacteria by the end of the twentieth century, and that the antibiotic approach of poisoning these organisms is no longer going to work because the poisons will have to be so strong they will kill the host along with the invader. In that scenario, medicine was going to have to have developed new approaches. But in the 1970s, when such alarms were being raised, there was little interest in immunology and little profit apparent in seeking a whole new approach to fighting infection. AIDS has changed all that. And perhaps now the world will be prepared when the antibiotic-resistant plagues appear. If so, AIDS could still prove to have been a godsend—a horror that is the foreground of a wonder.

In some ways, of course, AIDS is the first of the new plagues. How fortunate, however tragic, that the first such disease was a disease of the immune system—one that is relatively difficult to pass from person to person and that appeared first, in the industrialized world, in a relatively enclosed group. How much more tragic would it have been if the first such plague had been an antibiotic resistant air-borne staphylococcus that caused suppurating sores that oozed contagion onto everything its victims touched? Such a disease would have spread rapidly and would have caught the medical and pharmaceutical industries totally unprepared. But, in part because of discoveries in the wake of AIDS, now when that disease appears—say in the subways of New York City—immunologists are likely to have a whole new handle on how to control it.

Perhaps AIDS will also have helped refine our religious sensibilities. It is certainly true that after its first bad showing the Christian religious establishment has come around to offering help and solace to people with AIDS. Where the refining of religious sensibilities has been most obvious is among the first activist victims of the disease. Among gay men a major transformation of identity is underway. Perhaps because of the dramatic experience of human mortality and the fragility of life, perhaps because of the constellation of powerful archetypal forces in the collective mind of the human race, gay men are constructing and reclaiming an identity their homosexual forebears sometimes possessed in hunting and gathering cultures. Historical research into previously taboo topics has discovered that among shamanistic cultures—certain Amerindian tribes, for instance—sexual deviation was perceived as a sign of divine election. Individuals who didn't fit into the normal lifestyle of childrearing were assigned other social roles and revered as spiritual beings and powerful healers. (This dynamic has been true also in Roman Catholicism, though, of course, the aspects of sexual deviation were played down: children who didn't show an interest in dating and sexual courtship were advised they might have a call to the monastery or convent. After all, since the Middle Ages, such religious institutions have provided a social role for non-reproducers that revered them, even if it slightly marginalized them.) The blending of traditionally male and female traits into a spiritual identity outside the norm promises to give gay people a special perspective on society and culture, and may demand of them a change in the way they've existed as sexual outlaws so that they can fulfill a special role in the evolution of consciousness.

AIDS has certainly affected how people have sex. In that respect, it may function as an inhibitor of population growth at a time when overpopulation is becoming a major threat to Earth's survival. (Plague has always been one of nature's means of controlling population.) It would seem that the function of homosexuality in planetary ecology also has something to do with population control. (I assume it evolved in the species for a "reason.") That AIDS first attacked gay men, at least in America, may simply be a freak of history. Though one might wonder if there's some deeper relationship between these two facts.

As the research of Yale classics scholar John Boswell in *Christianity, Social Tolerance, and Homosexuality* suggests, the cultural and religious condemnations in the West of homosexuality and nonprocreative sex, in general, seem to have derived from population control needs in the fourteenth century. Before that time, even the Sodom and Gomorrah story was not particularly interpreted to be about homosexual sex. But following the Black Death and the devastation of the Hundred Years War, the Church and society had to explain the disasters in a way that would encourage population growth, and vilifying nonprocreative sex was just such a way. The issue is obviously the opposite today. And a kind of backhanded consequence of the tragedy of AIDS is likely to be the general acceptance of homosexuality as a reality of human life, like left-handedness. This may, in the very long run, assist its population control function.

The answer to how a loving God or beneficent Nature could wreck such misery is revealed in the myths of the Black Mother. In Hinduism, for instance, the wrathful manifestation of Mother Kali drinks blood from a human skull while she dances, with garlands of skulls swinging from her girdle, amid flames licking at the bodies of her burning children. In Christianity this image appears also, but only in the most attenuated form: the Blessed Mother receives down the body of Christ from the cross as the Pietà in which the Mother bears the suffering of her child as her own. The Western God is, in the words of Alfred North Whitehead, a "fellow-sufferer who understands" (i.e., who compassionates but also who stands under).

As Joseph Campbell said repeatedly in one way or another, "All life is sorrowful is the first Buddhist saying. And it is. It wouldn't be life if there were not temporality involved which is sorrow, loss, loss." Whitehead had summarized this fundamental experience of evil in two holy but horrible propositions: Things fade and alternatives exclude. The image of the Black Mother reminds us this isn't just a cruel joke played on us, but is indeed an attribute of the life of God. Time and perspective are the very bones of the body of God in manifestation. And they hurt. They hurt.

At any rate, in the language of the reincarnation, an enormous number of Buddhist monks who over the centuries had daily been making the vow to take on the world's suffering and to transform that hurt are bound to have ended up as homosexuals in the time of AIDS. It is not surprising then that AIDS should result in a new attitude toward life, suffering, and death, and that the gay men victims of this virus and their compassionate succorers should be leaders in this new attitude.

⟍

The world is a prison and a chamber of tortures and yet it can imprison us only so long as we take it seriously. It begins instead to entertain us and amaze us when we cease our seriousness and begin to embrace life, whatever happens in it. For the very appearances that seem to imprison us are the signs that can lead to this too-solid world's undoing.

I suspect that one of the reasons that God seems so often unreasonable and demanding, thwarting our carefully made plans, answering our prayers sometimes but seldom in the way we had hoped for, and expecting the impossible of us, is that such a God does not reinforce our assumptions of the everyday world. The God, on the other hand, who takes the world as seriously as we, who tends to give us the things we think we need, who answers prayers, who works miracles, who intervenes on our behalf, only keeps us complacent within the prison of our illusion.

The point of God is, after all, to shake us free of our belief that things matter, that one way is better than another, that life ought to be this way instead of that. For as long as we are still trying to make things over to suit our notion of values, we are not open. We are placing our faith in the illusion from which we are trying to wake. It is also for this reason that serious questions about the proper conduct of the spiritual life hinder us. When we think that we should, perhaps, be Zen Buddhists or should join the Church or give up sex or eating meat or observe such and such a discipline in order to be freed, we are reinforcing the imprisonment, which is our dependence on the notion that there is a separate and individual ego that needs to be freed.

As Eckhart said, all paths lead equally to God and God is on them all equally. The vocation of the wanderer, perhaps much more than that of the committed adept, accomplished and righteous, keeps us open. Our wanderings may make us adept. They should, in fact. But we must avoid the temptation to be self-righteous, to want to be adept more than to be open to life.

CHAPTER EIGHT

The Virtues of Emptiness

*Anyone who has had an experience of mystery knows
that there is a dimension of the universe that is not that
which is available to his senses. There is a pertinent
saying in one of the Upanishads: "When before the
beauty of a sunset or of a mountain you pause and
exclaim, 'Ah,' you are participating in divinity." Such a
moment of participation involves a realization of the
wonder and sheer beauty of creation.*
(Power of Myth, p. 207)

The myth of the Secret guides us in the development of an epistemology
with which we can begin to understand the modern predicament and
rise above the malaise. And, as we earlier recalled Plato had discovered,
an epistemology allows us to develop an ethics. But what kind of ethics
can we devise based on secrecy and emptiness? The secrecy seems to
suggest that the only basis for behavior comes from within the life. But
from within the life, how can one determine goodness? And the emptiness seems to suggest that nothing really matters anyway. There are no
values. Ideas and valuations of human behavior are arbitrary and have
no external basis. There are no standards. Things are good only insofar
as they produce their desired ends, and there is nothing about those
ends that demands they should be produced any more than that they
should not be.

In the face of such propositions, how can we lead "good" lives? What
is to prevent one of us from murdering his mother in acting out the myth
of Orestes or throwing tantrums in emulation of the Incredible Hulk?

Of course, no ethics prevents anyone from acting in any particular way. And indeed, even matricide and raging paroxysms ought to be incorporated mythically into a life. But the function of ethics is to teach us how to live. The secrecy does not mean that no actions are proscribed. The proscriptions come not from moral commandments, but from intuitions about the nature of behavior that derive directly from the experience of emptiness and that suggest certain qualities of goodness. The aim of an ethics is to provide a reason for good behavior, so that it flows naturally from the experience of being fully alive.

We must realize that, contrary to most of our past moral upbringing, goodness is not a goal that includes specific kinds of behavior people can seek to develop in themselves—like modesty, punctuality, efficiency, or humility. Quite the reverse: goodness is the way in which certain recognized, respected, and beloved people do, in fact, behave. Good deeds are those that good people do, which communicate to others the sense of what it is like to live vitally, to affirm and love life, and to cherish the variety of ways that life is manifested in all people.

Michael Novak, who has dealt incisively with the modern malaise in a book titled *The Experience of Nothingness,* found such a notion in Aristotle. Novak explains that Aristotle used as models of the ethical life the athlete and the artist who do not choose their actions from duty to law but from a sense, derived from seeing other persons' lives, of skill and craftsmanship. Novak says that ethics is not concerned with analyses of abstract forms, laws and general principles, or with conceptual and linguistic puzzles, but rather with concrete actions. The criterion of acting well is not a set of objective, universal laws, which, for instance, forbid matricide or throwing tantrums, but the actual behavior of human beings, whose names can even be mentioned. And in identifying such specific persons, what is recommended for imitation is not their actual behavior, but the process of living and acting that is demonstrated by their lives. The point of an ethics is not to define the limits of behavior, but to draw forth from the lives of imitable people the qualities that make their lives attractive.

What makes lives attractive, especially in today's world, I would argue, is openness and the willingness to confront the experience of emptiness that is so much a part of the modern sensibility. For the experience of emptiness can produce a keenness, an intensity of awareness of being alive in the indeterminate present, that allows people to shape their lives according to aesthetic principles that manifest "grace and beauty." This awareness can influence the actions of those who experience it, so that the rest of society take their lives for examples and name and categorize as particular virtues what these people do without thinking about virtue. In the past these people were the mystics and visionaries, the desert anchorites, and the wandering mendicants from whose experience and teaching the patterns of myth were generated. Today they must be each of us.

Contemporary theologian John S. Dunne proposes for imitation the lives of those who have ceased to assess the contents of actions and instead cultivate an attitude toward them of "renunciation." In *The Way of All the Earth* he cites the great Indian epic the *Bhagavad Gita,* which describes the ethical dilemma of Prince Arjuna, preparing to lead his armies into civil war, yet horrified by the senselessness of what he is about to do. Lord Krishna, after manifesting himself as Supreme Lord of the Universe, admonishes Arjuna on the field of battle to renounce the "fruits of action." Dunne takes this advice as still applicable today, for, he suggests, by such renunciation violence is transformed into action, and passion and pleasure-seeking into love and compassion.

Dunne follows Gandhi's argument that some actions, certainly all those that entail violence, cannot be performed at all if their fruits are renounced. Such actions are intrinsically goal-oriented: No one fights a war without any hope of winning; no one rapes another without hope of gaining some emotional release or satisfaction from it; no one robs a bank, embezzles from an employer, or rips off the supermarket without at least expecting to increase his or her possessions or self-repute. Renouncing the fruits of action, choosing to act in a certain way because it responds to a real life situation or because it is an act of skill or craft (like the work of an athlete or artist), acting for no other reason than the grace and beauty of the act itself—and of the life of which that act is a part—is electing the quality of life over the gains that may be derived from it.

One of the strongest and most effective motives for renouncing the fruits of action may be the awareness of valuelessness. Nagarjuna's articulation of emptiness had concluded that there is no discernable difference between samsara and nirvana, between time and eternity, between the world and heaven. In the face of that emptiness the enterprise of living and behaving becomes centered not on a valuable goal or on results and achievements, but on the quality of actions. Action is not rejected—there is no naive or spiteful repression of human activity—

but is transformed into graceful, which is to say life-affirming, activity consistent with the story one is living.

Thus the loss of external values does not have to hurl us into a chaos of cruelty and rapaciousness. Quite the contrary, it can help us see that the possibility of cruelty and rapaciousness arises only when we begin to believe in values and to think that there are things worth being cruel or rapacious to achieve. Finally, of course, the crucial question has to be what effect the consciousness of emptiness and ultimate secrecy and open belief will have in one's life. For, as Aristotle learned from his teacher, if the study of ethics does not lead to acting well, then it has no point.

~

There are certain qualities of attitude and action that can be identified in the lives of the good people who, because their awareness of emptiness renders them unaware of not being in heaven, are the models of ethical behavior. Six "operative virtues" can be identified that make their lives appear attractive, full of grace and beauty. Following the example of Teilhard de Chardin, I call the virtues "operative" because they describe, rather than prescribe, behavior. They cannot be willed, nor can they function as the object of choice or decision—as can, for instance, the virtues of celibacy, material poverty, or sobriety. What can be chosen is the willingness to be frank about one's experience of self and to structure one's life on the emptiness that choice compels one to confront. Then these virtues, which are qualities of disinterest, derive directly from the consciousness of emptiness.

The first and most important virtue is wonder. Wonder produces a high and liberating consciousness from which the other virtues flow. But because it arises from the sense of emptiness and because people tend to flee or resent that sense, at first appearance it may produce despair. For emptiness requires that one set aside individual ego, with all its demands and need for self-affirmation and aggrandizement and hankering after the objects of desire. Emptiness declares that no object of desire can ever really be achieved, that even if it is, it will be found paltry and unsatisfying—like dust in one's hand or mouth—and that even desiring it is painful, and yet there seems no way out, no exit. The response to such a condition is despair.

Such despair can cause one to set aside all hope of success or accomplishment, all aims and ambitions. Then the motive of acting has to cease to be for oneself. What one has has to be accepted as all that one has. Life has to be accepted just the way it is—since it can't be any other way. If this almost always difficult ordeal is successfully passed, then the blinders may be removed, the scales fall from the eyes, and the world may begin to shine brightly, if mysteriously, as unconditionally positive. The experience of despair can begin to buoy one up and make apparent that for all its indifference and unknowableness—and just because of them—the universe is ultimately benign. Thus despair may transform into wonder.

Wonder can sometimes come without the despair and the darkness of the soul's night. Sometimes it can invade the soul suddenly, and everything limited, or merely self-serving and shallow, is burned away. That is how it is finally experienced anyway—during moments when it is fully experienced—as an absolutely unconditioned gift from life itself that makes that life altogether fresh and new.

Wonder is the ability of the mind at certain moments to pierce through the "curtain of everydayness" and to see meaning inherent in the very substance of space itself. Of course, that meaning, rather than being perceived radiating from some inherent external quality, is, in a certain sense, projected outward onto objects and events in space. Yet it is really neither perceived nor projected. Indeed, *it* seems to give rise to both the experience of the perceiving self *and* the perceived external world. For, at least in the state of consciousness in which the meaning is discovered and wonder and awe felt, this consciousness seems more basic than either the perceiver or the perceived world. It is the experience of the creative intention at work. And that is why this state of consciousness is so often called God and why God is said to be the creator and maintainer of the world. For when God is experienced, it seems to precede all distinctions between subject and object.

Colin Wilson in *The Occult* calls the ability to achieve this consciousness "Faculty X" and sees it as responsible for marvels and supernormal powers. Wilson cites a number of instructive descriptions of the experience of wonder; they point to the qualities of this experience. One such quality is the sense of transcending time. Historian Arnold Toynbee, for instance, had the experience of suddenly rising above his particular place in time and seeing, stretching out into both past and future, the activity that for us ordinarily is focused into the tiny moment of the present actuality.

A second quality is a paradoxical sense of knowingness. For even as the mind realizes that it knows nothing very firm, since its attention has shifted from specific events to universal truths, free of content, it feels as though all knowledge is very clear and available. In a fictionalized autobiographical sketch cited by Wilson, "The Abominable Mr. Gunn," Robert Graves recounts the feeling he had one day, while sitting in a school yard, that he "knew everything": " . . . though conscious of having come less than a third of the way along the path of formal education, . . . I nevertheless held the key of truth in my hand, and could use it to open the lock of any door. Mine was no religious or philosophical theory, but a simple method of looking sideways at disorderly facts to make perfect sense of them." This "sideways looking" is the apprehension of the patterns out of which individual facts arise. To know the patterns is somehow to know something incommensurably deeper than actual facts.

Yet a third quality of the experience of wonder is physical sensation. There is often, in the moment of wonder, as in that of recognizing beauty, a roaring in the ears, an involuntary catching of the breath, a tingling in the fingers, a quivering of the extremities, a feeling of energy—grace—pouring into and through the body. Wilson cites a description of a mystical experience exemplifying this:

> I had one of those strange experiences of "rising up within oneself," of "coming inwardly alive." . . . First there is the indescribable sensation in the spine, as of something mounting up, a sensation which is partly pleasure and partly awe, a physical sensation and yet one which, if it makes sense to say so, is beginning to be not physical. This was accompanied by an extraordinary feeling of bodily lightness, of well-being and effortlessness, as if one's limbs had no weight and one's flesh had been suddenly transmuted into some rarer substance. But it was also, somehow, a feeling of living more in the upper part of one's body than the lower, a certain peculiar awareness of one's head as . . . the most important and intelligent of one's members. There was also a realisation that one's facial expression was changing; the eyes were wider open than usual; the lips were involuntarily smiling. Everything was becoming "more," everything was going up to another level.

A fourth quality, Wilson suggests, is not unlike the "insight" that theologian Bernard Lonergan has written so extensively about. An example of such insight is the experience of brain researcher Kenneth Pelletier, who spoke several times at the Mann Ranch. He recounted his work to develop a biofeedback program with which to learn to bring the wave patterns of electrical activity in the right and left hemi-spheres of his brain into symmetry. Ordinarily, he explained, the hemispheres operate, to some extent, independently. They go into syn-chronization, however, in several specific instances: during deep medi-tation, just before orgasm (at that moment referred to in the male as "ejaculatory inevitability"), and at the moment of insight when the so-lution to a puzzle is recognized.

Pelletier described his own experience with the biofeedback equip-ment of a feeling of the world turning to translucent crystal, the top of his head opening up, and light pouring into him from above. Indeed, if the hemispheres of the brain correlate, as neurophysiological research seems to indicate, to the yin and yang, nonverbal/verbal, feminine/masculine, wholistic/sequential polarities, then it is not surprising that wonder, as pattern recognition, would bring together what otherwise seems disconnected or conflicting.

Wonder, which of course begins with the experience of beauty—often of nature but also sometimes of human things—is the sense that one's life is not trivial, but is interconnected with all of the patterns of meaning that people have created. It reverses terror and anxiety, for it results in the acceptance of things just as they are. And thus it is the bliss that is the source of the other virtues.

꒳

The second virtue is transparency or, as Teilhard named it, "purity." It is the openness to the world and to other persons that allows for compassion and identification with the others. It is, in fact, freedom from the fear and desire which make life seem somehow always unsat-isfying, for these are blanched into unimportance in the fierce Clear Light of wonder. Then one can respond spontaneously to others and let oneself be accessible to them. Transparency breaks down the walls of persona and compulsive role-playing which build up between people, locking them out of one another and locking them into themselves in a state of alienation and loneliness. It frees people from the ego, which the spiritual masters have always said was only an illusion anyway and one that we are best freed of. For such an ego means feelings of self-consciousness, loneliness, and isolation.

Transparency is what, in other contexts, is called authenticity and telling the truth—in the sense of reporting accurately one's own experience and behaving accordingly. Such moment-by-moment honesty, free from guile, is possible when one sees that, in the face of emptiness, dissimulation and vanity offer one no more gain than honesty, and certainly promise to complicate and confuse one's life. If, indeed, consensual reality is being continuously invented through the interaction of conscious beings, then one can only move smoothly along the texture of that invention when one acknowledges openly one's involvement in the process. Being honest suggests taking responsibility for one's role as author of one's own story.

‿

The third virtue is the quality of transparency as it is perceived within and then projected into the outside world. It is innocence. It is the guilelessness which perceives one's own motives as exquisitely pure, since they spring immediately from the sense of being alive, and recognizes that same goodness in the world. Remember the Buddhist saying that the unenlightened see the world as unenlightened and hostile, while the bodhisattvas see the world as all-informed with compassion, and the buddhas see that even the grass is enlightened.

Innocence is not gullibility; it is not stupidity or imprudence. But it is a kind of intelligently informed defenselessness and vulnerability. It seems strangely true that it is often difficult to dupe a really good person. Somehow guilelessness is infectious. Perhaps that is because even a criminal cannot help but respond to being trusted. Or perhaps it only appears that the good person is less vulnerable because the impure man is so much more so, since he so easily trips over his own guile, which is often what gets him involved with criminals in the first place. This is one of the most immediate and obvious senses of the myth of karma: that the more defensive a person is, the less trusting and more embittered and unbending, the more will that person be treated by others in that same untrusting, embittered way.

Those whose lives are imbued with innocence are "disinterested" in Eckhart's words. In more modern parlance, the language of *est* and the New Age, they don't "make other people wrong." Recognizing their own basic innocence, they can see the basic innocence of those around them. While of course it's true that there are "bad people," most of the bad things that happen in the world happen not because of really evil intentions, but because of conflicting goals, value systems, and needs. Most of the bad things that happen are a result of people's having differences of opinion. And in the long run—and in the spirit of democracy and freedom—the problems that result from these differences of opinion are most likely resolved best by allowing different people to have different opinions. At any rate, intolerance of other people—especially when it's done in the name of what's really good for them—causes many more problems than it solves. The "war on drugs" is an obvious example. The metaphysical principle is stated: "What you resist persists . . ."

The spiritual teaching—on both an ethical *and* an epistemological level—isn't that things aren't right and wrong ($2 + 2 \times 4$ is right and $2 + 2 \times 5$ is wrong), but that holding the opinion that it matters is spiritually debilitating. Nagarjuna and Eckhart taught that enlightenment and salvation came from overcoming views and opinions. It is actually quite a difficult discipline to keep oneself from holding opinions and thinking that it matters whether one's right. As a discipline, in fact, it's almost impossible to maintain, if only because the major motivation for disciplining oneself so is because "it's right." Overcoming views and opinions succeeds far more simply from wonder and appreciation of the size and scope of life and of nature. We probably all understand that the thought of the Milky Way can be a great anodyne to concerns about what other people think. The thought of God—and of God beyond God and the emptiness beyond that—is intended to be such an anodyne and a great font of holy disinterest.

The innocent and disinterested can see all that comes to them as equal, so that even their vulnerability cannot hurt them, because even when they feel the direct pain and anguish of having been betrayed, everything seems to wash over them and leave them still standing. Indeed, they can see that the betrayal and the pain have taught them lessons in some way and helped make their lives more virtuous. Accepting all things as equal is also called submitting to divine will and is the essence of the prayer Jesus taught: *Fiat Voluntas Tua.* Accepting God's will is also loving life. The *Lazy Man's Guide* says:

> Love is the only dimension that needs to be changed. If you are not sure how it feels to be loving, love yourself for not being sure of how it feels . . . The way to raise your vibration level is to feel more love . . . If you try to close your mind, you will drop back to a lower vibration. But if you

look calmly at undesired events, absorb them mentally, and *love yourself
for disliking them,* you will keep going higher . . . You may not want to
love what you feel or see, you may not be able to convince yourself
that you could love it at all. But just decide to love it. Say out loud that
you love it, even if you don't believe it. And say, "I love myself for hating
this."

   And if you end up seeing so much around yourself that you don't like
and that you think is wrong, say to yourself, *"Well, what did you think it
was that needed to be loved."*

Loving and not making others wrong calms the sea of turmoil in
which we all live our lives. That sea is set in tumult by the bad intentions
we intentionally or unintentionally hold for others. Making others
wrong stirs the complex web of interactions between human beings—
on both an apparent, practical, psychologically modulated basis and,
perhaps, a mythic, coincidental, karmically modulated basis.

Everyone who has driven on a freeway has had the experience of
being overtaken by someone driving at breakneck speed, recklessly
shifting from lane to lane to get ahead. Many of us have, almost un-
wittingly, thought to ourselves: I hope he gets a ticket. It'd serve him
right. Or worse, we might have thought: I hope he has an accident. We
could have thought: I hope he or she gets to their destination safely.

Our intention may not cause that driver to get a traffic citation or to
have an accident. But it does affect us. It sets our mood for a while. It
makes us angry people instead of loving people. And, perhaps, in the
larger scheme of things, those intentions resonating from person to person actually generates a world in which bad things happen. And they
happen not just to those who are the object of the ill-wishing. For if the
accident happens, there are liable to be innocent victims. Since we are
all potentially innocent victims of the turmoil in the world, it's always
in our own best interest, and in the best interests of all those around us,
to wish well instead of ill. And this well-wishing arises directly from our
sense of being innocent.

Innocence, then, is that strangely knowing light in the eyes that
makes such people beloved of all who meet them. It makes them trust-
worthy because they radiate trust. And it causes them to see themselves—if they would look upon themselves—as wonderful and lovable
because they see themselves as reflections of the divinity of life.

This innocence and disinterest appear in modern mythology in the
psychotherapist's practice of non-judgment. For all psychologists, therapists, and even psychoanalytically oriented psychiatrists learn to listen

nonjudgmentally in order to create an environment in which clients or patients can honestly report their experiences and feelings. Such an attitude necessarily flows into every area of the therapist's life. And since the therapist operates as a kind of role model for his or her clients, in a psychologically sophisticated society the practice of nonjudgment and even "unconditional positive regard" (in the terms of Carl Rogers) is perceived as virtuous.

I am pleased to report that in my own life my religious ideals and training lead me toward the profession of psychotherapy. Religion urges us to become healing persons in society, making things better by our way of living. Training in psychology and mental health service teaches almost exactly the same. My work then in community mental health and psychiatric emergency proved a practical way of living the virtues I'd learned. Psychotherapy training taught me to connect with other persons in a healing way. And the presence of healing persons in the world heals the world. Gift waves go out from such a one.

～

The fourth virtue is adventure. It characterizes the life of one who lives open to experience. Adventure is not merely having fun or doing exciting things. As a virtue, it is an attitude of willingness to risk one's life, one's fortune, indeed even one's destiny on that which seems wonderful. It is the willingness to allow one's religious beliefs to change one's life, to allow oneself to follow one's bliss.

The hero's journey, which is the prototype of all myth patterns, is the ultimate adventure. This adventure is specifically aimed at dealing with the figures of the mythical world. For true adventure goes on at levels beyond the merely physical. Although, since the spiritual is manifested in the physical, the spiritual adventure may have dramatic, even threatening, effects on the material life. The spiritual adventure must consist of facing the moral dilemmas that rise up all around us. What is important is not so much that we resolve the dilemmas in specific ways as that we are willing to wrestle with the issues.

Perhaps the greatest problem with conventional religious ethical systems is that they seem to begin with clear statements of what must be avoided, thus obviating the need for wrestling with issues, and then suggest that religious accomplishment comes merely from avoiding what they have forbidden. Such simplistic moralities may be useful for social control, but they do not further spiritual growth.

In our lives we find that there are issues facing us that do not have easy solutions. Clear-cut moral issues are clear-cut. Few of us find a dilemma in whether we should murder people around us; the question of matricide is not one we have to wrestle with. The spiritual adventure does not consist merely of behaving correctly in such situations. It consists rather of willingly facing situations that are not clear-cut, that demand that we think and think, pray for guidance, and look for indications around us about what to do.

Adventure means carrying one's innocence into real life, trusting transparency, going to the extreme. It means setting aside the obvious and socially popular solutions based on naive realism. It means basing decisions on spiritual qualities and realities, not merely on those material and apparent.

But beyond the difficult and compelling aspects of adventure, the virtue describes the joy of pursuing life vitally and enthusiastically, trying new experience, embracing the future, loving the past but letting go of it, lest it create a drag on one's flight into life. For adventure, like the other virtues, is not an object of intentional behavior. One cannot choose to be adventurous in this sense. But one can face the emptiness out of which wonder initially arose and, accepting and affirming that, put it into practice.

❧

The fifth virtue differs from the others in being a quality of action rather than a quality of attitude. It is gentleness, by which is meant an active respect for life. It results from the collapse of the barriers between people, so that each person realizes that the life in him or her is the life that lives in all the others, and that the will for one's own life includes the will for life for all other beings. Such a will for life is not a clinging to life or grasping after it, but a detached attitude of joy, gratitude, and surprise. This is true compassion. A Mahayana mantrum summarizes this bodhisattva attitude: May all beings be happy, may all beings be well.

Campbell often told a story he'd read about a policeman in Hawaii who saved a young man who'd fallen from a cliff, risking his own life so that he had to be rescued by yet another. He cited Schopenhauer's question: "How is it that a human being can so participate in the danger of another, that forgetting his own self-protection, he moves spontaneously to the other's rescue? . . . His answer is that this is a metaphysical impulse that is deeper than the experience of separateness. You realize you and the other are *one*. And the experience of separateness is simply a function of the way we experience in the field of time and space." (*Hero's Journey*, p. 41)

In the face of total emptiness, heavy-handedness seems foolish; ambition, pride, and vanity dissolve; life is transformed with the beauty, grace, and delicateness of a Zen painting. Gentleness is the mark of the life lived aware that there is no ascertainable difference between samsara and nirvana, that the present existence is no different from heaven. For heaven is the symbol for life lived well. Such a life is not therefore weak or ethereal. It is not unaware or unconscious, but vital and sensitive.

All the traditions indicate that, while meditation and retirement from the world form one possible way, another way of the spirit is that of vitality and action. In persons like Thomas Merton, Dorothy Day, Martin Luther King, Gandhi, Aurobindo, and countless others known and unknown, gentleness, wonder, and respect for life enhanced their social involvement. For gentleness is not resignation or naive quietism. Out of meditation flows action. The action may be ungrasping, but is no less ardent. Arjuna could go into battle even though he did not seek victory; the Buddha could preach the way to nirvana even though he had seen all was illusion. The actions of gentleness seek to enhance life for all human beings. In that sense, gentleness is rightly and spontaneously indignant at injustice, murder, and the violation of life.

Campbell cited Ramakrishna's story of a young student who, having just learned from his teacher that God reveals himself in all things, was walking down the road, right into the path of an elephant. He decided not to step out of the road, believing that God was in the elephant and knowing that God would not hurt him. And so he ignored the driver sitting upon the neck of the great beast, shouting at him to get out of the way. After the elephant had thrown him off the road with its trunk, the boy returned bedraggled to confront his master. He demanded to know how God could have treated him so if indeed the elephant were God and God was all good. His guru only laughed and asked the well-

meaning youth why he hadn't obeyed the voice of God calling from behind the elephant's head, telling him to get out of the way. (*Myths To
Live By*, p. 150)

Emptiness and wonder are not excuses for narrowness of vision or
simple foolishness. There is injustice in the world. Bombs are dropped
daily on innocent people in the name of political ideologies. Human
rights are denied to countless numbers in the interests of religion or racial, even sexual, dominance. Gentleness produces, first, an attitude
whereby persons would not themselves commit injustice and, second, a
proper indignation whereby they would expend great effort to put an
end to injustice, which they see as arising from the illusion that "things
matter." Thereby they work to create a world in which injustice does
not exist.

The enlightened see that all beings live in heaven, but this is not an
excuse for maintaining the status quo. Just as heaven contains its conservatives, it also contains its radicals clamoring for justice. Gentleness
detaches the radicals from the object of their political endeavor and focuses their attention on the quality of the effort. And it encourages the
conservatives to respect the right and the obligation of those who differ
with them to pursue their own paths. For that attitude is enjoined on
conservatives and radicals alike by the recognition of the pluralism that
the modern world has forced upon human consciousness.

⌘

The sixth virtue is precisely that pluralism. For pluralism is a virtue
as the acceptance, in the spirit of innocence and adventure, of the variety of ways in which the divine is manifested in—and as—the human.
Pluralism, as an epistemological category, may seem new, but in fact it
has long been an element of Western thought. Indeed, it is found in one
of the most purely Western myths, the Arthurian legends. While the
story of the quest of the Holy Grail has obvious Christian roots, the sensibility out of which it sprang was far less orientalized than that which
spawned Christianity.

In *The Masks of God,* Campbell cites the episode from one of the
Grail stories which, he says, identifies the uniquely Western understanding of the spiritual life: As the knights set out on their common quest,
each pursued his own distinct path, for they had agreed that it would
not be seemly to follow the way of another, and so each one went the

way upon which he had decided, and "entered into the forest, at one point and another, there where they saw it to be thickest, all in those places where they found no way or path . . ." (*Masks of God,* Vol. IV, p. 540)

That myth speaks directly to us. We are, as we face the emptiness of our religious, philosophical, and even scientific explanations of life, at that thickest point in the forest, where the way is most difficult to discern. And, like each knight, we must each choose our own path. The clues that each person finds in life may lead one down paths that others have taken before and yet, so long as one is true to the clues of life, one is being guided by one's own life and not by the path. That is to say that the final hallmark of the life lived well today must be a tremendous tolerance of difference—not only tolerance, indeed, but respect for and active encouragement of human diversity.

Since each of us is on his or her own journey, responding to the promptings of life we find in day-to-day experience, each of us must respect each of the others. In the face of emptiness, self-righteousness has no place. We may work to assist our fellow travelers, we may suggest directions and help others interpret clues to their own paths, but we may never insist that another follow ours.

The crisis in religion today is only aggravated by the tendency of many who jealously claim divine authorization to denounce the behavior of those who do not live as they do, for thus they wish ill about themselves. That sectarian God whom they hope to placate by denouncing other styles of life is a God who cannot stand up to the onslaughts and criticisms of modern life. It is, on the other hand, the God who created man because he loves stories who can rise above the modern malaise, because he incorporates it all into his fascination with the life of each person.

That fascination with each life is manifested in the myth of the bodhisattva agreeing to live everybody's life in order to free them from suffering. I think the most important thing I learned about life from Joseph Campbell was the message he conveyed in his telling of the bodhisattva story. Truly, the central feature of Joe Campbell's spirituality is the bodhisattva vocation. Campbell called it "the way of joyful participation in the sorrows of the world."

In some ways, Joseph Campbell himself manifested the bodhisattva identity. I can remember him describing, with a certain glee, a Japanese statue of the bodhisattva he'd seen during a trip to the East. He explained the statue looked just like a modern businessman with a little mustache. "You could easily imagine him with a drink in his hand at a cocktail party, thoroughly involved in the affairs of the world."

In that regard, in *The Hero's Journey: Joseph Campbell on His Life and Work*, editor Phil Cousineau tells a story in which he recognizes the identity behind the man:

> Over a final glass of Glenlivet [in the Redwood Room of the Clift Hotel in San Francisco] I confided to him a favorite story of my own. A few years before I was drifting across the country on a motorcycle trip when, like a wayward traveler in an Arabian Nights tale tripping over a gold nugget hidden under a tree root in the dark forest, I discovered an uncanny scene that struck me as being at the heart of the hero's journey.
>
> It was that of a crumbling tombstone in Boothill Cemetery in Tombstone, Arizona, the gravemarker of an old gunslinger. The epitaph read: "Be what you is, cuz if you be what you ain't, then you ain't what you is."
>
> I can hear Joe's hearty bodhisattva laugh now and the clink of our glasses over the soothing sounds of the late-night jazz piano in the old redwood-paneled bar.
>
> "That's it!" he cried out with that eternal look of wonder in his eyes. "That's what it's all about: the mystery of the journey. That's just marvelous!
>
> "Now, how did that go again? 'Be what you is . . .' " (*Hero's Journey*, p. xxii)

Curiously, Joe's individualism was consistent with the spirituality. And that's a curiosity because the spirituality is basically monistic, whereas the American classical conservative individualism seems so radically pluralistic. But, indeed, then Campbell's embrace of both sides transcends the polarities.

Joe had a slight stutter which came out, paradoxically, as part of his eloquence, as part of the drama in his voice. It was occasionally noticeable in words beginning with the letter "G." I can hear him saying, "People ask me. 'What about all the evil and suffering in the world?' And I say, 'It's great just the way it is.' " That slight stutter of his on the word "great," and the force with which he spoke behind it, have the word sound almost like the cartoon advertising character Tony the Tiger. And that's precisely the meaning of Joe's spirituality of joyful participation.

As the epilogue of Cousineau's honorific to Campbell, he cites the story of the Tiger and the Goat. Says Joe:

There's a moral here, of course. It is that we're all really tigers living
here as goats. The function of sociology and most of our religious education
is to teach us to be goats. But the function of the proper interpretation of
mythological symbols and meditation discipline is to introduce you to
your tiger face. (*Hero's Journey*, pp. 230–231)

When you look at the world with all its suffering and pain and lashing
about, what you say is "Yes, it's great just the way it is." And you throw
yourself into life like a tiger going after its prey.

Campbell believed that a source of some of the very first frankly religious feelings in primitive human beings was the sense of guilt at killing other sentient beings for food. In paralleling Zorastrianism with its
worship of fire and turn-of-the-millenium Hinduism with its command-
ment of vegetarianism, Campbell distinguished two approaches to the
horrible reality that life feeds on life. This "feeding frenzy" within
which we live is like a blazing fire, consuming everything. One approach is to feed the fire. This is the way of sacrifice and burnt-offering.
(Judaism and Christianity embraced and then stylized this approach.)
The other is to quench the fire. This is the way of abnegation and world-
renunciation. Joe was fond of quoting Schopenhauer: "Life is something which should not have been." (Hinduism and Theravada Buddhism embraced this approach.)

Mahayana Buddhism with its myth of the compassionate bodhisattva Avalokitesvara and Christianity with its account of the loving
and forgiving Jesus hint at a middle way, i.e., the way of joyful participation, which is the way of the Campbellian hero.

This hero sees the horror of life, but neither joins in nor shirks from
it. Instead this hero participates with the awareness, from an overarching perspective, that the horror is an illusion and that the way to quench
the fire of suffering is to embrace the suffering and by loving it transform
it.

Campbell's dictum for how to do that is his aphorism: Follow your
bliss. The one who follows his or her bliss throws themselves into life—
like the tiger pouncing on its prey—in order to find in the participation
the joy that will lead them out of the suffering and out of encouraging
and sanctioning the blood-bath. "Gift waves go out from such a one for

the liberation of us all," wrote Joe in his account of the bodhisattva's apotheosis. (*Hero,* p. 166)

Perhaps because of his fascination with James Joyce and the idea of the Joycean artist, Campbell seemed to believe that the presence of artists—and heroes—in the world helped to change the world. People who follow their bliss instead of buying into the advertising propaganda of the world, who choose, for instance, as Joe did, to wander the world in search of gods instead of to struggle to make money, people who put their art or their curiosity or their contribution before their security and their egos—these are the people through whom the world is transformed.

At the end of *The Hero With a Thousand Faces,* Campbell wrote, " . . . a transmutation of the whole social order is necessary, so that through every detail and act of secular life the vitalizing image of the universal god-man who is actually immanent and effective in all of us may be somehow made known to consciousness." (*Hero,* p. 389) The hero throws himself or herself joyfully into the fray in order to discover their bliss.

Today we are long since past the time when the immediate issue is vegetarianism and ahimsa versus carnivorousness and blood-sacrifice. There may be major ecological reasons to eschew the business of meat-production: the destruction of the rain-forest, for instance, in order to provide short-term grazing land for cattle to feed the golden-arched maw of McDonald's, or the heart-stopping effects of saturated animal fats in the human diet. But they are no longer based in our horror in seeing the slaughter of other sentient beings. Flesh meats come so sanitized and hermetically sealed in plastic wrap that they might as well have been manufactured in a factory. We neither blanch at the horror nor participate in the slaughter in any real way.

But the issue of participation in the whole activity of the world remains. If we throw ourselves into the world for the gratification of our egos—for wealth and fame and success and power—while, in fact, we may win, we are liable to be burned by the fire. If we renounce the world for the avoidance of suffering, while we may achieve solitude, by that very act, we are liable to have fallen victim to ego gratification and be burned by the fire anyway.

The only way out is to go in, the only way to avoid the game is to play the game—but with the awareness that you are not your ego and that your motivation cannot be for ego, but must be for the bliss of the universal god-man. "I will participate in the game. It's a wonderful, wonderful opera—except that it hurts. . . . The hero is the one who comes to participate in life courageously and decently, in the way of nature, not in the way of personal rancor, disappointment, or revenge." (*Power of Myth*, p. 66)

☙

The reason we can endure life—can say yes to the ordeal, can say to the suffering and unfairness: It's great just the way it is—is because we do it for the bodhisattva, for the Christ, in us. We do it for the consciousness that has so loved the world that it has become the world in order to experience itself.

When we remember who we really are, then we can walk through the fire unsinged—or at least keep reminding ourselves when the fires begin to burn us that we have to refine our motivation and renew our vision of the goal. It is instructive that in the Roman ritual of the Office of Choir which monks sang throughout the day, in the first hour of Lauds, was regularly sung the Canticle of the Three Young Men in the Fiery Furnace (from the Book of Daniel). Perhaps in the words of the canticle is the reminder of how to accomplish this difficult task of walking through the furnace.

> *All the works of the Lord, bless the Lord; praise and exalt God above all*
> *forever.*
> *Angels of the Lord, bless the Lord; All the heavens, bless the Lord.*
> *Sun and moon, bless the Lord; stars of heaven, bless the Lord.*
> *Every shower and dew, bless the Lord; spirits of God, bless the Lord.*
> *Fire and heat, frost and cold, Light and darkness, bless the Lord.*
> *Let the earth bless the Lord, praise and exalt God above all forever.*
> (Daniel 3: 57–66, edited)

The secret of walking through the fiery furnace is to sing alleluias, to say yes, to say thanks. Do the thing that praises and exalts life through you. Follow your bliss. Make a difference.

Of course, it's just a story—and a pretty far-fetched one at that. But the Biblical young men in the furnace didn't walk around saying: "O woe is me," or "The fire can't hurt me" or "I'm above it all" or "I'm a vegetarian." What they said was: "Ain't it great to be alive," "Look at the sun, look at the moon, ain't it grand! Bless the Lord," "It's hot, it's cold, ain't it grand! Bless the Lord."

What the bodhisattva discovered and what Jesus taught—and what revealed itself to me that Sunday at the castle—is that this life happening to us right now *is* God. Bless the Lord.

The bodhisattva attitude is that the horror is the foreground of a wonder. From the perspective of that wonder, the bodhisattva feels compassion for all beings and holds a positive intention for each one in spite of—or because of—the fact that each being fails to recognize its true nature and so, identifying itself with its individuatedness, suffers the horrors as though they were meant for it personally.

When we—as reflexes of the bodhisattva, for that is what we really are—raise our sights above the foreground to the immense wonder, and for a moment perhaps transcend our egos, we discover everything's okay.

Werner Erhard summarizes this wisdom—and its blissful consequence—in an aphorism: "If God told you exactly what it was you were to do, you would be happy doing it no matter what it was. What you're doing is what God wants you to do. Be happy." This only can make sense, of course, to those who have remembered who they really are, who have remembered that they are God choosing to experience themselves as the world.

> Two degrees of initiation are to be distinguished in the mansion of the father. From the first the son returns as emissary, but from the second, with the knowledge that 'I and the father are one.' Heroes of this second, highest illumination are the world redeemers, the so-called incarnations, in the highest sense. Their myths open out to cosmic proportions. (*Hero,* p. 349)
>
> The aim is . . . to realize that one *is,* that essence; then one is free to wander as that essence in the world. Furthermore: the world too is of that essence. The essence of oneself and the essence of the world: these two are one. Hence separateness, withdrawal, is no longer necessary. Wherever the hero may wander, whatever he may do, he is ever in the presence of his own essence—for he has the perfected eye to see. (*Hero,* p. 386)

When Joe drew the moral of the story of the tiger raised as a goat whose hero quest was to discover his true tiger identity, he added, only partly tongue-in-cheek:

> . . . don't let them know that you are a tiger!
> When Hallaj or Jesus let the orthodox community know that they were tigers, they were crucified. And so the Sufis learned the lesson at that time with the death of Hallaj, around 900 A.D. And it is: You wear the outer garments of the law; you behave like everyone else. And you wear

the inner garments of the mystic way. Now that's the great secret of life. (*Hero's Journey*, p. 231)

There are no normative standards that can be set that all people must obey. What is right for one may not be right for another. Truth, after all, has no content. There are attitudes, not specific actions, that affirm life, that allow us to joyfully participate in the activity of the world. These are: wonder, which fills the heart with love; transparency, which opens the heart to other beings; innocence, which cherishes and fosters the goodness that is the life in all of us; adventure, which opens us to that life; gentleness, which demonstrates love; and pluralism, which recognizes the respect for each other that we must have if we are to face the thickness of the forest through which we must all wander, alone and together.

CHAPTER NINE

The New Myth:
Gaia Awakes

*[The idea of reincarnation] suggests that you are more
than you think you are. There are dimensions of your
being and a potential for realization and consciousness
that are not included in your concept of yourself. Your
life is much deeper and broader than you conceive it to
be here. What you are living is but a fractional inkling
of what is really within you, what gives you life,
breadth, and depth. But you can live in terms of that
depth. And when you can experience it, you suddenly
see that all the religions are talking of that.*
(Power of Myth, *p. 58*)

The natural evolution of biological species is primarily an historical issue. Divine creation is a religious issue. They are not in conflict, because
they are about different things. God's act of creation could have included a vast history, within which species evolved just the way the bi-
ologists say. In fact, all of us, in being born, create a world with a vast
history that precedes us. Yet it only came into being as "our" universe
within our lifetimes. Its history is always included in our act of creation.

Creation as an activity of God, and of the individual consciousness,
calls the mind to rise above space and time to an eternity wherein the
Great Secret manifests itself as the world of individual perspectives
seeking to find the solution to the puzzle of their own consciousness.
Within a religious system of metaphors, that activity is what generates
the evolution of species. Indeed one might say that the evolution of human consciousness which can ask questions and seek clues is a direct
manifestation of the divine, seeking solution to its own inherent secrecy.
Religionists needn't object to biological evolution, thinking it a denial

of God's role in the universe. And scientists need not deny creation, thinking it violates historical fact, for true creative activity goes on in dimensions unmeasurable by sensory observation and so has nothing to do with factual representation.

Religious scholar Huston Smith, another regular lecturer at the Mann Ranch, has mustered evidence and the testimony of scientists and philosophers of science to discredit the principle of natural selection. In *Forgotten Truth: The Primordial Tradition,* he points out that natural selection is tautological, i.e., it merely states what it claims to explain, that those species and individuals who are fitted for survival survive. Since this gives no basis for determining fitness other than survival, the principle holds only that the survivors survive.

Certainly, as the fossil record indicates, simpler forms preceded more complex forms. But, Smith argues, what is missing from the theory of evolution is a mechanism by which it happened. Can our "guiding myth" of secrecy provide this? Can it be that there is a life force which propels life forward toward intelligence? And can it be that the compulsion to pursue the Great Secret and the experience of wonder is the human perception of this force?

Perhaps wonder and awe are the significant religious experiences they are *because* it was the asking questions and experiencing wonder that forced the mind to expand, to organize information in new ways, and to develop complex neural pathways in primate brains. The experience of mystery and the response of wonder then could be seen as one of the mechanisms of the evolution of consciousness and intelligence. *Homo sapiens,* then, is a "religious animal" because what is experienced as the religious sensibility is what made the primates human.

❧

But today God—if the notion is to have any sense at all, any relevance to modern life—must be realized as a metaphor, an anthropomorphism for the human experience of self. And this is no derogation of God, for it frees the image of God from a naive realism that is no longer tenable and invests it with the mystery of human consciousness that daily confronts us in our own experience of being. Thus it makes God more real to us and makes us more real to God. For it suggests that the human self creates the universe of experience—from the tiniest wavelike particle of energy to the stars like dust scattered through a cosmos that eludes comprehension—and arises out of a stratum of reality that is every-where revealed but remains always mysterious. This image for God is, indeed, far more exalted and wonderful than the old notions we have outgrown.

This awareness is the radical basis for recasting religion and recon-ciling religion and science. For it suggests that our goal should not be to bring the two accesses to knowledge into agreement, but to find a new focus of wonder, a new metaphor for God, in relation to which the conflict between them does not exist. And that new metaphor for God is the consciousness that invents images for itself in order to know itself. The clue to that metaphor for God is the emptiness of all truth. Curi-ously, the very skepticism that seems to threaten faith is the source of the attitude of openness that saves it.

We may, in some ways, have already begun to feel that we, conscious human subjects, are the source of the mythic images that have come down to us as the gods. We may have thought that this invalidated re-ligion and left life bereft of meaning. Yet at the heart of our experience of ourselves we find the sense of mystery. When we look deep within ourselves to find the source of the myths—as if by finding it we could somehow solve all the riddles of life and free ourselves from the domi-nation of the gods—we encounter mystery. We encounter emptiness.

But rather than leave us alienated and confused with no way to find Truth, we discover in the secrecy the truth beyond truth. After all, what we are seeking, it seems, is not the truth but the openness to levels of being that stretch out around us infinitely. This openness to greater real-ity, more than naive certainty, has the power to transform human life and to save the individual. And the urge toward that greater reality, ex-perienced in the psyche as the feeling that there is something we ought to know but don't, a great secret that we are searching for, is the essence of spirituality.

The most difficult step in such an open and evolving spirituality is getting beyond the personal God. We seem to want to believe that God cares for each of us, that God is somehow friendly and concerned. It is easier to settle for God as cosmic pal than to search beyond the image for deeper spiritual reality.

We rightly personalize God in order to grapple with the idea. In much the same way, we personalize our pets in order to understand their be-havior. I have a cat. I watch her behavior and I project meaning into it. I call the cat by a human name and imagine that she actually knows who

I am and what kind of relationship exists between us. It is satisfying for me to imagine she's almost a person. That is why I have a cat instead of a vial of hydrochloric acid into which I could pour cat food each day to watch the chemical reaction. The cat is easier to anthropomorphize.

So is the personal God. Yet divine reality is beyond the pettiness we think of as personal. The personality I attribute to my cat is really just my own. The personality I attribute to God is also my own. Though, strangely, we attribute to and permit in God's personality traits we would never permit acted out in ourselves or our friends. We allow God to be monstrously egotistical, cruel, and conniving. For the God that we know and imagine *is* like us—except that he seems more complacent and self-satisfied. He is only a projection of our own egos—sometimes of the worst characteristics—into the cosmos.

The God behind that projection calls us to something deeper. We are engaged in a journey from God to God—from the God we know and understand but who is not real to a God who is real but whom we do not know and cannot understand. Like Meister Eckhart we must pray God that we be rid of God. We must take responsibility for the image of God that we allow to dominate and guide our lives. For there is a way that God is intensely personal, and that is the way that God exists immanently, deep in the heart of each of us. God is individualized in the sense that each human person is individualized. And so each individual lives with his or her own God.

And that God can be a trap. We can settle for our comforting images. We can start taking them seriously. Then they are no longer sources of wonder. Then God becomes petty indeed, concerned with my individual behavior, fretting over sinfulness (more often other people's), getting involved with politics and foreign policy, doing tricks at the beck and call of television preachers. If God is to have any meaning at all today, it has to be as the lure for our sense of transcendence. And that is the image of God that we must select for ourselves.

God is a figure of speech. The myths and doctrines of religion that deal with God's reality are figures of speech. "God," as a word, communicates something regardless of the actual existence of God. When Einstein said that God does not play dice with the universe everyone understood what he meant. He was not uttering a theistic credo, and the import of what he said did not depend on the actual existence of God.

But to see that God is a figure of speech does not demean God. After all, everything (including "actual existence") really is a figure of speech. All that we know are words. The aim of words about the spiritual reality is the transcendence of ego, so that we rise above limited perspectives and see the divine patterns which are, in Thomas Merton's evocative phrase, the "dance of the Lord in emptiness." God is a convenient image to pull us beyond ourselves, an always Other who forces us to confront the unknowable on which all experience rests. God and the gods are sources of wonder that force open the mind, signposts leading us on a journey through darkness into light.

This God is the symbol for the vast consciousness we experience as the universe. And this universe, we must see—that is the point of the gods—is but the three-dimensional surface of a cosmos that stretches out beyond matter into *n* dimensions.

In *2001: A Space Odyssey*, Arthur C. Clarke's fable of human apotheosis, the monolith that functioned as both the instrument and the symbol of the transmission of consciousness was a rectangular solid, like a door, with the dimensions $1 \times 4 \times 9$. In his metamorphosis, the Star-Child that the human astronaut became through his confrontation with incomprehensibility realized that those were the first three digits of the quadratic sequence. "And how naive to have imagined that the series ended at this point, in only three dimensions!"

☙

Thus we must not lose sight of the traditional figures we are trying to explain, for our explanations always sacrifice richness and variety for familiarity and intelligibility. We may offer explanations to accompany the ancient figures, but we cannot totally supplant them. For, because they are of the nature of dream and carry overtones and harmonics that reverberate deep in consciousness, our explanations can never be exhaustive. Just as the description and explanation of sexual functioning can never substitute for the experience of making love, so the explanation of mythological symbols can never substitute for the experience of belief.

Understanding religion in this way allows us to appreciate the significance of human decisions and forces us to assume the necessary responsibility for the dismaying future we are bringing about. It declares that the individual's life is the instrument of revelation. The pages of dusty scripture handed down from antiquity may be rightly revered as the record of many lives, but they cease to have absolute authority when compared with the life here and now. They remain guides—not because they come from God on high, but because they come from the depths of human beings. The focus of belief in God becomes the patterns of individual lives and, within a single life, the patterns of events made intelligible by the myths we have inherited as our own culture and as the world's culture.

As we see that the point of religious belief is to alter patterns of consciousness within the individual and to push individuals toward more expansive, multidimensional interpretations of their lives, we see that we can use myths judiciously to bring about personal transformations. That is, we see that the patterns of mythological thought describe high cultural and artistic achievements, that they are powerful and efficacious factors in the psyche which can transform and renew experience, that they have been used by human beings since time immemorial to describe their most sublime moments and to facilitate them in others, and that the myths contain instructions for how to live well, how to achieve a certain transcendent, visionary consciousness, and how to deal with the challenging emptiness of the foundations of reality.

☙

Joseph Campbell was frequently asked what the "new myth" would be. That is, now that humankind had achieved a perspective on religion and so in some ways debunked religion, at least as a literal description of the cosmos, what would follow?

Campbell usually answered that in the same way that one cannot predict tonight's dream, so one cannot predict tomorrow's myth. Often he was pessimistic about the future of myth and belief, saying that modern-day people simply have nothing to believe in. On the other hand, he was often quick to observe that one of the great mythological events in human history has happened in our time and that is it is likely that this event is a precursor of the new myth.

That event, of course, was the landing on the moon and the achievement of a perspective from which the Earth could be viewed from outside and above. We've all become familiar with the image of Earth from space. Technology and science have given us a vantage point no human beings before us have ever had and revealed to us a universe beyond the scope of the imagination of any people before us. And that vantage point is not only in space, but also in mind.

This is the point we've been making over and over again as together we've thought about what religion is in the spirit of Joseph Campbell's investigations. Today we have a whole new way of understanding the universe: we see with historical perspective; we understand from above, from a critical distance; we can view the evolution of life on the planet; indeed, we can view the evolution of the planet out of the nothingness of space. We are discovering whole new models of what space and time and matter and energy are. And herein is the new myth.

Over the years of my correspondence with Joe, I pursued this topic frequently. I observed that he seemed himself to be one of the spokespersons of a new kind of mythic consciousness. He was always polite and accepted my praise and adulation, though he always humbly "pooh-poohed" the notion. In the same way, when Bill Moyers asked him if he were a hero, he laughed, deflected the accolade, and said he preferred to call himself a maverick.

But, of course, being a maverick *is* being a hero. And Joe did do battle, at least in mind, with the guardians of the past. He threw aside the tradition he grew up with. He chose a path no one had taken before. He discovered a worldview and a transcendent Truth. And he came back bringing boons. The immense popularity his ideas have achieved demonstrate that.

I certainly don't mean to suggest that Joseph Campbell was a world savior, like Jesus or Buddha or even Mahatma Gandhi. There will probably never be such figures in history again. The modern epistemology has seen to that. There's been a shift away from individual heroes to the content of their accomplishments. Case in point: we no longer know the names of the inventors of the technological devices that have changed our world. We all know Thomas Edison invented the incandescent light bulb, but who knows who invented the compact flourescent bulb that modern ecological concerns is going to make replace Edison's invention? Who knows who invented the television? Or the computer? Or the microchip? The heroic act is no longer being accomplished by single individuals, but in movements in the consciousness of the race itself. And it was such a movement that Joe Campbell was a part of.

The understanding that there are such movements in the conscious-ness of the planetary mind, I believe, comes directly out of what is the "new myth." And that myth has four aspects:

First, that mythic consciousness has moved up a notch and the new myth is a meta-myth (which Joseph Campbell manifested by his very style of storytelling);

Second, that the meta-myth implies a collective mind, which is me-taphorized as the consciousness of the planet itself (which ecological bi-ology and popular imagination call Gaia);

Third, that the notion of a collective planetary mind demands a new scientific paradigm (which can be exemplified in both the Gaia Hy-pothesis and the holographic model); and,

Fourth, that, like all myths, the new myth projects into the future and offers a vision of transformed human/planetary consciousness (which was hinted at, for instance, in the mystical evolutionary theory of Pierre Teilhard de Chardin).

ॐ

In the conclusion of *The Hero With a Thousand Faces,* Campbell traces the evolution of myth. He says that what determines a guiding myth is how it manifests and explains the place of human life in the mysterious universe. Primitive men and women worshipped plants and animals, the presence of which both as food sources and as independent and sometimes dangerous life-forms made them mysteries to be ap-peased and understood, for on them survival depended. Later they wor-shipped the stars and planets that move through the sky and that were associated with the seasons of fruiting and harvest upon which agrarian society depended. As people found themselves having to make decisions and manipulate natural forces, human concern shifted to the elements of mind and will; the gods were symbolized as invisible beings who in-fluenced experience through truth and moral imperatives.

Today, with the development of psychology and the social sciences, what Campbell called "the focal point of human wonder" has shifted beyond the *contents* of consciousness to the *nature* of consciousness. The subject matter of myth is no longer as fascinating as the fact that the mind creates and uses myths. What has the power to fascinate us is our awareness of the mythologizing faculty itself, that is, of the ability of consciousness to invent a world for itself to experience, and to reveal through its invention that very inventive power. (Cf. *Hero,* pp. 390–391)

The mythic ladder has carried us from God as plant and animal, to God as the stars and geometric principles that guide celestial movement, to God as high abstraction and moral responsibility, and now to God as the human ability to create the gods. Thus the focus of religion today must no longer be God, but consciousness. For the modern person who has some sophistication in psychology, theoretical physics, and anthropology can no longer believe in God as an "other," out there in the sky somewhere, making blustering commands known by divine interventions and magic signs. Such a person looks for a god within, a higher power in the self that reveals its longings and intentions as human feelings and insights.

෴

The Gaia Hypothesis was developed by James Lovelock and Lynn Margulis. Originally it only meant to suggest that planet earth exhibits homeostatic processes that have kept it suitable for life. The most obvious and familiar of these is that evolution produced plants that process carbon dioxide into oxygen in their metabolism and then, in a complementary way, produced animals that process oxygen into carbon dioxide. We've all come to understand that there's a complex ecological balancing act going on all around us all the time, of which we human beings are apparently a part but by which we've often failed to abide—and are currently endangering the planet because of this failure.

Over the 1980s the Gaia Hypothesis has gradually been given more and more metaphysical and mystical implications. In *The Rebirth of Nature* new paradigm biologist Rupert Sheldrake proposes that our modern understanding of ecology reassimilates such ancient, pre-scientific ideas as the Platonic forms and animistic souls as science recognizes and acknowledges that nature is alive and follows ecological and evolutionary processes that just can't be explained by a materalistic, mechanistic view.

Sheldrake is creator of the evolutionary theory of formative causation, known popularly as the theory of morphogenetic fields and even more popularly (and somewhat inaccurately) as the Hundredth Monkey Effect.

The theory of formative causation holds that evolution takes place not as mutations in individual creatures, but as changes in fields that surround the earth (perhaps even extending throughout interstellar space) and that influence the development of organisms much the way electromagnetic fields influence the path of electrons moving through them. Magnetic fields cause atoms of iron to line up; the gravitational field of the earth controls the motion of virtually every object on the planet. High energy physics is committed to the notion that a so-called unified field theory can be developed which will explain the structure and motion of everything in the universe. Life is part of the universe; why wouldn't there be fields that influence how it grows and evolves?

Among other things, the theory explains how certain learned traits can be passed on to offspring. For it hypothesizes that the behavior of individual organisms gradually, through repetition, alters the shape of the fields associated with that particular type of organism. In his first book, *A New Theory of Life,* Sheldrake cites, as example, an early behavioral experiment on rats at Harvard that challenged the orthodox Darwinian model of evolution through random mutation: the rats seemed to pass along learning from one generation to the next. When scientists in London set out to replicate the experiment in order to disprove the Harvard study, to their dismay they found the rats (of the same species, but across the Atlantic and in no way related genetically to the Bostonian rats) began their learning of the particular behavior just where their American cousins left off. Somehow, it appeared, the activity of the American rats had influenced the whole species.

Sheldrake proposes that the behavior of Earth itself including all the life forms that have grown up on it—and *as* it—is controlled by nonmaterial fields and that perhaps evolution is following a well-determined pattern. Just like an acorn somehow "knows" how to become an oak, so the Earth "knows" how to grow from a rock to an intelligent and self-aware mind. And we're somewhere in the middle.

Perhaps the most interesting and mind-boggling dynamic he describes in *The Rebirth of Nature* is that over the history of life on Earth the salinity of the oceans has remained virtually constant. That doesn't sound so mind-boggling at first glance. But consider that rainwater is constantly carrying minerals salts off the land into the oceans. Like the

Dead Sea, they should be becoming saltier and saltier. If they had, also like the Dead Sea, they'd have become uninhabitable and life would have died out. But somehow they didn't. Somehow the oceans discharged salt. How?

This has happened primarily in two ways. One involves life: corals grow in the water off-shore and gradually wall bodies of water off from the ocean; the water evaporates and the salt is left on the edge of coral atolls. The other involves geology: the continents float on the surface of the mantle; this movement occasionally causes some water to be trapped on-shore where it evaporates. The central U.S., for instance, was once under water, and all the salt ended up in Great Salt Lake, Utah. Was it just chance that caused the American continent to tilt a little so the water ran to Utah instead of back into the Gulf of Mexico? Or was some evolutionary process overseeing this whole thing to keep the planet livable?

Such phenomena suggest that the unit of life is not the individual organism, but the planet. The Earth, according to this myth, is a great organism growing upward through the stages of its growth toward some kind of planetary reflection and carrying on its own life cycle on a level above the human. This is the mystical biological perspective of Teilhard de Chardin. And it was such an explanation that Arthur Koestler suggested in his critique of evolution, in which he proposed the notion of "Janus-faced holons." According to Koestler's idea, the units of each order of reality are composed of many particles (holons) of the next *lower* order and, in turn, compose with many other holons the units of the next *higher* order. Thus, just as the interaction of many individual neurons in the brain of a single person results in a thought, so the interaction of many individual thinking persons results in the great thoughts of the planet.

This image, in turn, suggests an "etheric DNA" that determines the pattern of growth followed by the planet. The myths and archetypes are the appearance in human thought of this DNA. They are the great thoughts of the planet itself. And the thoughts that are the most wonderful are those that cause the planet to ask questions and experience wonder. The actual thoughts of this planetary mind go on at a level that is totally alien to human beings; and for that reason, its truth, which is the Truth of religion and metaphysics, is incomprehensible, which is to say that it is a Great Secret.

And because this planetary mind is growing and developing, its projection into our world will be changing. That is why religion must be allowed to grow, and why we are always having to seek new guiding myths, and why the new myth must be evolutionary and ecological.

The basis of this new myth is the great paradigm shift of modern times. What founds modern consciousness, we've all heard again and again, are the ideas of the three great influential thinkers of modern times: Darwin, Freud, and Marx. Though, in fact, the specifics of each man's system have been supplanted, they prepared the way and what they taught us is that life is evolving, directed by unconscious factors, and moving toward the collective.

❧

A new model of the physical universe is called for. And technology has just recently gotten one ready for us. This, of course, may not turn out to be the actual model that's embraced, but it is certainly the precursor for whatever that one's going to be. This is the holographic model.

Holograms, most of us have come to understand, are a sort of peculiar photograph taken with laser light which seems to produce a difficult-to-focus-on, but obviously three-dimensional image. The term is also applied to hypothetical three-dimensional projections that look like free-standing statuettes. The latter doesn't yet exist outside science fiction movies, but is certainly consistent with the technology. Holograms differ significantly from photographs in several important ways. The most obvious is that to produce the image the light must pass through the hologram, not be reflected off its surface. In a true hologram (which is not necessarily the kind of holography one finds for sale at kiosks in airports), there is no image as such. Under normal lighting the hologram shows only crisscrossing interference patterns, like the surface of a pond into which one had thrown a handful of pebbles. The information for producing the image is contained in the interference patterns; and that information is only interpreted into the image when a laser beam passes through the film.

For our purposes here, the technology of holography is not as important as the qualities that make the hologram a potential model for the universe of experience. These are:

First, holography produces an image that demonstrates full three-dimensionality and parallax. If you are looking at an object in a hologram and move your head to the side a little you can see around behind the object to what's in the background;

Second, the image is contained in the patterns of interference which are spread throughout the hologram. If you cut a hologram in half, you don't get half the image; instead you get the whole image, but half your vantage point is gone (and the image is a little fuzzier). It's as though you were looking out a window and then the window were "cut in half," say, by putting a piece of cardboard over it. The whole view outside is still there, but you can see it only by looking through the half of the window that's unobstructed. In technical terms, the image in a hologram is non-localized;

Third, the image only comes into being when a proper light source shines through the hologram.

In the fascinating and wonderfully readable *The Holographic Universe,* science reporter and mystic Michael Talbot explains at length how modern brain research is showing that holography provides a model for how memory and thought are "stored" in the human brain, and how high-energy particle physics is beginning to use the holographic model to make sense of the behavior of sub-atomic phenomena. Talbot reports on the work of Karl Pribram and David Bohm, one a brain physiologist, the other a theoretical physicist.

Pribram and others have discovered that memory and experience do not seem to be not localized in the brain. In spite of long efforts to do so, researchers have not found where specific memories are stored. In the effort to do so they've cut out parts of animals' brains to see what learned behaviors they could destroy. But when they cut out part of a cat's or a rat's brain, the learned behavior wasn't eradicated, though it became slower and "fuzzier" (i.e., the animal took longer to run the maze, for instance, but it still remembered how). What they've found is that the learning seems to be not in any specific cells at all but in the patterns of electrical activity throughout all the brain cells—stored, as in a hologram, in interference patterns.

Bohm observed that physicists have long been trapped in a dilemma about whether sub-atomic particles are things or waves. Depending on the vantage point of the observer and the type of experiment, they seem to behave as either or both particles of matter and waves of energy. But the two models are, in theory, logically exclusive of one another. An electron can't be a wave if it's a particle and vice versa. The pebble tossed into the pond is not the waves and the waves don't behave like a pebble. But in experiment after experiment, physicists have found sub-atomic particles are both.

It has been observed that two photons moving apart from each other at the speed of light seem connected to one another so that a change in the polarization angle of one of them "causes" a change in the polariza-tion angle of the other. But since nothing can travel faster than light-speed, there is no way the two particles can communicate with one an-other. Called the Einstein-Podolsky-Rosen paradox, this phenomenon was supposed to discredit the series of theories called Quantum Me-chanics. In fact, it challenged the nature of physical experimentation it-self. It simply didn't have an answer unless the two particles aren't really separate from one another or aren't really in different locations.

Following Bohn, Talbot offers an example to resolve the problem. Two cameras are set up televising the movement of a fish in an aquar-ium, one is directed at the aquarium's front, the other at its side. An ob-server who has never seen a fish or an aquarium and is watching this on two television monitors might well presume he or she is watching two separate creatures. The fish both swim around; they look different, but there's a certain similarity to their movements. After a while the ob-server might wonder how the two creatures manage to communicate with one another in order to synchronize their motion. Until the ob-server discovers the arrangement by which the television images are generated, the whole process seems a mystery, not unlike the Einstein-Podolsky-Rosen paradox. There aren't two fish and there aren't two particles—they are actually different aspects of an event happening at another level of reality.

David Bohm has offered the hologram as a model for space that ex-plains how things can be non-localized. What the model suggests is that our whole cosmos really is a maze of interference patterns which are projected into "reality" by our observing minds. Like the images in a hologram, things aren't here or there, they are non-locally spread throughout the patterns that make up the cosmos. Consciousness itself is something like the laser that, shining through interference patterns in the brain, brings into being the three-dimensional universe in our minds which, in turn, is a reflection of the interference patterns outside us— which are, in fact, our interaction with other minds.

Talbot's presentation of the model demonstrates how it can "explain" a whole raft of strange events—many of which I've earlier pointed to as indicators of the Great Secret—from telepathy to healing and from UFOs to apparitions of the Blessed Virgin Mary.

෯

If we combine Sheldrake's notion of morphogenetic fields with Pribram and Bohm's notion of the holographic model, what we get is a universe of interacting, living fields, of which we are part, which bring themselves into being—in us—as the universe of experience and to which we have ecological obligations. Each thing is everything and everything is each thing. "Each thing" and "everything" are just different aspects of an event happening at another level of reality.

This, of course, is what the bodhisattva myth talked about: each being and every being is a different aspect of Avalokitesvara entering nirvana. And this is what we saw the Christian myth of Incarnation could be construed to mean. These turn out to be metaphorical ways of talking about something very difficult to focus on. The holographic model itself, of course, is just another metaphor, but it's one that is articulated in the scientific and techological language of today.

෯

Teilhard de Chardin declared, a little precociously, that in humankind evolution—and, consequently, ecological dynamics—has become conscious. We are responsible for overseeing the planet or at least for participating in the process if something even bigger than us is overseeing it. And, if only for survival reasons, ecological concerns *have* to become part of our mythology and morality. And they are becoming so.

Teilhard championed the notion now referred to as "punctuated evolution" in which evolutionary steps occur at crisis times in order to resolve problems resulting from previous evolutionary adjustments. To repeat the example I just used, according to Teilhard, when the atmosphere became choked with oxygen from plant respiration a crisis resulted and the evolutionary process produced animals to breathe the oxygen and convert it back into CO_2. (This, of course, is parallel to the homeostatic notion in the Gaia Hypothesis: like an air-conditioner thermostat that cools down the room after it gets "too" hot, homeostasis responds to extremes.) He hypothesized that the whole process was driven toward greater complexification and consciousness. In the long run, Teilhard saw evolution moving toward the creation of God, at what he called the Omega Point.

At any rate, Teilhard predicted that the next step in evolution, after the achievement of individual consciousness in human beings, would be a collective consciousness. In such a collective consciousness, individuality would not be lost, but individual persons would experience directly their participation in the planetary mind. Teilhard distinguished between "individuality," which is what separates us and walls us off from each other, and "personality" which is what constitutes our talents, skills, and interests and contributes to our interactions with others. In the collective consciousness—experienced, I suspect, as bliss, harmony, and compassion—it's easier to fulfill the potentialities of one's personality because one doesn't have to be afraid. One understands instinctively that one's own behavior affects others and so shapes one's moral life as one would have others shape theirs—all for the betterment of the planetary ecology, both of matter and of mind.

Of course, there'll still be different kinds of people, but perhaps they won't fight each other. As individuals, they might get angry, but as personalities they could freely show their anger and release it. As individuals, they might feel needy or insecure, but as personalities they could know how to negotiate satisfaction without conflict. What, perhaps, all the different people will share will be a common experience of wonder and goodwill.

Teilhard, of course, was predicting this as a mystical phenomenon, perhaps a little like telepathy (and certainly like intense compassion). In fact, we might imagine that this sense of participation in the living dynamics of Gaia is starting with today's sense of ecological awareness and could grow into actual collective consciousness through technological invention.

Marshall McLuhan told us television was creating a planetary mind. At this point, perhaps, what such a planetary mind is thinking about is trivial—if not down-right counterproductive. But as ecological awareness, in response to real crises, pushes us all toward a sense of being part of the planet, television, telephone, and computer modem hook-up is liable to help us all participate and contribute to the growing self-awareness of the planet.

The new myth, I think, hypothesizes that one day (perhaps soon) the network of human minds and technological links—interacting in a great maze of interference patterns—may wake up. Then not only individuals, but the planet itself will enjoy the rapture of being alive.

The contribution that each person makes to this great network is his or her own unique lifestory. Earlier I mentioned Joseph Campbell's citing Schopenhauer's essay "On the Apparent Intention in the Fate of the Individual" in which he observed that "when you reach an advanced age and look back over your lifetime, it can seem to have had a consistent order and plan, as though composed by some novelist." He goes on to say:

> Schopenhauer suggests that just as your dreams are composed by an aspect of yourself of which your consciousnes is unaware, so, too, your whole life is composed by the will within you. And just as people whom you will have met apparently by mere chance became leading agents in the structuring of your life, so, too, will you have served unknowingly as an agent, giving meaning to the lives of others. The whole thing gears together like one big symphony, with everything unconsciously structuring everything else. And Schopenhauer concludes that it is as though our lives were the features of the one great dream of a single dreamer in which all the dream characters dream, too; so that everything links to everything else, moved by the one will which is the universal will in nature.
>
> It's a magnificent idea—an idea that appears in India in the mythic image of the Net of Indra, which is a net of gems, where at every crossing of one thread over another there is a gem reflecting all the other reflective gems. Everything arises in mutual relation to everything else, so you can't blame anybody for anything. It is even as though there were a single intention behind it all, which always makes some kind of sense, though none of us knows what the sense might be, or has lived the life that he quite intended. (*Power of Myth*, p. 229)

In ages past, human beings only knew about the lives of a few people: their families and close friends, of course, and then neighbors and townsfolk with whom they were acquainted, and also figures from the past whose lifestories were recounted in myth, legend, and history. In the course of a human lifetime, these didn't change very much. A person only connected with others' lifestories a small number of times in a lifetime.

Today, television and the media give us access to the lifestories of hundreds and thousands of people. We are kept abreast instantaneously of news and important events around the world. We are made privy to the private lives of both the famous and the common who reveal their deepest secrets on human interest talk shows. We are taken into the lives and adventures of detectives and attorneys and doctors and soldiers in movies and television series. We are allowed to participate in the emotional and sex lives of the rich and the beautiful and the desperate and the wanton in soap operas and dramas. The exposure to other lifestories that used to happen only rarely in a lifetime, can now happen to us hourly.

And this is changing our consciousness. The great political shift that has happened at the opening of the 1990s is an example. It almost seems obvious that the pictures that began appearing on American television of the Russian people—looking surprisingly "normal"—have been as effective in bringing peace and reconciliation with the Soviets as all the talks between political leaders or our government's gloating over the collapse of the Russian communist system. We are now living in a world in which the network of interacting lifestories is becoming more and more complex and, simultaneously, more and more apparent and conscious.

ॐ

The spiritual dilemma of human beings in the centuries around the time of Zoroaster and Gautama Buddha, the time Campbell called "The Great Reversal," was how to respond to the horror of life. Feed the fire. Quench the fire.

In our day, twenty-five hundred years later, the fire is still burning. In the early 1990s, singer Billy Joel used the image of that fire that's been burning since the world's been turning in the song "We Didn't Start the Fire" to capsulize the history of the late twentieth century. We live in the midst of that fire. Time rushes by us in a dizzying pace. Modern technology has got everything moving at breakneck speed. Our computers have to be superfast and accelerated. We fax our letters over the phone so we don't have to wait for the mail. And the faster it all happens the more it gets all boggled up in errors and confusion. Nothing seems to work right.

The fire licks at our hearts and minds. The raging fire of everyday business burns our lives away as we die victims of stress and hypertension and psychologically-induced cancers.

But the new paradigm promises to recast the experience of this world. Can it slow it down? Is that the solution? Who knows?

Can it reexplain what all this is about? Yes. And can it augur and facilitate a real change in human nature to help us adapt? I think we have to hope so. That's how the new scientific paradigm becomes the new myth, the vision of reality that brings itself into being by its being believed.

In this vision, the issue is no longer feeding or quenching the fires either of suffering or of sacrifice. We do not feed the fire. We feed Earth. In this new paradigm coming down to us in which the planet, not the individual flower, fish, beast or human being is the basic unit of life, our role as conscious beings is to supply Earth with richness of experience, compassion, joy, indignation, affection—fullness.

The human contribution to Earth is organization and consciousness. Along with the cetaceans, perhaps, we are the only beings on the planet capable of having complex, organized, self-aware experience. We have a duty to use that capability for the sake of the planet. In doing so— and in understanding ourselves as organs of the mind and body of Gaia—we change what we are and how we stand in relation to the whirlwind of modern life.

ఞ

What this new myth tell us, like the myths of old, is that the universe isn't what we think or perceive, that we live in a world of interacting factors (they used to be spirits and demons, now they're fields generating holograms), and that we have moral and behavioral obligations to the greater whole.

In such a universe—especially one experienced directly (not just conceived rationally) through conscious links with other beings—the experience of being human changes. We cease to be individuated egos clashing with one another and begin to seem like aspects of each other. As this awareness grows and evolves into a state of consciousness that we simply can't imagine now (just as a cat is simply unable to imagine what human intelligence is like), the religious and moral issues that face us now change drastically. When each person actually experiences that other persons are aspects of him or herself, the relationship between persons changes. Morality is different.

We can begin to imagine what these changes would be like. And indeed we can see that they make sense today, even without the immediate experience of oneness with others, if only because we're capable of conceiving of and extrapolating from the notion that we're all aspects of the single organism of the planet.

Compassion obviously becomes the source of decisions, instead, say, of greed, fear, or self-aggrandizement. I can't do something to another that I know I wouldn't want done to me because I'd know the other *is* me. Theft, murder, and war simply disappear as possibilities. Rules change from the relationship of individuals to a natural law to the relationships within a natural ecology. To offer an obvious example, the criteria for assessing the morality of non-reproductive sex (from masturbation to homosexuality to contracepted intercourse), however "unnatural" one might think it to be, shifts from obedience to natural law to its consequences in the global ecology. When population control is demanded by the practical limitations of the planet's resources, the rules that govern reproduction have to change.

In fact, many of the rules about sex—that have so hobbled Christians—simply fade away, because the rules about sex have always been commandments under law rather than instructions about natural ecology. The traditional rules of sexual behavior have been about the relationship between individuals—males and females—in the present, even though, in fact, sex itself is about the relationship between individuals and the race in the future. Rising to a higher perspective reveals this.

From such a perspective, the moral questions appear different. In the abortion debate, for instance, the two polarities so fiercely debated now—the life of the unborn and the right of a woman to choose—are both superceded. Neither of these issues is as important as the life of the planet. When the perspective moves up a notch, the unit of life does not seem the individual but the mystical organism of which the individual is but a single flower. Jesus offered the image of the vine and the branches. Then abortion—as well as euthanasia and rational suicide—do not seem like the destruction of the vine as much as the pruning of the branches to help the greater organism grow stronger. On the other hand, as a method of population control, abortion seems too invasive a medical procedure, perceived by too many as killing—even when they accept that it may be necessary. Pregnancy is such a powerful image of life surviving through time that it should not be cavalierly violated with the conflicting image of killing.

Pornography—the representation of sex in the mass media—now too often seems to objectify and alienate individuals. When each can somehow live in the lives of all, erotic photography may instead seem to offer opportunities for all to experience vicariously the sexual, physical joys of others. Then the beauty and sexual prowess of the few become available to the many. Both the acts of being photographed and of looking at the photographs is an experience of sharing with other persons who, in fact, are aspects of oneself in other bodies and other places. Sex itself shifts from the pleasuring of one person with another to the pleasuring of the collective as it perceives itself embodied.

In fact, I suggest, the rules about sexual behavior—that have seemed the keystone of traditional religious morals—need to, and will, be superceded by rules about distribution of resources, exchange of information, cooperation and contribution to the smooth operation of society. Rules about traffic flow and money exchange, for instance, are far more salient today and in the future than rules about personal behavior.

The point of this future ethics—as well as of current ethics—is to achieve a perspective above and beyond individual acts. And that is what the meta-myth of what I've been calling the Great Secret does. Because we are able—and required—to see from the higher perspective, this myth points to a transcendent reality and offers us the possibility of mystical perception which, in turn, enhances and deepens our experience of being alive. And that, after all, Joe Campbell said, is what religion is really about.

࿔

As I am extrapolating an ethics for the future based on what I argue is the new myth suggested by the work of Joseph Campbell, I have to wonder what he'd have thought. To my recollection, Joe and I never discussed these issues, especially the aspects of avant-garde sexuality. Joseph Campbell was such an academic, cultured, private, and traditional gentleman that he seemed above such discussions. He occasionally joked about teaching at Sarah Lawrence, a women's college, and being surrounded by attractive young women, and there was always a certain ribaldry in those jokes. But still they were very tame. He lectured about sexuality, and enjoyed pointing out that in the Middle Ages adultery was the highest form of love (since it required risk-taking and daring). But those sentiments seemed to come more out of his gentle sarcasm about the Church and traditional society than out of an advocacy of the sexual revolution. At any rate, for all that he was a handsome and fit man, to me, he simply seemed to transcend sexuality.

I visited with Joe and his wife, Jean Erdman, while I was in New York researching teenage prostitution for the study for the Department of Health and Human Services that I wrote about in *In Search of God in the Sexual Underworld*. We discussed my work over dinner at a restaurant on Avenue of the Americas near the high-rise apartment building he and Jean lived in on Waverly Place. He certainly knew my personal concerns, even if we never talked about my private life. And he was ever gracious and welcoming.

Joseph Campbell lived in Greenwich Village. His apartment building overlooked Sheridan Square and Christopher Street, where riots in 1969 initiated the modern gay-rights movement. His wife, Jean, was a dancer and celebrated choreographer. Together they established the Theater of the Open Eye. Joe was certainly familiar with gay people, and with a whole class of non-traditional individuals. I suppose he laughed at homophobic jokes (he lived before the heyday of political correctness), but I don't think he could have been seriously homophobic or judgmental.

He prided himself on being a true conservative and a maverick, which in a way made him also an open-minded progressive. He respected human diversity. In *The Hero With a Thousand Faces,* in the closing section which describes the new mythic consciousness he advocated, he wrote: " . . . the ideals and temporal institutions of no tribe, race, continent, social class, or century, can be the measure of the inexhaustible and multifariously wonderful divine essence that is the live in all of us." It was life that fascinated Joseph Campbell.

☙

In this new consciousness that I am hypothesizing, life and death take on altered meaning. That is partly why the rules of morality change, since morality so often deals with controlling the issues of life and death. Death no longer seems to mean facing the particular judgment before being cast into an afterlife of unending joy or unrelievable pain. We've come to say casually these days that "death is a part of life." Perhaps when individuals begin to sense themselves as aspects of a larger consciousness, they will cease to fear the end of one manifestation and the start of the next. Perhaps they will concern themselves with ego less. That, after all, is the message of death.

Death came to Joseph Campbell on October 30, 1987, in a hospital in Honolulu. I cannot report on the details of his death. I have politely declined from inquiring. Joe was a private person—even as he was an open mind. Besides, I don't think the details of the actual dying of his body belong in books about the implications of his ideas. Suffice it to say he remained active until close to the very end. He still had projects going. *The Historical Atlas of World Mythology* was unfinished. He loved life and cooperated with modern medicine to give him what time was possible. When that time was up, Joe died the death of a modern cancer patient.

My own mother died recently just such a death. She cooperated with radiation and chemotherapy treatments until they—and the cancer—exhausted her. And when pneumonia set in, she passed quickly and simply. I had the opportunity to attend her dying and to be there to repeat over and over, "let go, go into the light." It was a difficult, though marvelous and profound, experience for me. I don't know how she experienced it. She was drugged and feverish. I imagine though that some part of her, a part already transcending her ego, was hearing me and waking up to the light.

Who knows what Joseph Campbell was experiencing when that part of him transcending ego woke to the light? I can remember him laughing warmly when I switched to the next slide during his lecture on *The Tibetan Book of the Dead* and forsook the Clear Light. I'd like to think that, however drugged and medicated his physical body was, at the moment of his death, when a part of him beyond ego connected to the transcendent, eternal consciousness, he laughed warmly, remembered fondly, and then went right into the Light.

At any rate, the message of Joseph Campbell's wisdom was not about dying or even about getting to the end. He never stopped working, never stopped the journey. In his final conversation with Bill Moyers, he quoted Karlfried Graf Dürckheim, "When you're on a journey, and the end keeps getting further and further away, then you realize that the real end is the journey." Joe went on to say, "The Navaho have that wonderful image of what they call the pollen path. Pollen is the life source. The pollen path is the path to the center. The Navaho say, 'Oh, beauty before me, beauty behind me, beauty to the right of me, beauty to the left of me, beauty above me, beauty below me, I'm on the pollen path.'"

Moyers answered, "Eden was not. Eden will be."

Joe rejoined, "Eden *is*. The Kingdom of the Father is spread upon the earth, and men do not see it." (*Power of Myth*, p. 230)

The "new myth," the "new consciousness" that is coming and that is growing up in us now is the awakening to that Kingdom, to the pollen path that is the life source, to our oneness with Gaia. In that network, who we are is what we contribute and how we further the process of the world's growing awareness.

Perhaps it goes without saying that Joseph Campbell made a major contribution.

Polytheism

*I once heard a lecture by a wonderful old Zen
philosopher, Dr. D. T. Suzuki. He stood up with his
hands slowly rubbing his sides and said [regarding
Christianity], "God against man. Man against God.
Man against nature. Nature against man. Nature
against God. God against nature—very funny religion."*
(Power of Myth, p. 56)

The religion that is not naive, that is open to the multidimensionality of
the cosmos and of the consciousness that underlies the experience of
each of us human beings, is ultimately polytheistic. Not polytheistic in
the sense of the primitive religions that superstitiously feared a multitude of gods and appeased them with numerous sacrifices, but in the
sense of the modern plurality of secular and religious symbols. For all
of these can be recognized as metaphors for the powers of human consciousness beyond the limited ego.

The heroes are all metaphors for the self struggling to come to grips
with the problems of life. The heroes who are world-saviors, like Jesus
or Buddha, are metaphors for the eternal transcendent Self struggling,
in each of us, to perceive the reality of life. That is, after all, the essential
problem: how to so affirm the day-to-day problems of life that they appear as merely the foreground of a much greater wonder against which
the little problems disappear.

Each of us is the eternal transcendent Self gathering experiences for its own delight and everywhere revealing to itself that it is itself and yet everywhere hiding that truth. In religion we find the clues to our identity as God, and yet in order to learn the language in which the clues are given—which are the metaphors of myth—we have to take the myths seriously. And so we are on a journey—a hero's journey—from having no knowledge of divine reality to learning about it to transcending what we have learned. "The end (goal) of religion is the end (transcending) of religion."

For men and women of the past, the aim of religious discipline was most often to help them overcome their individual needs, fears, and desires, so that they could fit into their tribe or village. For us, the conquest of the ego cannot mean the annihilation of the individual. We revere and cherish the contribution that the individual, in his or her sacred uniqueness, makes to society. The ego that must be conquered is that which demands that one set of beliefs be chosen over another, that one race be granted hegemony, that one nation or one ideology prevail over the others. And that conquest is accomplished precisely by the recognition of the plurality of ways in which the nature of humanity is expressed. Polytheism is the conquest of the ego. And the place of the gods in such a polytheism is to manifest and give substance to the powers with which human beings create and mold their universe and their future.

The forms of the spiritual teachings, according to the "new consciousness" of religion that is developing today and that has founded the discussion in this book, are not mere projections from the individual mind outward, but are rather projections upon it by a transcendent reality that is the object of mind just as physical forms are the objects of the senses. This transcendent reality, we have seen, is of course itself such a form; the awareness of it is always mediated through the symbols and clues that one finds as the substance of one's own life; and the only inclusive metaphor for it is secrecy.

Over the years of my life as a counterculturalist, first as a monk and mystic then as a hippie, a scientist, a psychologist, a mythologist, a researcher, a sexual rights activist, a community organizer, a gay rights advocate, an AIDS educator, and also a bookseller and a writer, I have sought a mystery. It has seemed like that has been the central point of my life. And I have discovered the gods as metaphors and symbols of fundamental qualities of consciousness that bring me to a state of wonder before that Great Secret.

The world, pervaded by a sense of secrecy that calls to us to question our presumptions about our lives, is shot through with divinity. It is a world in which it is possible to see God everywhere. It is what Teilhard called the "divine milieu." For as we see, God is not simply another thing in a universe of things, but is the symbol for the intimate perception that the experience of each of us is constituted by a vast array of interweaving patterns of meaning. Consciousness rises through these patterns, observing and selecting, highlighting and neglecting, assembling and creating a world.

That world is full of God. The mountains are holy. The waterfalls, pouring life-giving water into the parched deserts, resound with the voices of the gods within them. The sun is God (everyone can see that). The forests reach up their branches in prayer to receive its living, radiant grace. In the cities, men and women toil to renew the face of the earth. In each person, if one has the eyes to see, divinity resides. Each in his or her turn manifests the personalities and qualities of the gods. This whole world can be invested with spiritual significance, if we open up the scope of our experience and shift our focus from individual things to the patterns of interaction that give rise to them.

This spiritual presence does not come from outside us as doctrines or moral imperatives preached by the leaders of churches. It is found in each person's own heart as he or she examines life, affirming it with love. And love has always been said to be the highest virtue. Love, as Joseph Campbell pointed out repeatedly in his treatment of courtly love and romance (in Program V, for instance, of "The Power of Myth"), is making oneself vulnerable to one another's sorrow. When Jesus said "Love another," what he meant was "Open yourself to recognize other people's feelings, feel with them, affirm their life and your own, even with all the sorrows and all the joys. Say 'Yes' to life." For by that love we transform the suffering and pain and confusion. Recognizing our divine identity and loving the world we have created just as it is transforms it so that it becomes a source of bliss.

For thus each one finds roots that sink deep beneath the consciousness of the solitary individual self into some shared awareness and subjectivity which is always beyond the search of knowledge and the intellectual faculties, but which is found in the grace and beauty of a life story well lived and in the still meditation that observes that all that is, is holy and worthy of the highest affection, affirmation, and love. For we discover then that the secret which veils from us the nature of our own consciousness is that there is only radical subjectivity: only you and I and the multitude of subjects with whom we share the gift of life.

We live in a universe, finally, that is ultimately empty: The voices of the gods have fallen silent, God has absconded, the heavens above us have proven to be only sky. We create the gods, you and I. We create the universe of our experience. We are alone. We have only each other. And, for that reason, we are responsible for each other. We have one another—and Earth which is our common identity—to care for and cherish.

And we are far more than we have ever realized. The gods before whom we once groveled and with whom we have rejoiced in ecstasy are aspects of our own selves as we, in turn, are aspects of the self of Earth. The space-visitors awaited by some to announce an end to fears of loneliness, the divine companion some look to for redemption, the hints at an occult, esoteric reality known only by some initiates—these turn out to be clues to our own incomprehensible depths and heights.

The awareness of emptiness impels us toward the conclusion that the true religious act is to become aware of the stories we are living and to shape those stories, through attention, according to archetypal forms that give them meaning and grace in the face of a universe which is forever outside our minds' grasp, but from which can flow bliss.

For we, conscious beings, are the universe. What we worship and adore and love in its multiplicity of forms is the reality, as ungraspable and elusive as it is, of our own lives. The gods have ceased to speak, because we hear them as inflections of our own voices. The gods have disappeared, because they have left us in their place. We are the divine beings we have been searching to meet.

CITATIONS

Joseph Campbell wrote fifteen books and edited another nine. He lectured prolifically, and his words and manner have been videotaped and are available in several video series. His words cited in this book have been gathered from the following:

The Hero's Journey: Joseph Campbell on His Life and Work, edited and with an introduction by Phil Cousineau, San Francisco: HarperCollins, 1990

The Hero With a Thousand Faces, Joseph Campbell, New York: Bolligen Foundation, Princeton University Press, 1949

The Masks of God, Vol. IV: Creative Mythology, Joseph Campbell, New York: Viking, 1968

Myths To Live By, Joseph Campbell, New York: Bantam, 1973

An Open Life: Joseph Campbell in conversation with Michael Toms, edited by John M. Maher and Dennie Briggs, New York: Harper & Row, 1989

The Power of Myth, Joseph Campbell with Bill Moyers, edited by Betty Sue Flowers, New York: Doubleday, 1988

The Power of Myth video, on six videocassettes, S. Burlington, VT: Mystic Fire Video, 1988

BIBLIOGRAPHY

Anonymous. *A Course in Miracles.* New York: Foundation for Inner Peace, 1975

Blakney, Raymond B., editor and translator. *Meister Eckhart.* New York: Harper, 1941

Boswell, John. *Christianity, Social Tolerance, and Homosexuality.* University of Chicago Press, 1980

Capra, Fritjof. *The Tao of Physics.* Berkeley: Shambala, 1975

Clarke, Arthur C. "The Nine Billion Names of God," in *Star Science*

Fiction Stories, No. 1, edited by Frederik Pohl. New York: Ballantine, 1953

Clarke, Arthur C. *2001: A Space Odyssey.* New York: Signet, 1968

Dunne, John S. *The Way of All the Earth.* New York: Macmillan, 1972

Golas, Thaddeus. *The Lazy Man's Guide to Enlightenment.* New York: Bantam, 1972

Harding, Douglas. *The Hierarachy of Heaven and Earth,* cited in *On the Psychology of Meditation* by Claudio Naranjo and Robert E. Ornstein. New York: Viking, 1974

Hofstader, Douglas. *Gödel, Escher, Bach: An Eternal Golden Braid.* New York: Random House, 1980.

Jaynes, Julian. *The Origins of Consciousness in the Breakdown of the Bicameral Mind.* Boston: Houghton Mifflin, 1976

LeGuin, Ursula K. "Myth and Archetype in Science Fiction," *Parabola Magazine,* Fall 1976.

Lewis, C. S. *Perelandra.* New York: Macmillan, 1965

Merton, Thomas. *Seeds of Contemplation.* New York: Dell, 1959

Needleman, Jacob. *The Heart of Philosophy.* New York: Knopf, 1982

Novak, Michael. *The Experience of Nothingness.* Evanston: Harper Colophon, 1971

Pearce, Joseph Chilton. *The Crack in the Cosmic Egg.* New York: Pocket Books, 1973

Peck, M. Scott. *The Road Less Traveled.* New York: Simon and Schuster, 1978

Ramsey, Ian T. *Religious Language, an Empirical Placing of Theological Phrases.* New York: Macmillan, 1963

Roszak, Theodore. *Where the Wasteland Ends.* Garden City: Grove, 1972

Schekley, Robert. "Ask a Foolish Question" in *Six and the Silent Scream.* New York: Belmont, 1963

Sheldrake, Rupert. *The Rebirth of Nature: The Greening of Science and God.* New York: Bantam, 1991

Simak, Clifford. *A Choice of Gods.* New York: Putnam, 1972

Smith, Huston. *Forgotten Truth: The Primordial Tradition.* New York: Harper & Row, 1976

Streng, Frederick J. *Emptiness: A Study in Religious Meaning* (includes text of Nagarjuna's *Mulamadhyamakakarikas*). Nashville: Abingdon, 1967

Strieber, Whitley. *Communion: A True Story.* New York: Morrow, 1987

Strieber, Whitley. *Transformation: The Breakthrough.* New York: Morrow, 1988

Talbot, Michael. *The Holographic Universe.* New York: Harper-Collins, 1991

Teilhard de Chardin, Pierre. *The Divine Milieu.* New York: Harper, 1960

Teilhard de Chardin, Pierre. *The Phenomenon of Man.* New York: Harper, 1961

Twain, Mark. *The Mysterious Stranger.* New York: Signet Classics, 1962

von Daniken, Erich. *Chariots of the Gods?* New York: Bantam, 1971

Watts, Alan. *The Book (On the Taboo Against Knowing Who You Are).* New York: Collier, 1967

Weil, Andrew. *The Natural Mind.* Boston: Houghton Mifflin, 1972

Wilson, Colin. *The Occult.* Random House, 1973

ABOUT THE AUTHOR

Edwin Clark (Toby) Johnson, Ph.D., is a writer and psychotherapist now in semi-retirement. He is author of two spiritual autobiographies and three novels. His 1990 novel *Secret Matter* received a Lambda Literary Award in the science fiction category.

With Kip Dollar, his partner since 1984, Johnson is co-owner of Liberty Books, a specialty bookstore in Austin, TX. The mailing address of Liberty Books is 1014-B North Lamar Blvd., Austin TX 78703.

Other books you may enjoy

QUANTUM SOUP by Chungliang Al Huang
Praised by Joseph Campbell as "a gourmet preparation . . . to tickle the sophisticated palate and provoke happy, healthful belly laughs," Huang's artful series of philosophical essays and anecdotes link Eastern wisdom and Western thought in a lively, thought-provoking collage. $17.95 paper, 144 pages

CRAZY WISDOM by Scoop Nisker
This glorious romp through human history celebrates the fools, prophets, madmen, and teachers who have found wisdom on the other side of convention. Lighthearted lessons are punctuated with quotes from crazy wisdom practitioners like Chuang Tzu, Jesus Christ, Mark Twain, and Albert Einstein. $12.95 paper, 240 pages

LOVE IS LETTING GO OF FEAR by Gerald Jampolsky, M.D.
The deceptively simple lessons in this very popular little book (over 1,000,000 in print) are based on *A Course in Miracles;* working with them will teach you to let go of fear and remember that everyone's true essence is love. Includes daily exercises. $7.95 paper or $9.95 cloth, 144 pages

JOURNEY WITHOUT DISTANCE by Robert Skutch
The fascinating story behind *A Course in Miracles* is told by a man who witnessed it firsthand and knew Helen Schucman at the time she began hearing a mysterious "voice" dictate the *Course* to her. A fascinating and inspirational true story. $7.95 paper or $12.95 cloth, 160 pages

I KNOW FROM MY HEART by Jack Schwarz
A collection of essays, meditations, and teachings that draw on both Eastern and Western spiritual traditions. "What most delights and amazes me in the life, the wisdom, and the teachings of my friend (Jack Schwarz) is the way in which his words so often illuminate for me the sayings of the greatest master."—Joseph Campbell $12.95 paper, 160 pages

THE HEART OF HEALING by Bruce Davis, Ph.D., and Genny Wright Davis
The real-life spiritual odyssey of two professional healer-therapists begins in California when an Alaskan shaman initiates Bruce into the mysteries of psychic healing. This path leads him to his soul mate, Genny, and together they explore the sacred world of faith, healing, and love. $8.95 paper, 208 pages

Available from your local bookstore, or order direct from the publisher. Please include $1.25 shipping & handling for the first book, and 50 cents for each additional book. California residents include local sales tax. Write for our free complete catalog of over 400 books and tapes.

Celestial Arts
Box 7123
Berkeley, CA 94707
For VISA or MasterCard orders call (510) 845-8414